Diaspora Missiology

Other Books in the EMS Series

No. 1   *Scripture and Strategy: The Use of the Bible in Postmodern Church and Mission*, David Hesselgrave

No. 2   *Christianity and the Religions: A Biblical Theology of World Religions*, Edward Rommen and Harold Netland

No. 3   *Spiritual Power and Missions: Raising the Issues*, Edward Rommen

No. 4   *Missiology and the Social Sciences: Contributions, Cautions, and the Conclusions*, Edward Rommen and Gary Corwin

No. 5   *The Holy Spirit and Mission Dynamics*, Douglas McConnell

No. 6   *Reaching the Resistant: Barriers and Bridges for Mission*, Dudley Woodberry

No. 7   *Teaching Them Obedience in All Things: Equipping for the 21st Century*, Edgar Elliston

No. 8   *Working Together With God to Shape the New Millennium: Opportunities and Limitations*, Kenneth Mulholland and Gary Corwin

No. 9   *Caring for the Harvest Force in the New Millennium*, Tom Steffen and Douglas Pennoyer

No. 10 *Between Past and Future: Evangelical Mission Entering the Twenty-first Century*, Jonathan Bonk

No. 11 *Christian Witness in Pluralistic Contexts in the Twenty-first Century*, Enoch Wan

No. 12 *The Centrality of Christ in Contemporary Missions*, Mike Barnett and Michael Pocock

No. 13 *Contextualization and Syncretism: Navigating Cultural Currents*, Gailyn Van Rheenen

No. 14 *Business as Mission: From Impoverished to Empowered*, Tom Steffen and Mike Barnett

No. 15 *Missions in Contexts of Violence*, Keith Eitel

No. 16 *Effective Engagement in Short-Term Missions: Doing it Right!* Robert J. Priest

No. 17 *Missions from the Majority World: Progress, Challenges, and Case Studies,* Enoch Wan and Michael Pocock

No. 18 *Serving Jesus with Integrity: Ethics and Accountability in Mission,* Dwight P. Baker and Douglas Hayward

No. 19 *Reflecting God's Glory Together: Diversity in Evangelical Mission,* A. Scott Moreau and Beth Snodderly

No. 20 *Reaching the City: Reflections on Urban Mission for the Twenty-first Century,* Gary Fujino, Timothy R. Sisk, and Tereso C. Casino

No. 21 *Missionary Methods: Research, Reflections, and Realities,* Craig Ott and J. D. Payne

No. 22 *The Missionary Family: Witness, Concerns, Care,* Dwight P. Baker and Robert J. Priest

ABOUT EMS
WWW.EMSWEB.ORG

The Evangelical Missiological Society is a professional organization with more than 400 members comprised of missiologists, mission administrators, reflective mission practitioners, teachers, pastors with strategic missiological interests, and students of missiology. EMS exists to advance the cause of world evangelization. We do this through study and evaluation of mission concepts and strategies from a biblical perspective with a view to commending sound mission theory and practice to churches, mission agencies, and schools of missionary training around the world. We hold an annual national conference and eight regional meetings in the United States and Canada.

Evangelical Missiological Society Series no. 23

Diaspora Missiology

Reflections on Reaching the Scattered Peoples of the World

Michael Pocock and Enoch Wan
Editors

WILLIAM CAREY LIBRARY

Diaspora Missiology: Reflections on Reaching the Scattered Peoples of the World
Copyright © 2015 by Evangelical Missiological Society
All rights reserved.

No part of this book may be reproduced, stored in a retrieval system, or transmitted in any form or by any means—electronic, mechanical, photocopy, recording, or otherwise—without prior written permission of the publisher, except brief quotations used in connection with reviews in magazines or newspapers.

Unless otherwise noted, Scripture quotations are from The Holy Bible, New International Version®, NIV® Copyright © 1973, 1978, 1984, 2011 by Biblica, Inc.® Used by permission. All rights reserved.
Scripture quotations marked (ESV) are from the ESV® Bible (The Holy Bible, English Standard Version®), copyright © 2001 by Crossway, a publishing ministry of Good News Publishers. Used by permission. All rights reserved.

Scripture quotations marked (NASB) are taken from the New American Standard Bible®, Copyright © 1960, 1962, 1963, 1968, 1971, 1972, 1973, 1975, 1977, 1995 by The Lockman Foundation. Used by permission. (www.Lockman.org)

Published by William Carey Library, an imprint of William Carey Publishing
10 W. Dry Creek Circle
Littleton, CO 80120 | www.missionbooks.org

Melissa Hicks, editor
Brad Koenig, copyeditor
Hugh Pindur, graphic design
Rose Lee-Norman, indexer

William Carey Library is a ministry of Frontier Ventures
Pasadena, CA 91104 | www.frontierventures.org

Library of Congress Cataloging-in-Publication Data

Diaspora missiology : reflections on reaching the scattered peoples of the world / [edited by] Michael Pocock, Enoch Wan.

   pages cm. -- (Evangelical Missiological Society series ; 23)
Includes bibliographical references and index.
   ISBN13: 978-0-87808-045-8 (alk. paper) -- ISBN10: 0-87808-045-7 (alk. paper) 1. Missions. 2. Church work with migrant labor. 3. Church work with immigrants. 4. Church work with aliens. I. Pocock, Michael, 1942-, editor.

23 22 21 20 19 Printed for Worldwide Distribution

Contents

Introduction 1 xv
MICHAEL POCOCK

Introduction 2 xix
ENOCH WAN

Part One: *The Current Phenomenon of Global Diasporas* 1

Chapter One 3
Global Migration: Where Do We Stand?
MICHAEL POCOCK

Chapter Two 21
Mapping the Diaspora with Facebook
TREVOR CASTOR

Chapter Three 37
The Muslim Diaspora
MARK HAUSFELD AND JOSHUA FLETCHER (PSEUDONYM)

Part Two: *Theory and Models of Diaspora Missiology* 57

Chapter Four 59
Assessing the Value of Diaspora Community Input in Missiological Research
FRED FARROKH

Chapter Five 77
Mission by and beyond the Diaspora: Partnering with Diaspora Believers to Reach Other Immigrants and the Local People
STAN DOWNES

Part Three: *Biblical and Theological Guidelines* 89

Chapter Six 91
Diaspora Ministry in the Book of Acts: Insights from Two Speeches of the Apostle Paul to Help Guide Diaspora Ministry Today
LARRY W. CALDWELL

Chapter Seven 107
God's New Humanity in Diaspora: A Church of the Nations and for the Nations
DAVID STEVENS

Part Four: 127
Strategy and Models

Chapter Eight 129
Three Models of Acculturation: Applications for Developing a Church Planting Strategy among Diaspora Populations
DAVID R. DUNAETZ

Chapter Nine 147
The "With" of Diaspora Missiology: The Impact of Kinship, Honor, and Hospitality on the Future of Missionary Training, Sending, and Partnership
JACQUES HÉBERT

Part Five: 165
Case Studies in Diaspora Missions

Chapter Ten 167
Mission and the Palestinian Diaspora
ANDREW F. BUSH

Chapter Eleven 183
The Ethiopian Diaspora: Ethiopian Immigrants as Cross-cultural Missionaries; Activating the Diaspora for Great Commission Impact
JESSICA A. UDALL

Part Six: 197
The Way Forward

Chapter Twelve 199
Organizing to Reach the Diaspora: A Case Study of The International Mission Board, SBC; Changing Its Overseas Structure from Geographic Components to Global Affinity Groups
JERRY RANKIN

Chapter Thirteen 215
Diaspora Missiology and Beyond: Paths Taken and Ways Forward
ENOCH WAN

Appendix 1 227

Appendix 2 229

Appendix 3 231

Selected Bibliography 233

Contributors 255

Figures

Figure 1: Muslim Americans 66
Figure 2: Predictable Sociological Process 123
Figure 3: Determinants of Group Identity 124
Figure 4: Four Acculturation Strategies 137
Figure 5: Emic Diaspora: The Jewish Diaspora 153
Figure 6: Etic Diaspora: Foreigners in the Land 154
Figure 7: Emic Diaspora as a Bridge to the Natal Land 155
Figure 8: Etic Diaspora as a Bridge to the World 156

Tables

Table 1: The Push and Pull Forces that Move People 41
Table 2: Muslim Population in NY 68
Table 3: Common Misconceptions 149
Table 4: Current Diaspora-natal Integration 150
Table 5: Types of Exogenous Networking 151
Table 6: The Landscape of Relational Networks 160
Table 7: Affinity Groups 210
Table 8: Diaspora Missiology 216

Acknowledgments

The editors wish to acknowledge the authors contributing to this volume and many others who presented papers related to the theme of diaspora missions during the regional conferences of the Evangelical Missiological Society in 2014. They also recognize the invaluable work of their administrative assistants, Karen Hedinger for Enoch Wan and Jennifer Bugos for Mike Pocock. Their assistance in standardizing the formats of diverse authors and chapters and aligning them in a single manuscript was invaluable. Thanks to the staff of William Carey Library for their patient and expert advice at every stage of the production of this volume, in particular, Melissa Hicks for her supervision of this project, Brad Koenig for copyediting, and Jeff Minard for managing William Carey Library.

Introduction 1
MICHAEL POCOCK

This book deals with what today is called *diaspora missiology*, an emerging discipline focusing on ministry to the millions of people who live and work in areas far from their birthplace. *Missiology* combines biblical and theological studies with insights from the social sciences including cultural anthropology, sociology, communication, and diagnostic tools. We should never let this discussion be coldly scientific, however, because we are dealing with human beings, marvelously made, but subject to many weaknesses and stresses. This is evident in the pictures we often see of people struggling for a better life. They move in a search of better opportunities, security, peace, education, or business. But to encounter the *shalom* that Scripture talks about, they need the God of peace in their lives.

Looking more like a soaked pile of clothes than a human being, he lies collapsed on the sands, waves lapping at his outstretched feet. He is alive, but barely. All the strength of his young life has been used up just to get here. Around him, other young men are staggering to their feet on land they have never trod before. Where is this happening? Who are these people? Is this the American side of the Rio Grande? The shores of Florida? The beaches of Italy or the Andaman Sea between Thailand and Malaysia where thousands of tribal people from Myanmar have desperately sought for some kind of relief in 2015?[1]

No, but it could have been. Actually it was happening on the shores of the Canary Islands. The exhausted new arrivals had survived six hundred miles in a wooden boat on the open Atlantic. They are *Subsaharianos*, Sub-saharan Africans from Senegal, Mauritania, and Morocco. They were part of a desperate struggle to get to Spain and Europe. The Canary Islands are the closest Spanish territory. Over twenty thousand arrived in the islands during 2006. If they can stay and find work in Spain, they will send money home to help their families.

The governor of the Canary Islands was desperate. What should she do? The numbers were overwhelming their resources. What should the Spanish government do? Bring them to the Spanish mainland? Take them back to Africa and leave them on the shores? Like many other European governments and those of the United

---

1 "Flight from Myanmar and Bangladesh leaves thousands adrift at sea." Jonathan Kaiman and Shashank Bengali. *Los Angeles Times*, May 20, 2015.

States and other countries receiving so many undocumented immigrants, Spain struggles to deal with the challenges to their administrative capabilities, their culture, and their values.

In Barcelona, Spain, Pastor Guillem Correa sits in his office at Solidarity Initiatives hard at work to help new arrivals like those above. He has organized a ministry that brings health, business, and housing professionals together to help new arrivals. They give orientation, health checkups, temporary housing, job training, employment, and spiritual guidance. While the government wrings its hands, pastors and churches moved by the love of Christ are already organized to help meet needs.[2] This became clear during the hurricane Katrina in the United States and Indonesian tsunami emergencies of 2005, the Japanese tsunami of 2011, and the powerfully destructive earthquakes in Nepal, 2015. African governments face similar human crises born of war, famine, AIDS, and unemployment. These governments need help. International assistance from private and faith-based initiatives and churches are often the most immediate, organized aid available.

A common phenomenon of our globalized era is that governments seemingly have less power to handle major emergencies than private and often faith-based initiatives. Not only that, but national boundaries have become increasingly irrelevant. Huge numbers of people, some 232 million, do not live in the countries of their birth. Many are desperate, undocumented migrants, legal refugees, or contract workers. Still others are global entrepreneurs capitalizing on growth opportunities in rapidly growing newer markets like China. While many in the United States worry about some 2 million (half documented and half undocumented) immigrants who arrive each year, contract workers in countries like Kuwait, Saudi Arabia, and United Arab Emirates constitute more than 80 percent of the total population.[3]

Human migration is a phenomenon occurring throughout human existence. Joseph Henriques and I have documented this in *Cultural Change and Your Church*.[4] But the process has greatly accelerated as a component of globalization. Douglas McConnell and I explained the impact of globalization and changing demographics

---

2   Rev. Guillem Correa is a Methodist pastor in Barcelona, Spain, and General Secretary of the Evangelical Council of Cataluna. He founded and directs Iniciatives Solidaries (Catalan)— www.iniciatives. entitatsbcn.net, www.actualidadevangelica.es (accessed March 22, 2012).
3   Human Rights Watch, "I Already Bought You," www.hrw.org/zh-hans/node/129797/section/5 (accessed May 21, 2015).
4   Michael Pocock and Joseph Henriques, *Cultural Change and Your Church* (Grand Rapids: Baker Books, 2002).

on Christian ministry worldwide in *The Changing Face of World Missions*.[5] There has been hardly a day in 2014 in which the *Dallas Morning News* has not contained an article dealing with migration issues. Pick up a copy of *La Nacion* or *El Pais* in Spain, the *Manchester Guardian* in Great Britain, or a major newspaper of almost any world-class city and one will find the same: migration is a constant concern. Migration solves the problems of many who immigrate to find safer conditions and meaningful employment, and it serves the needs of the countries to which they move. But the increased *rate* of migration also overwhelms and frightens many who have to deal with the consequences. This is true at the global level and in the United States.

It seems that God is orchestrating global migration with a view to blessing humanity, populating his creation, and drawing people to himself. The chapters in this book clearly show from the creation mandate in Genesis to the explanations of Paul in Acts 17, God meets individuals and nations in the midst of their journeys, alternately blessing, showing himself, protecting and sometimes disciplining his people through movement. We are all human beings made in the image of God, "fearfully and wonderfully made," as the Psalmist says (139:14). Every person has unimaginable worth, whether he or she is a well-established citizen of a wealthy nation, or a seemingly powerless refugee, or a contract worker far from home. But human depravity mars what would otherwise be a delightful adventure, introducing difficulties, danger, exploitation, and loss.

Until recently, mission agencies and individual missionaries tended to regard displaced or migrating people as secondary to their chief object of reaching those who were indigenous to nations to which they felt called to minister. A missionary in France might have considered immigrant Muslims secondary to indigenous French people, but that began to change by the turn of the century. Now many agencies can see that diaspora peoples are indeed a legitimate focus of Christian missions, and that is evident from a number of world conferences addressing the needs. In 2014 the Evangelical Missiological Society made diaspora peoples the focus of its regional and national conferences. It quickly became evident that ministry to diaspora peoples is now on the "front burner" for Christian missions. This book is evidence of this awakening.

Christians *should* be in the vanguard of those who reach out in love to people on the move. As Christians themselves move, they should make disciples among all

---

5   Michael Pocock, Gailyn Van Rheenen, and Douglas McConnell, *The Changing Face of World Missions* (Grand Rapids: Baker Academic, 2005), chs. 1–2.

the nations. But individuals, churches, mission agencies, communities, or nations will fail to "do the right thing" unless we take time to understand migrating, or what we prefer to call *diaspora* peoples, and what God is telling us through Holy Scriptures. This book will help readers understand and respond to global diasporas in the ways God intended.

Diaspora Missions is not a comprehensive treatment of all the factors and kinds of people involved in diaspora missions; it is a selection of key issues which should aid us in understanding and interacting ministerially with the scattered peoples of the world.

Introduction 2
ENOCH WAN

As an emerging topic for research and as an agenda for ministry application, *diaspora missiology* had a humble beginning with just a few published pieces as listed below:
- Enoch Wan, "Mission among the Chinese Diaspora: A Case Study of Migration and Mission," *Missiology* 31, no. 1 (January 2003): 35–43.
- Enoch Wan, "Diaspora Missiology," *Occasional Bulletin* of EMS (Spring 2007).
- The booklet "The New People Next Door" (Lausanne Occasional Paper 55), produced by the Lausanne Committee for World Evangelization (2004), is a significant document in that it helped placing the topic of diaspora missiology on the global agenda of the church.

Since then diaspora missiology was covered at national and international conferences in Japan, Korea, Thailand, and South Africa prior to 2014 as shown in appendix 1. Research conducted recently and the resultant publications are listed in appendix 2. Personal efforts and sample publications can be found in appendix 3.

In 2014, diaspora missiology was the focus of the Evangelical Missiological Society both at regional and national levels, leading to the publication of the present volume, which is different from other recent publications on the same topic[1] for the following reasons:

a) it is a joint effort of experts in biblical, theological, and missiological studies;

b) it is a collection of juried papers from regional and national conferences of EMS in 2014;

c) it includes contributions from seminary professors, professional researchers, and practitioners;

d) the broad scope of phenomenological, theoretical, biblical, and strategic studies;

e) the logical organization in six parts as shown in the Contents; and

f) it includes a review of paths taken (see the last chapter), past efforts (see the three appendices), and a forecast of future development.

---

1 Several recent publications are listed below:
Enoch Wan, ed., *Diaspora Missiology: Theory, Methodology, and Practice*, rev. ed. (Portland, OR: Institute of Diaspora Studies, 2014); J. D. Payne, *Strangers Next Door: Immigration, Migration and Mission* (Downers Grove, IL: InterVarsity Press, 2012); Sadiri Tira, ed., *The Human Tidal Wave* (Manila: LifeChange, 2014); S. Hun Kim and Wonsuk Ma, eds., *Korean Diaspora and Christian Mission* (Oxford: Regnum Books International, 2011).

"Diaspora missiology" as a focus of missiological research and a contemporary strategy of Christian mission is promising due to the following factors: the changing landscape in Christian missions (i.e., the shifting of Christendom from the West to the rest, and from the Northern Hemisphere to the Southern Hemisphere,[2] increasing impact of globalization on Christian mission,[3] the emergence of majority mission,[4] and the ever-increasing size and scale of the phenomenon of diaspora.[5] From the broad scope of Christian mission and in light of factors listed above, the present volume is a significant contribution to the ongoing studies on diaspora missiology.

---

2   See extensive discussion in Wan, *Diaspora Missiology* (2014), chs. 2, 12.
3   Ryan Dunch, "Beyond Cultural Imperialism: Cultural Theory, Christian Missions, and Global Modernity," *History and Theory* 41, no. 3 (October 2002): 301–25; Peter van der Veer, *Conversion to Modernities: The Globalization of Christianity* (Psychology Press, 1996); Joel Robbins, "The Globalization of Pentecostal and Charismatic Christianity," *Annual Review of Anthropology* 33 (2004): 117–43; Donald M. Lewis, ed., *Christianity Reborn: The Global Expansion of Evangelicalism in the Twentieth Century* (Eerdmans, 2004); P. L. Wickeri, "Mission from the Margins," *International Review of Mission* (2004), Wiley Online Library.
4   Enoch Wan and Michael Pocock, *Missions from the Majority World: Progress, Challenges, and Case Studies*, EMS 17 (Pasadena: William Carey Library, 2009).
5   See Wan, *Diaspora Missiology* (2014), chs. 2, 9, 10.

Part One:

The Current Phenomenon of Global Diasporas

Chapter One

Global Migration: Where Do We Stand?

MICHAEL POCOCK

ABSTRACT

The pace of global scattering of peoples beyond their original countries of birth has accelerated, creating opportunities for ministry both to and by Christians in this phenomenon. People in these diasporas and their families both benefit and are threatened by separation from family, culture, and country. Christian ministries that earlier regarded immigrants, refugees, international students, and nomads as peripheral to their foci increasingly direct their attention to these people as their primary focus.

As he opened the sixteenth annual Iberian-American Summit in Montevideo in November 2006, then–UN General Secretary Kofi Annan proclaimed: "International migration is one of the greatest issues of this century . . . We have entered a new era of mobility."[1]

This was not an overstatement. Developments since have proved him prophetic! Two hundred and thirty-two million people lived outside of their country of birth in 2013.[2] As we shall see, "migration is as old as the Bible, but it has accelerated to an amazing and often confusing extent. This chapter will help us understand the current levels of migration, the categories of people on the move, the direction in which migration flows, and the forces that influence this phenomenon.

We shall also look at the fears of Christians and non-Christians in receiving countries, and the reasons why an old book like the Bible can give us a framework for understanding human movement and God's agenda in and through it. Understanding reduces fear. Discovering a purpose within a phenomenon like human migration prepares us to engage it rather than ignore or flee from it.

---

1 Annan, Kofi, "Opening Address" (speech, 16th Annual Ibero-American Summit, Montevideo, Uruguay, November 3, 2006), PressZoom, http://presszoom.com/story_120578.html (accessed November 28, 2006).

2 United Nations Department of Economic and Social Affairs and the Organisation for Economic Co-operation and Development, "World Migration in Figures," October 3–4, 2013, http://www.un.org/en/development/desa/population/publications/pdf/migration/migration/World_Migration_Figures_UNDESA_OECD.pdf, 1.

In speaking with the Greek philosophers in Athens, the Apostle Paul gave a classic explanation for why people are where they are, spread over the globe. At the conclusion he said, "In him [God] we live and *move* and have our being" (Acts 17:28, italics mine). Paul's contention is that God is at work in human migration, and those that move, whether they know it or not, are under his providential, even salvific, care. In the same passage, Paul explains that God places people where they are to help them reach out to him and find him (Acts 17:26,27). This takes migration out of the world of mere economic, political, or environmental dynamics and puts it into a grander scheme of God's design and purpose for humanity.

Around the world, Christians are waking up to the reality that the massive movement of peoples in migration presents an unprecedented opportunity for spreading the gospel. Among the hundreds of thousands on the move to find work or a better life are highly committed Christians. Many are effectively living a life that witnesses to the presence of Christ. Others would be more effective if they had some basic preparation in cross-cultural living and how to share the gospel and lead small group Bible studies, and in fact saw themselves as instruments in the Great Commission calling of the Lord Jesus Christ. They also need pastoral care to maintain their own spiritual vitality while they are away from home.

Both evangelicals and Catholics can clearly see this point. There are, for example, 10.5 million Filipinos serving as contract workers outside the Philippines who send home $21 billion a year to their families.[3] Lorajoy Dimangondayao says of the Filipino diaspora workers:

> With Filipinos found in almost every industry, at every level of management, and in every strata of society, Christian Filipinos are positioned to be effective witnesses for Jesus Christ wherever they are situated. Christian Filipinos recognize God's providence in placing them in all corners of the globe to serve people of all sorts. They become like the Apostle Paul who became all things to all people . . . for the sake of the gospel.[4]

---

3   National Statistics Office of the Philippines, http://www.census.gov.ph/ (accessed May 18, 2014).
4   Lorajoy Dimangondayao, "To All People: Samples of Diaspora Filipinos Making a Kingdom Impact," in *Scattered: The Filipino Global Presence*, ed. Luis Pantoja, Sadiri Joy Tira, and Enoch Wan (Manila: LifeChange, 2004), 291.

A Catholic symposium entitled "Faith on the Move: Towards a Theology of Migration in Asia," was held in Quezon City, Philippines, in July 2006. Participants called for pastoral care for the thousands of Filipinos working abroad, but also showed we can get insight into how God works, and in fact how Jesus worked when we reflect on the situation of people on the move.[5] This same conference examined victimization of migrants and family disintegration caused by migration. These are the kinds of problems, among many, needing reflection and action by Christian laypeople and missionaries today.

Global migration in the United States and around the world presents awesome possibilities and perplexing challenges. This chapter attempts to show how we can build on the opportunities while resolving the difficulties of global migration. The first order of business is to grasp the size and shape of this phenomenon. *National Geographic*, which focused an entire issue on migration, emphasizes the dramatic reality of migration:

> Migration is big, dangerous, compelling. It's Exodus, Ulysses, the Battle of Agincourt, Viking ships on the high seas bound for Iceland, slave ships and civil war, the secret movement of Jewish refugees through occupied lands during World War II. It is 60 million Europeans leaving home from the 16th to the 20th centuries. It is some 15 million Hindus, Sikhs and Muslims swept up in a tumultuous shuffle of citizens between India and Pakistan after the partition of the subcontinent in 1947. . . But it is much more than that. It is, as it has always been, the great adventure of human life. Migration . . . drove us to conquer the planet, shaped our societies, and promises to reshape them again.[6]

Migration to the United States

There were 40 million foreign-born people in the United States in 2010. The largest percentage, 53.3 percent, were from Latin America and the Caribbean, followed by 28 percent from Asia, 12 percent from Europe, and 7 percent from other regions

---

5 Scalabrini Migration Center, "Faith on the Move," http://www.smc.org.ph/symposium.htm (accessed August 8, 2006; page discontinued).
6 Michael Parfit, "Human Migration," *National Geographic*, October 1998, 11.

of the world.⁷ Of these, approximately 12 million are unauthorized migrants. They include those who entered without valid documents and those who entered legally but overstayed the expiration date of their visas.⁸

The United States has been in an accelerated period of migration since 1965 when a new US Immigration Act was passed removing the national quota system that had been in place up to that time. From 1965, immigration, which had been predominantly European, changed. Significantly more Asians, Africans, and Latin Americans began moving to the United States. The foreign-born population now constitutes 13 percent of the population. Although the actual numbers are significantly greater than at other periods, foreign-born people have historically constituted greater percentages of the total population in 1890 (15 percent) and 1910 (14.7 percent).⁹ Immigrants increased by 57.4 percent between 1990 and 2000 alone.¹⁰

The arrival in the United States of approximately 1 million legal and 1.5 million unauthorized immigrants each year is a great concern to many and to the US government. The pressure is on to enforce existing measures against illegal migrants and to enact more effective legislation. This is happening at the national and local level. The US Congress in 2006, while failing to pass comprehensive reform legislation, did pass a measure to build a wall seven hundred miles along parts of the southern border with Mexico. Six hundred and fifty miles had been built by 2013. Volunteer "Minutemen" began patrolling certain border ranch lands.¹¹ Communities like Farmers Branch, Texas, passed laws forbidding landlords to rent housing to undocumented persons and have authorized police to routinely check the documents of any person they believe may be undocumented. Arizona passed and began implementation of similar laws. Most recently Texas governor Perry authorized one thousand National Guardsmen to help control the Texas border

---

7   American Community Survey, "The Foreign-born Population of the United States: 2010," United States Census Bureau, http://www.census.gov/prod/2010pubs/acs_19.pdf.

8   Dimangondayao, "To All People."

9   Jie Zong and Jeanne Batalova, "Frequently Requested Statistics on Immigrants and Immigration in the United States," http://www.migrationpolicy.org/article/frequently-requested-statistics-immigrants-and-immigration-united-states (accessed June 23, 2015).

10 Ibid.

11 "Thirty Days to Change a Mind," editorial, *Dallas Morning News*, July 29, 2006, 24A. The U.S. Border Patrol stated that 56,547 unaccompanied and undocumented minors entered the U.S. southern border during the year up to June 30, 2014. U.S. Customs and Border Protection, http://www.cbp.gov/newsroom/stats/southwest-border-unccompanied-children (page discontinued). The border fence mandated in 2006 has never been finished, primarily due to high costs and failure of Congress to fund the project completely. *Wikipedia*, s.v. "Secure Fence Act of 2006," http://en.wikipedia.org/wiki/Secure_Fence_Act_of_2006 (accessed May 2014).

area. 85,131 unaccompanied minors have arrived on the Southwest U.S. border between October 2014 and June 2015.[12]

Americans are conflicted over what to do about migration, and, more particularly, unauthorized workers and their families. Columnist Steve Blow has likened our attitudes over immigration to the game "Red Rover," where children form a chain, hand to hand, and challenge anyone on an opposing team to break through the chain. If they can, they become part of the chain.[13] In similar fashion, Americans seem united in opposition to the *entry* of illegal migrants, but expect them to become part of society and that government and communities will provide many services to them once they *are* here. He and others have pointed out the plain fact that the United States needs the labor and benefits from the spending power of migrants, legal and illegal. The combined spending power of US Hispanics alone surpassed 1 trillion dollars in 2010 and is projected to be 1.5 trillion in 2015.[14]

Attitudes among Christian church people reflect national patterns. Some see undocumented migrants as a threat and as criminals who have broken the law to enter the country. At the same time, many other Christians believe that the history of God's people in Scripture and its teaching about the treatment of aliens and the reality of America as a nation of immigrants compels us to deal graciously with those who so desperately want and need to be here.

The Global Picture of Migration

Americans often feel their country is the special object and attraction of the world's immigrants, but migration is actually occurring at high levels to Canada, Europe, the Middle East Gulf states, and the more prosperous cities of Asia. The movement of the world's peoples has been likened to weather patterns swirling constantly and forming changing patterns all over the planet.[15] Movement is a constant feature of human life. Societies come into possession of particular areas and come to think of themselves as permanently in place. This may continue for lengthy periods, but eventually migratory forces will bring others into their territory or take themselves

---

12 "Southwest Border Unaccompanied Alien Children," U.S. Customs and Border Protection, http://www.cbp.gov/newsroom/stats/southwest-border-unaccompanied-children (accessed June 23, 2015).
13 Steve Blow, "Migrant Policy Is a Puzzler," *Dallas Morning News*, July 16, 2005.
14 "Hispanic Buying Power," *The Shelby Report*, http://www.theshelbyreport.com/2011/07/01/hispanic-buying-power/#.U_5EaWMic0k (accessed May 2014).
15 Pocock and Henriques, *Cultural Change*, 59–60.

to other regions. We have dealt with the historical picture of migration patterns in other sources.[16] Here we are looking at a snapshot of the situation today.

International migrants worldwide amounted to 232 million persons in 2013. About a third of these have moved from one developing country to another, and a third have moved from a developing country to a more developed country.[17] Thirty-four percent of all migrants have moved to Europe, 23 percent to North America, 28 percent to Asia, 9 percent to Africa, 3 percent to Latin America, and 3 percent to Oceania.[18]

These figures reflect only *international* migration. *Internal* migration, generally from rural to urban areas, is also a major consideration. Urban centers everywhere in the developing world are surrounded by millions of such internal migrants. They are usually poor, yet hopeful. Mexico City grows by about eighty thousand each month. Nairobi, Kenya; Lagos, Nigeria; Beijing; and Kolkata are in similar situations. Movements on a grand scale are changing cities, countries, economies, and societies worldwide. These international and national changes constitute an immense challenge to governments and municipalities struggling to find jobs and form infrastructures to manage this wave of humanity. But human migration is not simply a challenge for governments, it has major implications and opportunities for Christian churches and missions.

Although international and internal migration bring problems to many in receiving nations and cities, migrants themselves are materially contributing to the growth, economy, and national life of the countries to which they go. The population of Kuwait, Saudi Arabia, and United Arab Emirates ranges from 48 percent to 80 percent nonnational.[19] They are there with contracts to perform work desired by the host country.

Immigrant workers help solve not only their own economic challenges, they help their countries and families back home. Foreign workers remitted an estimated

---

16   Ibid., 59–77. See also Pocock, Van Rheenen, and McConnell, *Changing Face*: Pocock, ch. 1, "Globalization," 21–44; and McConnell, ch. 2, "Changing Demographics," 45–78.

17   United Nations Department of Economic and Social Affairs and the Organisation for Economic Co-operation and Development, "World Migration in Figures," October 3–4, 2013, http://www.un.org/en/development/desa/population/publications/pdf/migration/migration/World_Migration_Figures_UNDESA_OECD.pdf (accessed May 20, 2014).

18   "United Nations Report Trends in International Migrant Stock: The 2013 Revision"; *Wikipedia*, s.v. "List of Countries by Foreign-born Population," http://en.wikipedia.org/wiki/List_of_countries_by_foreign-born_population (accessed May 2014).

19   Kasim Randeree, "Workforce Nationalization in the Gulf Cooperation Council States," Center for International and Regional Studies, Georgetown University School of Foreign Service in Qatar, Occasional Paper 9, http://www12.georgetown.edu/sfs/qatar/cirs/KasimRandereeCIRSOccasionalPaper9.pdf, 2–3.

$500 billion to their home countries in 2013. This is a huge transfer of wealth amounting to the single major source of the gross domestic product in countries like the Philippines.[20] If we are concerned about international aid, surely this is one of the most effective forms, one that better than any other puts the assistance into the pockets of the actual families and communities in need.

Who Are Today's Migrating Peoples?

Refugees

Globally, 35.8 million people are considered "persons of concern," and 10.5 million are refugees according to the United Nations High Command for Refugees (UNHCR) worldwide.[21] The definition of refugee status dates to 1951 when the UNHCR met to formulate the Conventions and Protocol Relating to the Status of Refugees. The definition is considered fundamental and operative today. A refugee is any person who, owing to well-founded fear of being persecuted for reason of race, religion, nationality, membership of a particular social group or political opinion, is outside the country of his nationality and is unable, or owing to such fear, is unwilling to avail himself of the protection of that country, or who, not having a nationality and being outside the country of his former habitual residence as a result of such events, is unable or unwilling to return to it.[22]

Refugees, then, are people who are migrating by coercion rooted usually in violence, war, and civil unrest. They may be fleeing the regime in Myanmar (415,000 in 2014), Somalia (1.3 million), or they may be Sudanese fleeing to Chad, where there are 632,000 at the time of this writing (2014). Worldwide, 28.8 million more are *internally* displaced people within their own country.[23]

---

20 A helpful site for visual representation of remittance flows is Rich Harris and Claire Provost, "Remittances: How Much Money Do Migrants Send Home?—Interactive," *The Guardian*, January 31, 2013, http://www.theguardian.com/global-development/interactive/2013/jan/31/remittances-money-migrants-home-interactive.

21 UNHCR, "UNHCR Statistical Online Population Database," 2012, http://popstats.unhcr.or/PSQ_POC.aspx (accessed June 5, 2014).

22 UNHCR, "Convention and Protocol Relating to the Status of Refugees," General Provisions, Article 1, "Definition of the Term 'Refugee,'" 16, http://www.unhcr.org/protect/PROTECTION/3b66c2aa10.pdf (accessed December 1, 2006).

23 The Internal Displacement Monitoring Centre, Geneva, lists 28.8 million globally Internally Displaced People (IDPs) in 2012. These are those who are displaced within their own country. UNHCR, "Internally Displaced People Figures," http://www.unhcr.org/pages/49c3646c23.html (accessed June 5, 2014).

The immediate needs of refugees are food, shelter, and protection. In the long term they need relocation to a willing host country. Alternately they need repatriation to their own country if the situation permits, or to be integrated into the nation in which they have found immediate refuge. Refugees are routinely in temporary camps or centers for six to fifteen years before they are more permanently settled. Churches and individual Christians are a big assistance in helping refugees. In the United States, the Church World Service is one such group that coordinates resettlement. The UNHCR often works in partnership with church bodies or nongovernmental organizations (NGOs) to resettle the approximately 38.7 million refugees it serves worldwide.

Christian denominations, individual churches, and families can play a key role in solving the dilemma of the world's refugees. How to help will be discussed later.

Read more about refugees:

Church World Service, www.churchworldservice.org/resources.html. Refugee Council USA, www.refugeecouncilusa.org.United Nations High Commission on Refugees, www.unhcr.org.

Economically Active Migrants

The majority of people on the move worldwide are categorized by the International Labour Organization (ILO) as "economically active." 214 million strong, they constitute the largest single block of migrant people. Economically active migrants are often contract workers who have an employment agreement with an interested party outside their country and government authorization from both their own country and the host country. Over 50 percent of these are women.[24] They may also be business entrepreneurs.

Unauthorized migrants are also economically active, but less well-tracked, precisely because they are undocumented or only partially so. They may have a passport but not the appropriate visa. In the United States, Border Crossing Cards are issued that permit primarily Mexican and Canadian citizens to enter and leave

---

24   International Labour Organization, "International Labour Organization (ILO) and the 2013 High Level Dialogue on International Migration and Development," p. 3, http://www.un.org/esa/population/meetings/eleventhcoord2013/ILO_Paper_UN_11th_CM_on_Migration_2013_15022013.pdf (accessed June 5, 2014).

daily for work. Many overstay their permits. In 2012, estimates indicate a total of 11.7 million unauthorized immigrants in the United States.[25]

As noted earlier, economically active immigrants, generate a great deal of money, part of which is spent in the country in which they work. US$500 billion worldwide is remitted to home countries annually by overseas workers. If the remittances of unauthorized working people is added, the total is thought to be much higher.[26] These remittances to families in home countries constitute the main source of the national gross domestic product for many countries.

Among the economically active migrants are many Christians, a fact that has been documented by the Filipino International Network working to assist and network Christian Filipinos. Although the numbers are not certainly known, an estimated 6.32 million Americans work outside the United States. The figure may be two to three times higher. The US Census does not count citizens who live outside the country, but that may change.[27] The point we shall make is that economically motivated migrants constitute a powerful global reality with potential for ministry that flows along the lines of commerce. This is true for migrating Christians worldwide, and for those from the United States.

It's not a bed of roses for those who migrate to work. Large numbers of women are moved between countries for sexual exploitation. Many have been tricked by offers of legitimate work in other countries. There are plenty of challenges to be faced by governments that can be and in some cases are being addressed by Christian organizations. The chief problems listed by the ILO and the UN for both international and internal migrants are:

- Human rights violations
- Exploitation and low wages
- Poor working conditions
- Trafficking and sexual abuse
- Violence
- Lack of social protection

---

25 Migration Policy Institute (MPI), "Frequently Requested Statistics on Immigrants and Immigration in the United States," http://www.migrationpolicy.org/article/frequently-requested-statistics-immigrants-and-immigration-united-states#9 (accessed June 5, 2014).
26 International Labour Organization, "International Labour Migration and Development: The ILO Perspective," 2006, http://www.ilo.org (accessed December 5, 2006).
27 The Association of Americans Resident Overseas indicates this figure is an unofficial estimate by the U.S. State Department in late 2011.

- Denial of freedom to associate
- Discrimination, xenophobia[28]

One of the interesting facets that emerge when studying Scriptures for guidance on migration is how often the above difficulties are addressed, especially for foreigners. When Boaz permitted the foreigner, Ruth, to glean in his harvest fields, he instructed the other workers not to abuse her, and he told her precisely where to work (Ruth 2:9,15). This was not only an act of decency, but also in accord with the law in Israel (Deut 24:19–22). Women make up almost half of migrant workers today, so accounts of their protection in Scripture are highly relevant.

Read more about economic migrants:

Filipino International Network, www.fin-online.org. International Labour Organization, www.ilo.org. Luis Pantoja Jr., Sadiri Joy Tira, and Enoch Wan, eds., *Scattered: The Filipino Global Presence* (Manila: LifeChange, 2004).

International Students

Men and women studying abroad are dynamic components of contemporary globalization. Through educational exchanges, ideas, values, and technologies move rapidly to and from all sectors of the globe. An estimated 4 million students worldwide now study outside their own country. Universities in Great Britain supervise the studies of 140,000 students outside the United Kingdom. Australia and New Zealand are deeply engaged in international education.[29] The Technological University of Monterrey, Mexico, has more than 145,000 students studying online throughout Latin America. North American seminaries have considerable components of international students in residence programs and increasingly online around the world.

Over 819,000 foreign students studied in US institutions of higher education in 2013. As in many other countries, Chinese students formed the majority, followed by Koreans, Indians, and Japanese. Their primary interests are in the fields of business

---

28 United Nations Development Agenda, "Integrating Migration in the Post-2015 UN Development Agenda Position Paper," October 2013, http://www.ilo.org/wcmsp5/groups/public/---ed_protect/---protrav/---migrant/documents/genericdocument/wcms_242561.pdf (accessed June 5, 2014).

29 UNESCO Institute for Statistics, "Global Flow of Tertiary-level Students," http://www.uis.unesco.org/Education/Pages/international-student-flow-viz.aspx (accessed June 5, 2014).

management and engineering but include computer science and the biomedical fields.[30] Fifty-eight thousand US students study abroad.

Even though the number of international students seems great, they represent only a fraction of the people from their home countries. But they are very significant, "the cream of the crop." International students who return to their home countries have an impact disproportionate to their numbers. They return to head up government departments and major businesses, spearhead research and development in the sciences, and contribute to the fields of engineering, architecture, and society at large. Some become the presidents, kings, and premiers of their nations.

All do not return. Highly skilled and professional graduates also represent a large portion of permanent immigrants. Twenty million migrants with university or graduate school training live in the thirty well-developed and democratic nations that compose the Organization for Economic Cooperation and Development (OECD). Sixty percent of these migrants were from developing countries.[31] This is what is meant by "the brain drain" that has paralyzed many underdeveloped nations.

Low-income countries suffer disproportionately from the brain drain. In parts of sub-Saharan Africa and Central America, sometimes more than half of all university graduates migrate to OECD countries, with potentially serious consequences for critical sectors such as education, health and engineering.[32]

International travel and study is always a broadening experience. It is also more likely to become a vital, routinely anticipated component of US student development. Study abroad can even be a life-changing experience. Many non-Western students who knew little or nothing about Christianity while in their home country become Christians during their student days overseas. International Students Incorporated gives assistance and spiritual guidance to thousands of foreign students in North America. University-oriented ministries like Campus Crusade and InterVarsity Christian Fellowship as well as individual evangelical churches have significant ministries to international students.

International students, like other migrants, are either the *vehicles* or the *objects* of God's grace. The believers among them have a strategic impact for Christ in the

---

30   Institute of International Education, "International Education Matters," *Open Doors* 2005 Report, www.udel.edu/iepmedia/economy_opendoors05.html (accessed December 1, 2006).
31   UN International Migration and Development, "International Migration Facts and Figures," 2006, http://www.unmigration.org.
32   Organisation for Economic Co-operation and Development, "Migration and the Brain Drain Phenomenon," http://www.oecd.org/social/poverty/migrationandthebraindrainphenomenon.htm (accessed June 5, 2014).

countries where they study or settle. Those who are not believers have marvelous opportunities to investigate the claims of Christianity, often in a more open atmosphere than would have been possible at home.

Read more about international students:

Institute of International Education, "Open Doors 2014 Report," http://www.iie.org/en/Research-and-Publications/Open-Doors/Data/International-Students/Fields-of-Study/2011-13. International Students Incorporated, www.isionline.org.

Nomads

Nomads are a significant component of migrating peoples worldwide. They are an estimated 30 million in number.[33] They are marginalized in most of the countries where they are found, but taken together have a population smaller than only five nations. They range in percentage of population from 10 percent of the population in Ethiopia to 40 percent in Mongolia.[34]

Historically, nomads have influenced the formation or destruction of nations in Asia, the Middle East, and Africa.[35] They remain peoples of consequence, even though their number is being reduced by shrinking access to pasturelands; the encroachment of mechanized, technological cultures; and more sedentary forms of agriculture. Nomads differ from other migrants in that mobility is an ongoing aspect of their lives, as they move in seasonal cycles.

Nomadic peoples like the Fulbe, Turkana, and Masai predominate across the Sahel, a semiarid swath of land stretching from West Africa to the eastern Horn of Africa, on the southern border of the Sahara Desert. North of the Sahara, Berber Arabs still maintain a seminomadic life. Arab Bedouins move along the borders of the Saudi Arabian desert. Two layers of nomadic peoples, like the Inuits and Sami, inhabit the entire Arctic from northern Canada to Finland through Russia, and across the Central Asian steppe including the former Russian republics, the Tibetan region of China, and Mongolia.

---

33 The exact numbers of nomadic pastoralists can only be an estimate by the nature of their mobile existence. "Nomadic People World-wide," https://maps.google.com/maps/ms?ie=UTF8&t=m&msa+0&msid=210679661112179870040.0004bf3ca1f5f363c45df&dg=feature (accessed June 5, 2014; page discontinued).

34 Stefan Rhys-Williams, "Educating Nomads: Ethiopia's Afar and the Fight for Learning," Institute of Opinion, http://www.instituteofopinion.com/2013/11/educating-nomads-ethiopias-afar-and-the-fight-for-learning/; *Wikipedia*, s.v. "Mongolia," http://en.wikipedia.org/wiki/Mongolia (accessed June 5, 2014).

35 Victor Azarya, *Nomads and the State in Africa* (Aldershot, UK: Avebury-Ashgate, 1996), 4, 87.

Self-sufficiency is the chief identifying characteristic of all nomad groups. They are able to make systematic use of resources that are too difficult or too distasteful for others to utilize. Secondarily, their identity is closely related to their herds, in the case of nomadic pastoralists, or their trade in metal work, music, or entertaining among other peripatetic nomads like Gypsies (Romani) or "travelers" in Europe. Nomads may be periodically sedentary for reasons of drought, pastureland failure, war, or the provision of essential resources in a central location. A large part of their identity is tied to the idea that they *could* move at any time. Mobility is a preferred lifestyle for nomads. Generally, their movement is quite systematic.

The mobility of nomads poses challenges for traditional ministry to them. Malcolm Hunter has quoted African nomadic herders as telling him, "When you can get your Church on the back of a camel then I will think that Christianity is meant for Somalis."[36] Later we shall see the kinds of ministries that currently are having an impact among nomadic peoples. Indigenous movements to Christ among Gypsies are encouraging. In Spain alone, the Filadelfia Movement composed entirely of Romani Gypsies numbers some 200,000 believers.[37]

According to 120 pastoralist leaders from twenty-three countries at the Global Pastoralist Gathering of February 2006 organized by the United Nations, "The biggest concern was the loss of traditional rights to grazing land." They also expressed concern for access to education, health care, safe water, markets, economic progress, and legal protection.[38] These challenges are stepping-stones to ministry among nomadic peoples. There is evidence that such ministry is already being carried out by Christian agencies such as World Vision, International Justice Mission, Lifewater International, and a number of other Christian and secular NGOs.

Read more about nomads:

David J. Phillips, *Introducing the Nomads of the World* (Pasadena: William Carey Library, 2001). The Commission on Nomadic Peoples, http://users.ox.ac.uk/~cncp/. The Center for the Study of Eurasian Nomads, www.csen.org. Ahmed Kemil, Mary Fallon, and Doug Fallon, *A Nomad in Two Worlds*, Amazon Kindle, 2013.

---

36   Phillips, xiii.
37   Jason Mandryk, ed. "Spain," *Operation World*, 7th ed. (Downers Grove, IL: InterVarsity Press, 2010), http://www.hopemissiontrips.com/files/hopemissiontrips/International%20Information/spai.pdf (accessed June 5, 2014).
38   Afrol News, "Nomadic Pastoralists Meet in Addis Ababa," December 28, 2006, http://afrol.com/articles/15594 (accessed December 29, 2006).

The Causes of Migration

What causes people to migrate? The answers are as varied and complex as people themselves, but Philip Martin puts it down to *differences* between the migrant's original living context and the one towards which he or she is moving. "International migration is a result of demographic, economic and other differences between countries. These differences are widening, promising more international migration in the 21st Century."[39]

Martin divides the dynamics into *economic* and *non-economic* forces. Economic causes relate to labor supply and demand. Developed countries need and recruit labor from less developed countries where low wages or unemployment combined with agricultural failures make life untenable. The economic difference between two countries constitutes the "push" to migrate as well as the "pull." Mexican and Central American migration to North America and Pakistani contract workers in the United Arab Emirates are examples of *economic* dynamics.

Non-economic causes include flight from war zones, persecution, family reunification, and even adventure.[40] Always, a negative condition in one area *pushes* the migrant, and a more positive situation in the destination country *pulls* the migrant. Cubans in Miami or Sudanese in Chad and Burmese in Thailand are examples of flight from fear.

Others have divided the main causes of migration into the *security dimension* and the *economic dimension*.[41] Security factors include natural disasters, conflicts, threats to individual safety, and poor political prospects. Economic factors include a poor economic situation or a poor market in one country countered by better circumstances in another.[42]

Demographic factors enter into the equation. The direction of migration flows is almost always from an area of greater population density and higher birthrate to one of lesser population density. But the flow may also be from more rural areas with fewer jobs to more urban zones having greater employment possibilities.

Once a migration flow has been established, factors like communication media, availability of transportation, family members, friends, or community members

---

39   Philip Martin, Manolo Abella, and Christine Kuptsch, *Managing Labor Migration in the 21st Century* (New Haven, CT: Yale University Press, 2006), 9.
40   Ibid., 7.
41   *Wikipedia*, s.v. "Human Migration," http://en_wikipedia.org/wiki/Human_migration (accessed December 29, 2006).
42   Ibid.

who have migrated and serve as a network, help the migrant and encourage further migration.

Barriers to migration may be legal, logistical, or social. Barriers may be the dangers of the Atlantic Ocean for sub-Saharan Africans, the proposed wall across parts of the southern United States, rigorous enforcement of laws against undocumented immigrants in border states, or public hostility to migrants. What has become evident from several studies is that none of these barriers in the long term effectively impede migration where the individual or family is desperate.[43] Perhaps this is because forces larger than human motivation or resistance are at work.

Secular and Christian Opinions on Migration

As levels of migration have risen, antipathy towards migrants has increased. This can be seen in response to Muslim youth demonstrations in France during the summer of 2006 and towards Hispanic youth marches in favor of legalization of unauthorized immigrants in many United States cities in Spring 2006 and mixed response to the arrival of thousands of unaccompanied, undocumented minors in 2013–14. Sadly, only 7 percent of US adults surveyed in 2010 by the Pew Foundation said their faith affected what they believed about immigration. Personal experience, education, and the media all had greater impact on the public's thinking.[44] Fifty-five percent said that even legal immigration should be reduced.

So what are churches doing about immigration? The Church World Service has placed 450,000 refugees through churches in the United States since its founding in 1947.[45] The Chicago Council on Global Affairs in its Survey 2012 found Americans had become more favorable to immigrants over a period of twelve years and viewed immigrants as less of a threat than they did in 2002.[46] It is gratifying to see evangelical leaders advocating for comprehensive immigration reform through the Evangelical Immigration Table. Representatives including church and seminary leaders have personally met repeatedly with members of Congress urging them to enact a more

---

43   Francisco Checa and A. Arjona, *Las Migraciones a Debate: De las Teorias a las Practicas sociales* [The Debate about Migration: From Theories to Social Practice] (Barcelona: Institut Catala d'Anthropologia-Icaria, 2002), 5; and Cohen, among others.
44   Pew Research Center, "Catholics, Other Christians Support Immigration Reform, But Say Faith Plays Small Role," April 1, 2014, http://www.pewresearch.org/fact-tank/2014/04/01/catholics-other-christians-support-immigration-reform-but-say-faith-plays-small-role/.
45   *Wikipedia*, s.v. "Church World Service," http://en.wikipedia.org/wiki/Church_World_Service; see also Church World Service, http://www.cwsglobal.org.
46   The Chicago Council on Global Affairs, http://www.thechicagocouncil.org/UserFiles/File/Trade Force Reports/2012_CSS_ImmigrationBrief.pdf (accessed July 31, 2014; page discontinued).

just and comprehensive immigration policy. The Table's "I Was a Stranger" Challenge seeks to inform and encourage Christians to let the spirit of the Scriptures rule their thinking and response to immigration.

The heart of why evangelical Christians believe we should love, welcome, and seek justice for immigrants is our commitment to the authority of Scripture over every aspect of our lives. The Bible speaks clearly and repeatedly to God's concern for the immigrant, guiding the Christ-follower toward principles that we believe should inform both the interpersonal ways that we interact with our immigrant neighbors and the public policies that we support.[47]

At the global level, the World Evangelical Alliance, in addition to its initiatives to combat human trafficking, began the Refugee Highway Partnership (www.refugeehighway.net) linking churches and agencies around the world in concrete efforts to assist refugees and asylum seekers.[48]

Daniel Carroll Rojas has urged evangelicals to "think Christianly about immigration," and supplied the scriptural tools to do so.[49]

Conclusion

Does it matter what you think about global migration? Understanding any phenomenon promotes positive engagement. Faced with the momentous nature of global migration, ignorance is not an option. It is possible to allow history to pass us by while we complain about what makes us uncomfortable. We can and should be the instruments of God to respond to people in a movement that, in spite of its many challenges and hurts, God is using to draw men and women to himself.

The objective of this paper has been to present the facts about global migration; identify the various kinds of migrants and their contexts and challenges from a human perspective; later search the Scriptures for the principles that apply to migratory movements in history; and urge the adoption of appropriate attitudes, policies, and ministries to people on the move in North America and around the globe. It's time to discover where we stand!

---

47 Evangelical Immigration Table, "I Was a Stranger," http://evangelicalimmigrationtable.com/iwasastranger/; Religious News Service, "One More Time, Evangelicals Head to Hill in Immigration Reform," April 29, 2014, http://www.religionnews.com/2014/04/29/one-time-evangelicals-head-hill-immigration-reform/#comment-113818 (accessed July 31, 2014).

48 For example, World Evangelical Alliance, "Refugee Sunday 2009 Resource Pack," June 21, 2009, http://refugeehighway.net/downloads/wrs/refugee_sunday_resource_pack_complete.pdf.

49 M. Daniel Carroll R., *Thinking Christianly about Immigration* (Denver: Vernon Grounds Institute of Public Ethics, 2011). See also by same author, *Christians at the Border: Immigration, the Church and the Bible* (2008; repr., Grand Rapids: Brazos, 2012).

Discussion

With which specific categories of people on the move have you had personal contact? Under what circumstances?

In your context or community, which migratory category of people is deemed most controversial? Why?

In your experience, are you aware of Christian believers among the various categories of migrant people? In what context did you meet them?

Regardless of their religious persuasion, can you cite one or more human or spiritual virtues in a non-native-born person with whom you have had contact that have been instructive to you? How were these manifest?

How would you characterize your own response to those from other countries and cultures? Admiration? Interaction? Helpful? Fearful? Angry? Rejecting? Why?

Chapter Two

Mapping the Diaspora with Facebook

TREVOR CASTOR

ABSTRACT

This chapter demonstrates the efficiency of Facebook as an ethnographic field site and a migration-mapping tool. Computer-mediated communication is the primary medium for transnational practices of diaspora peoples. This virtual space is often where transnational identity is constructed through contesting, reinforcing, and renegotiating sociocultural boundary markers. These digital diasporas maintain a sense of collective belonging through frequent virtual returns to the homeland. Consequently, ethnic and nationalistic boundaries are broadened and relocalized. In addition to cultural insights, Facebook's new Graph Search allows users to search the more than 1.2 billion user social graph based on linguistic, ethnic, national, and religious identifiers. Users have a vested interest in keeping an up-to-date and accurate profile in order to be found and find others in the social network. This user profile information is public data and likely more current than other data used in migration mapping.

Introduction

A friend and five companions were planning a three-week trip to a West European city. The purpose was to conduct an ethnographic survey and find unreached people groups (UPGs) in the diaspora. This is standard practice in Christian missions but not the most efficient. Mapping a city in three weeks is costly, not to mention the fact that there are numerous cities to cover. This paper demonstrates a more efficient way forward via Facebook (FB). It will review current literature on immigrant social media practices, evaluate the context of virtual space, and discuss the significance of social media for the diaspora. Finally, through a step-by-step process, it will demonstrate how to use FB's Graph Search to find out exactly where diasporic UPGs live.

Virtual Scouting on Facebook

The advantage of a virtual scouting trip is that it draws from data already available on social media. In this arena, FB reigns supreme: with 1.2 billion users from over two hundred countries,[1] it is the second most visited Internet site, surpassed only by Google. If FB were a country, it would be the third largest and most diverse on earth. Of the seventy FB languages, Portuguese is growing fastest, followed by Arabic, German, Spanish, Indonesian, and Chinese.[2] This transnational landscape makes the world smaller as indicated by a recent study: within the FB social graph, there are only four degrees of separation between any two random users in the world. In other words, when considering another person in the world, oftentimes a friend of your friend knows a friend of their friend.[3]

FB is particularly useful for the diaspora, who, due to their transnational identity, need to stay connected with their social networks in their country of origin while simultaneously forming new social networks among the fellow dispersed.[4] Case in point: a recent Pew study shows that 73 percent of Latino-American Internet users are also on social media, primarily through FB (2013).

Digital diasporas often use virtual transnational social space to reinforce, contest, and renegotiate culture in order to create individual and collective identities.[5] In contrast to online forums and gaming, these virtual communities are primarily anchored in physical communities. Most research concludes that online social networks reinforce existing relationships, serving as a means to strengthen offline relationships in an online setting.[6] Certainly, this is true of the diaspora who generally "have an existing real network of relationships and grounded community before employing the Internet to connect with one another and build their digital communities."[7]

---

1 Alexa, "How Popular Is Facebook.com?," http://www.alexa.com/siteinfo/facebook.com (accessed December 12, 2013).
2 Socialbakers, "Top 10 Fastest Growing Facebook Languages," http://www.socialbakers.com/blog/1064-top-10-fastest-growing-facebook-languages (accessed March 14, 2014).
3 Lars Backstrom, Paolo Boldi, Marco Rosa, Johan Ugander, and Sebastiano Vigna, "Four Degrees of Separation," in *Proceedings of the 3rd Annual ACM Web Science Conference* (Evanston, IL, 2012), 33–42.
4 Andoni Alonso and Pedro J. Oiarzabal, eds., *Diasporas in the New Media Age: Identity, Politics, and Community* (Reno: University of Nevada Press, 2010).
5 Jennifer Brinkerhoff, *Digital Diasporas: Identity and Transnational Engagement* (New York: Cambridge University Press, 2009).
6 Francisco Javier Pérez-Latre, Ioia Portilla, and Cristina Sanchez-Blanco, "Social Networks, Media and Audiences: A Literature Review," *Comunicación y Sociedad* 24, no. 1 (2011): 63–74.
7 Padmini Banerjee and Myna German, "Migration and Transculturation in the Digital Age: A Framework for Studying the Space Between," *Journal of International and Global Studies* 2, no. 1 (2010): 23–35.

Given diaspora social media practices, it is feasible to create a virtual social network of UPGs without ever leaving home. Developing a cultural map, or surveying the land, is essentially what missionaries have always done on scouting trips or vision trips. The main difference in a virtual scouting trip is that the data, which normally takes weeks if not months to gather, can be gathered in minutes by data mining one of the world's largest data sets. Data mining FB in order to locate and learn about unreached people groups should be an initial step in diaspora mission strategies.

Admittedly, groups like the Joshua Project, International Mission Board (IMB), and Global Mapping International (GMI) are identifying UPGs. But since they only provide demographics at a country level, much time and money is spent obtaining precise locations. For example, the Joshua Project lists ninety-five UPGs in the UK. Additionally, the IMB informs us of 2,500 Berbers in the UK, but where exactly are they? Demographics provided by these groups do not provide geographical precision. Neither do they include details about international students. FB, on the other hand, can map diaspora UPGs in most cities, provide a list of restaurants they frequent, and even tell what schools international students attended. Finally, given transnational mobility, statistics by these groups are often outdated, whereas FB tends to be more current as users have a vested interest in maintaining current profiles.

Transnational Theoretical Framework

The perception of an immigrant uprooting themselves from their homeland, family, and culture and learning a new language in order to make a new life in their country of settlement is no longer sufficient.[8] Rather, they often maintain extensive social networks in their homeland, creating a "fluid continuum rather than a radical divide compartmentalizing life into two separated worlds."[9] Transnationalism or transnational migration "is the process by which immigrants forge and sustain simultaneous multi-stranded social relations that link their societies of origin and settlement."[10] "While back-and-forth immigrant movements have always existed,

---

8 Linda Basch, Nina Glick Schiller, and Christina Blanc-Szanton, eds., *Nations Unbound: Transnational Projects, Postcolonial Predicaments, and Deterritorialized Nation-states* (New York: Routledge, 1994).
9 Fernando Lima, "Transnational Families: Institutions of Transnational Social Space," in *New Transnational Social Spaces: International Migration and Transnational Companies in the Early Twenty-first Century*, ed. Ludger Pries (New York: Routledge, 2001), 77–93.
10 Nina Schiller, Linda Basch, and Cristina Blanc-Szanton, "From Immigrant to Transmigrant: Theorizing Transnational Migration," *Anthropological Quarterly* 68, no. 1 (1995): 48–63.

they have not acquired until recently the critical mass and complexity necessary to speak of an emergent social field."[11]

For much of the world, technology is rapidly becoming the primary way of communicating,[12] especially in the diaspora, who often use virtual space to renegotiate identity.[13] Bernal refers to the Internet as the "quintessential diasporic medium, ideally suited to allowing migrants in diverse locations to connect, share information and analyses, and coordinate their activities."[14] Thus ethnographic research should utilize a multi-sited approach, combining digital and physical field sites. Combining the online and offline worlds in ethnography may provide a richer account than either can provide on its own.[15] This can be accomplished through participant observation of virtual space, such as social media and ethnic forums, coupled with field research.

Social Media and Diaspora Literature

Digital diasporas often use computer-mediated communication as a virtual vehicle to return home. This virtual transnational social space allows digital diaspora peoples to create an imagined community[16] by broadening the boundary markers of ethnic, national, and collective identities.[17] Alonso and Oiarzabal define digital diasporas as "the distinct online networks that diasporic people use to recreate identities, share opportunities, spread their culture, influence homeland and host-land policy, or create debate about common-interest issues by means of electronic devices."[18] The Internet is a cheap and effective medium to maintain and develop cross-border social networks. A personal computer and the Internet are regular resources for transnationals, who "constitute webs of informational exchange and transfers of knowledge in both the physical and digital world."[19]

---

11 Alejandro Portes, Luis Guarnizo, and Patricia Landolt, "The Study of Transnationalism: Pitfalls and Promise of an Emergent Research Field," *Ethnic and Racial Studies* 22, no. 2 (1999): 217–37.
12 Dhiraj Murthy, "Digital Ethnography: An Examination of the Use of New Technologies for Social Research," *Sociology* 42, no. 5 (2008): 837–55.
13 Alonso and Oiarzabal, *Diasporas*; Brinkerhoff, *Digital Diasporas*.
14 Victoria Bernal, "Diaspora, Cyberspace and Political Imagination: The Eritrean Diaspora Online," *Global Networks* 6, no. 2 (2006): 175.
15 Murthy, "Digital Ethnography."
16 Bendict Anderson, *Imagined Communities: Reflections on the Origin and Spread of Nationalism* (1983; repr., London: Verso, 2006).
17 Bernal, "The Eritrean Diaspora Online."
18 Alonso and Oiarzabal, *Diasporas*, 11.
19 Ibid., 6.

Context of Virtual Spaces

Virtual transnational social space not only provides a medium for sharing information, but also a "forum for renegotiating and reinforcing diaspora identity."[20] The context of this forum is nonhierarchical, noncoercive, and may be anonymous, allowing participants to test liberal values and discuss topics otherwise culturally taboo.[21] That fact alone has important missiological implications: a social space without fear of government control, or personal danger, may quickly reveal persons of peace or community gatekeepers. Creating a FB group and monitoring discussions may unearth truth seekers.

The Internet also provides a global public sphere where unequal power relationships can be marginalized and magnified.[22] That is, gender and age can be veiled in a virtual setting, providing a place for women and youth. Without it, they may not feel free to participate. The unequal power relationship of income level and education, on the other hand, is harder to hide. Internet access tells something about social status, and the "digital divide"[23] must be taken into account when researching transnational virtual social space.

Imagined Virtual Communities

Additionally, the Internet provides social space "to sustain and re-create diasporas as globally imagined communities."[24] Although these communities are virtual, their intention is the transformation of the real world.[25] As noted above, most relationships on social media sites are supported by a "common offline element."[26] These digital diaspora communities utilize a variety of ways to reinforce collective identity, like social media, blogs, and forums. This identity exists within the actual community back home and among the fellow dispersed. Issa-Salwe differentiates virtual diaspora communities from typical virtual communities: "Generally, the shared identity, born of a virtual community, is temporal. A group of Somalis, for instance, using CMC [computer mediated communication] may create a virtual community, but it has

---

20   Brinkerhoff, *Digital Diasporas*, 235.
21   Ibid.
22   Jose Benitez, "Transnational Dimensions of the Digital Divide among Salvadoran Immigrants in the Washington DC Metropolitan Area," *Global Networks* 6 (2006): 181–99.
23   Ibid.
24   Alonso and Oiarzabal, *Diasporas*, 9.
25   Martin Sökefeld, "Alevism Online: Re-imagining a Community in Virtual Space," *Diaspora: A Journal of Transnational Studies* 11, no. 1 (2002): 5–38.
26   Dana Boyd and Nicole Ellison, "Social Network Sites: Definition, History, and Scholarship," *Journal of Computer Mediated Communication* 13, no. 1 (2007): 210–30.

another relationship: "a specific group identity—one, in turn, backed by the real world (or offline relationships)."[27] Research shows how activities and discussions of the virtual Somali community impacted the actual Somali community in real time and space. The Internet served as the vehicle for enforcing cultural homogeneity and the fragmentation of Somali society through political and social divisions.[28]

Similarly, Tynes observed as diaspora Sierra Leoneans created a "virtual nation— any community that communicates in cyberspace, whose collective discourse and/ or actions are aimed towards the building, binding, maintenance, rebuilding or rebinding a nation."[29] Diaspora Sierra Leoneans, through an online ethnic forum, Leonenet, effectively used virtual space to impact geographically bound Sierra Leoneans. After over a decade of civil war, Sierra Leone's government institutions were either ineffective or nonexistent. So the diaspora used online social space to generate, negotiate, and maintain ideas about Sierra Leonean identity. Ultimately, government structures were reinstituted and able to act on ideas generated online. Strangely enough, the virtual nation came first, and then the real nation.

Yabiladi ("my country" in Arabic) provides a parallel forum for Moroccan diaspora. This is the virtual space where the dispersed forge a sense of national belonging. Members use the forum to share struggles in their host societies as well as homeland memories. Talking about returning home someday, for example, helps them cope with feelings of displacement. Shared feelings of the dispersed provide a sense of identity that is being reconstructed through renegotiating aspects of Moroccan culture.[30]

Delocalized or Relocalized

A longing for home is the defining characteristic among diaspora. The Internet provides a virtual return that is often sufficient for maintaining a sense of collective identity. While the Internet is essentially delocalized, and often disembodied, this is not the case for the diaspora. Diasporic virtual space is typically "anchored in

---

27   Abdisalam M. Issa-Salwe, "The Internet and the Somali Diaspora: The Web as a Means of Expression," *Bildhaan: An International Journal of Somali Studies* 6, no. 8 (2008): 54–67.
28   Ibid.
29   Robert Tynes, "Nation-building and the Diaspora on Leonenet: A Case of Sierra Leone in Cyberspace," *New Media and Society* 9, no. 3 (2007): 497–518.
30   Amina Loukili, "Moroccan Diaspora, Internet and National Imagination: Building a Community Online through the Internet Portal Yabiladi" (paper presented at Nordic Africa Days, Nordic Africa Institute, Uppsala, Sweden, October 5–7, 2007).

offline contexts, rather than self-contained, disembodied universe."[31] Such was the case of Iranian diaspora who used virtual space to negotiate Iranianness, and at the same time form "mobile and dynamic, yet sustained, emotional connections to two distant and bounded nation-states."[32] The negative media coverage of Iran, and disillusionment with American Iranianness, led many to create an online diaspora community. This transnational community was embodied in memory, shaped by offline experiences, and rooted in geographical bounded territories of Iran and the United States. Transnational online identity is a pattern for the diaspora as they re-territorialize living space, often blending the old and the new.[33]

Some argue that transnationalism and digital diasporas reduce boundaries and move society towards a global identity in a borderless world.[34] Bernal disagrees. Her research among Eritrean diaspora reveals expanding boundaries, suggesting "what might have once been outside the margins (of the nation) is now more effectively included within a larger framework of imagined community."[35] She even suggests that the transnational nature and influence of online diaspora qualify them to be an "offshore citizenry or extension of the nation."[36]

Conclusion

"The Internet provides users with instantaneous and unlimited opportunities to connect with other users across both borders and frontiers and exchange information."[37] This "virtual space is a realm in which physical space, both proximity and distance, is of no importance."[38] Through digital social space diasporas try to renegotiate sociocultural features and basic value orientations that serve as ethnic and nationalistic boundary markers, essentially reconstructing a transnational identity. The Internet is often the context for renegotiating dynamic relationships between

---

31   Matthijs Van den Bos and Liza Nell, "Territorial Bounds to Virtual Space: Transnational Online and Offline Networks of Iranian and Turkish-Kurdish Immigrants in the Netherlands," *Global Networks* 6, no. 2 (2006): 201–20.
32   Donya Alinejad, "Mapping Homelands through Virtual Spaces: Iranian Diaspora Bloggers," *Global Networks* 11, no. 1 (2001): 43–62.
33   Javier Bustamant, "Tidelike Diasporas in Brazil: From Slavery to Orkut," in *Diasporas in the New Media Age: Identity, Politics, and Community*, ed. Adoni Alonso and Pedro J. Oiarzabal (Reno: University of Nevada Press, 2010), 170–89.
34   Arjun Appadurai, "Global Ethnoscapes: Notes and Queries for a Transnational Anthropology," in *Recapturing Anthropology*, ed. Richard Fox (Santa Fe, NM: School of American Research Press, 1991), 191–210.
35   Bernal, "The Eritrean Diaspora Online."
36   Ibid.
37   Banerjee and German, "Migration and Transculturation," 26.
38   Sökefeld, "Alevism Online," 111.

religion, culture, and politics.[39] Digital diaspora activity does not diminish ethnic boundaries or national borders. Instead, it tends to reinforce collective identity, territoriality, ethnicity, and nationalism,[40] and may even broaden its scope.[41] Through virtual returns the diaspora maintain significant influence in their homeland. The literature suggests that digital diaspora communities are anchored in two worlds via the Internet, with FB by far the largest platform for mediating transnational social space.

Facebook's Graph Search

Considering the value of social media to the diaspora, FB's latest innovation, Graph Search, has unique qualities. According to Zuckerberg, it will be a "pillar" of the company. Engineering director Lars Rasmussen puts it this way:

> In the past, Facebook has really been primarily about mapping out and staying in touch with and communicating with the people you already know in the real world. But now, we're building a product that can also be used in finding people maybe you should know.[42]

Finding people we *should know* are what scouting trips are intended to achieve. So how can Graph Search help us? Some FB user information is public: "name, profile pictures, cover photos, gender, networks, username and User ID . . . along with your age range, language and country." Searching this information, along with whatever other information is made public, FB can aggregate a list of people you should know. It does it by using a natural language query function to perform searches that are different from Google's keyword-based searches. Simply put, you search by asking questions like you would naturally to another human. Moreover, FB's searches relate to people, meaning users can generate helpful information based on certain criteria. For example, would you like to know what people in your city read the Qur'an? Would you like to know what restaurants these people frequent? How

---

39 Mark Graham and Shahram Khosravi, "Reordering Public and Private in Iranian Cyberspace: Identity, Politics, and Mobilization," *Identities: Global Studies in Culture and Power* 9, no. 2 (2002): 219–46; Rizwangul Nur-Muhammad, Giles Dodson, Evangelia Papoutsaki, and Heather Horst, "Uyghur Facebook Use and Diasporic Identity Construction," IAMCR 2013 Conference, Dublin, June 25–29, 2013; Sökefeld, "Alevism Online."
40 Van den Bos and Nell, "Territorial Bounds."
41 Bernal, "The Eritrean Diaspora Online."
42 Facebook, 2014.

about the mosque they attend? What about the languages spoken by people that live nearby? How about Africans and Asians in your city, or international students attending your local college? Finally, how about the city with the largest community of a specific diaspora people group? With Graph Search and a little tutoring, you can quickly find answers to these questions.

Method 1: Locating a people group

Step 1: Create a new FB account but do not give any profile information

Performing a Graph Search with your existing FB account will skew results. No two searches will be identical, because results generated are weighted, based on your profile and existing social network. For example, when I search "Turkish speakers" using my personal account, the results are listed in the following order:

First, current friends who speak Turkish.

Second, those who speak Turkish and with whom I share at least one friendship.

Third, the rest of FB listing Turkish as a language.

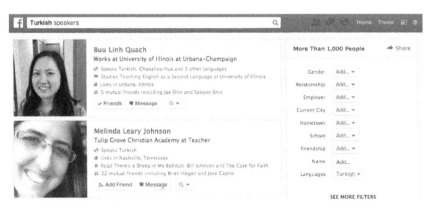

Even if you start with a clean profile, results can still be skewed as FB maintains information based on prior searches, and is aware of your location based on your Internet Protocol (IP) address. The IP address of the computer or mobile device you use to log in provides FB information about your location at a city level even if not in your profile. Thus your searches may be weighted based on your suspected location.

Step 2: Search by language

Type the language into the search bar and visit the language page to see how many FB users speak that language. "Fulani" in the search bar reveals 470,000 Fulani speakers. The "470,000 users speak this" is a link (see below), so click it and FB will aggregate a list of 470,000 Fulani speakers.

Step 3: Refine the list to countries

Type in: "Countries that Fulani speakers live in." A list is generated, accompanied by an impressive Bing map tagging forty-five countries. This map is a place to start but not an exhaustive list of Fulani-speaking host countries; in fact, it seems to be randomly selected. The countries are not displayed in any particular order, but you can easily check each country to see those with the largest Fulani populations. Click "Fulani speakers" under each country to see one of the following: "Less Than 100 People," "More Than 100 People," or "More Than 1,000 People."

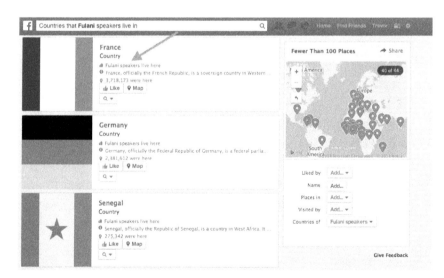

Unfortunately, for now FB does not provide an exact count. Current demographics provided by the IMB suggest a large Fulani diaspora in France. FB confirms this and also lists large groups in Canada, the United States, Italy, Belgium, and the UK. After choosing a country with a sizable diaspora, determine the country of origin to ensure you are identifying the right people. To do this, click "hometown" in the "refine your search" box. A drop-down list appears, giving countries of origin for diaspora groups. Belgium has over a thousand Fulani speakers from Senegal, Mauritania, and Guinea, but most are from Guinea.

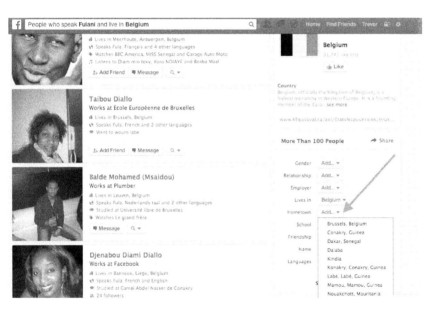

Step 4: Refine the list to cities

After determining a country with a significant diaspora, and finding where that group comes from, you can refine the search to cities within the country. For example, type in "cities in Belgium that Fulani speakers live in," and a list of cities will be generated. Again, this is not exhaustive or weighted on population, but you can manually check each city to find the one with most people.

Step 5: Start building your social network and collecting data

After choosing a city, begin building a social network and try to befriend a few Fulani speakers. FB will aggregate and recommend friends. These networks are very homogenous, and you will soon become part of the digital diaspora community. In order to collect data, here are a few possible search phrases: "Mosques in Belgium liked by Fulani speakers" or "Mosques in Belgium visited by Fulani speakers." By typing in "people who like [*name of the mosque*] and live in Belgium," your search will aggregate a fairly accurate depiction of mosque members.

"Restaurants that Fulani speakers visited in Belgium"

"Places in Belgium visited by Fulani speakers"

"Groups that Fulani speakers who live in Belgium belong to"

Each of these queries will reveal helpful information about the community you wish to locate. Also, remember people's networks are public information. In other words, the following query can aggregate an important list: "Friends of [*person's name*] that live in Belgium." All this reveals how networked someone is within the diaspora of a particular city and, again, could lead to persons of peace or gatekeepers in the community.

Method 2: Mapping a City

The easiest way to map a city is to begin searching spoken languages. So, for example, type in "Languages spoken by people who live in Columbia, South Carolina" (see appendix 2). This will give you an idea of the linguistic diversity of any global city. Once this is aggregated, click the link to see how many turn up. That said, not everyone puts a language in his or her profile, but you can move beyond language. FB can refine searches by religion, but few include this in their profile. They may, however, publicly like a religious text, such as the Qur'an. In fact, on FB, Islam is liked 2.9 million times, whereas the Qur'an is liked 12 million times. Now type "people in [*city*] who like the Qur'an," and this will help locate the Muslim population.

You can also search by continent of origin: "People from Africa who live in Columbia, South Carolina" generates of over one thousand from Angola, Zimbabwe, Burkina Faso, Nigeria, Liberia, Cameroon, Morocco, Ethiopia, Cote d'Ivoire, Egypt, Nigeria, Senegal, Sierra Leone, Libya, Uganda, Botswana, Ghana, etc. (see appendix 3). "People from Asia who live in Columbia, South Carolina" yields over one thousand: Pakistan, Afghanistan, Philippines, China, Syria, India, Bangladesh, Lebanon, Saudi Arabia, Turkey, etc.

Limitations of Graph Search

Admittedly, FB has limitations. For example, there is no way to verify the information is true. There is, however, little reason to lie as to language, current city, or country of origin, because misrepresentation makes it hard to connect with others. FB takes information users provide in order to suggest potential friends. Nevertheless, there are some who claim to speak thousands of languages. Take Mr. Benson, who claims to speak Wolio as well as 9,792 other languages, including Harry Potter!

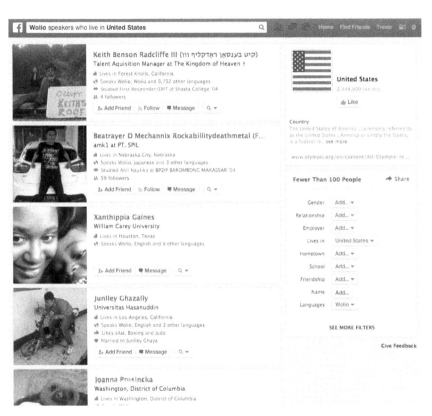

In addition to those who willfully misrepresent facts, some unwittingly give false information. For instance, according to FB, there is a small community of Pashtuns living in Dera, Democratic Republic of Congo. Upon further investigation it is clear users checked their current city as Dera, assuming it was Dera Ismail Khan, Pakistan—not Congo. When searches return peculiar results, there is reason to double-check.

Some languages like Pashto and Iraqi Arabic will include Westerners in the aggregated list. Generally they are military personnel who did tours in Afghanistan or Iraq and who add this to their profiles. Similarly, former missionaries and missionary children will show up as anomalies in aggregated lists, but these are few and do not skew data enough to discredit the method. Also, it should be noted that up to 10 percent of FB users are fake accounts.[43]

Another limitation is that not all FB users list language in profile settings, and this method is highly dependent on language preferences. Furthermore, even though FB is continually adding languages, some smaller dialects are missing. In fact, some languages that should be distinct are merged. Southern Pashto, Central Pashto, and Northern Pashto are combined into Pashto. Similarly, Dari and Farsi are joined into Persian.

But such language mergers are likely temporary because, since beginning this research, FB has already added more languages and differentiated between smaller languages once grouped together. Case in point: Berber now has the following dialects on FB: Kabyle, Rif, Tachelhit, Tamasheq, Shawia, Amazigh, and Nafusi (see appendix 1).

Potentially the most significant drawback of Graph Search as a mapping tool is a limited display of search results. Some searches give too much data for FB's map interface to display, forcing a manual check of data, so a script or plug-in must be written to specifically data mine FB's data sets of language and cities. This enables users to map current cities with the largest diaspora concentrations. Using FB's "More Than 1,000 People" category is a good beginning. And, as stated, knowing precisely where UPGs live will have a significant impact in mission studies.

---

43 Peter Aspinall, "Commentary on 'Trending Now,'" *Journal of Public Health* 36, no. 4 (January 12, 2014): 535–36.

Final limitations of Graph Search include the following: it is only in English, and it is not yet compatible with mobile devices. But the infrastructure of Graph Search is constantly being updated and indexing trillions of connections is a multiyear project, according to Zuckerberg. Though current methods may not always work, the idea of using FB as a migration-mapping tool will probably not change. Search indexes should become increasingly intuitive and more accurate and keep on expanding.

In addition to the quality of data collected, there are some concerns as to ethics, privacy, and consent of FB. That said, the methodology described above will help missiologists test current demographic information and build on it. Graph Search can find participants based on linguistic, ethnic, national, and religious identifiers. On a more practical level, FB reveals where people live and their numbers. Finally, it shows what UPGs are currently within one degree of separation—friends of their friends. Shrink the world by using the preceding method to map a people group. Completing the task of reaching UPGs with the gospel from every language may be closer than we think.

Suggestions for Further Study

Since everyone in the diaspora world is not on FB, and anecdotal evidence suggests that some groups may have a significant gender imbalance of social network subscribers (e.g., conservative Muslim groups), quantative analysis to determine the percent of users is necessary for accurate demographics. Furthermore, a script or plug-in that queries language preferences, current cities, countries of origin, and geotags is needed in order to data mine FB efficiently. Data can then be exported to an external program like Google Earth to display findings. Finally, other social media sites—Twitter, Instagram, LinkedIn, Pinterest, and Google Plus, as well as China's equivalents, Qzone and Sina Weibo—should be considered as potential field sites and mapping tools.

Acknowledgements

A special thanks to my wife for being patient with what likely appeared as an unhealthy obsession with social media. Thank you to Mark Szymanski and Kevin Mason with United World Missions (UWM) for raising funds and hiring CIU students to test and refine the theories put forth in this paper. Also, thanks to my PhD supervisors, Dr. Moyra Dale and Dr. Peter Riddell, at Melbourne School of Theology. Finally, thanks to my CIU colleagues, particularly Dr. Warren Larson and Dr. Mike Barnett.

Chapter Three
The Muslim Diaspora
MARK HAUSFELD AND JOSHUA FLETCHER (PSEUDONYM)

ABSTRACT

Turkmenistan is one of the world's most restricted access countries. The nominally Muslim post-Soviet government has been totalitarian to their people's freedoms, stagnant in economic development, and closed to foreigners residing in their country. Hence opportunities for missionaries to engage Turkmen people with the gospel are limited. However, Turkmen women and men are on the move. Diaspora Turkmen look to their neighbors to the west in related history and heritage for economic hope. Thus Turkmen are a growing diaspora people among one of Eurasia's metropolises. The Turkmen's diaspora classification from their perspective of financial need is that they are a "pushed" diaspora population. The lack of economic sustainability propels them from their homeland to the nearest viable and familiar nation and people that has possibilities to provide. Yet at the same time the economic strength of this metropolis is a diaspora "pull" that provides provisional hopes to Turkmen women and men. For each Turkmen that has their hope fulfilled, there are others that fail, fall into lifestyles of vice, and return to Turkmenistan if and when possible. This diaspora "push" and "pull" upon diaspora Turkmen in a relative context of freedom is a great missiological opportunity. That is happening through a unique partnership in mission.

Missionaries from the United States are in relationship with another diaspora people in Istanbul—Turkic Muslim-background believers (MBBs). This chapter will discuss how these unique partners in mission are engaging diaspora Turkmen Muslims with the gospel.

Introduction: A Foundation

Hagar, the Egyptian maidservant of a childless and desperate Sarai, has no choice but to comply when her mistress convinces her own husband, Abram, to sleep with Hagar to raise an heir (Gen 15:2) through her (16:2). When she becomes pregnant, a jealous and despised Sarai complains to Abram and invokes God's judgment on the situation (16:5). Abram preserves familial peace by authorizing Sarai to "do with her whatever you think best" (16:6a). Sarai then abuses Hagar, and Hagar flees (16:6b).[1]

Hagar finds herself by a desert spring when an angel appears and asks her, "Hagar, slave of Sarai, where have you come from, and where are you going?" (16:8). She answers that she is running from her mistress. The angel instructs her to return to Sarai and submit to her. The angel then delivers God's kindness to her in a promise:

> I will increase your descendants so much that they will be too numerous to count . . . You are now pregnant and you will give birth to a son. You shall name him Ishmael [meaning "God hears"], for the Lord has heard of your misery. He will be a wild donkey of a man; his hand will be against everyone and everyone's hand against him, and he will live in hostility toward all his brothers. (16:10–12)

Hagar returns to Sarai and gives birth to Ishmael. Ishmael is a young man when Sarah (Sarai) gives birth to Abraham's (Abram's) son Isaac. Ishmael's behavior toward Isaac irritates Sarah, who this time expels Hagar and Ishmael from the household. Abraham is bewildered, but God affirms that Isaac will carry on his lineage and promises to make Ishmael a nation as well (Gen 21:9–14).

In sadness, Abraham sends Hagar and Ishmael on their way with food and water supply. The two wander in the desert of Beersheba, and when they have used all their water, Hagar laments her son's impending death. God intervenes as Hagar and Ishmael weep. He calms her fears and repeats his previous promise: "Do not be afraid . . . Lift the boy up and take him by the hand, for I will make him into a great nation" (Gen 21:14–18).[2]

From its beginning, this lineage creates the historical and spiritual milieu that forms Islamic identity. Frederick Mathewson Denny identifies this connection:

> Then God shows Hagar a well of water, which saves the two. Ishmael grows up in the wilderness, becoming an expert archer . . . The Arabs, and through them, the Muslims, [trace] their spiritual lineage back to Abraham through

---

1 See Genesis 16:7–15.
2 See Genesis 21:8–18.

Hagar and Ishmael, regarding themselves as a great nation that God had promised to create.[3]

This lineage is rooted in flight and promise. Hagar and Ishmael are forced to leave home, but God personally attends to them on their journey, and he is present with them in their place of exile (Gen 21:20,21).

Islam and Diaspora

Muslims have been moving since Islam's inception, and when Muslims move, Islam spreads. Muhammad begins to receive the Qur'an through revelations from the angel Gabriel. His wife Khadija persuades him he is not insane, as he suspects; she convinces him that he is a prophet.[4] Muhammad proclaims his revelations that God is *One* to polytheistic leaders in Mecca who reject him. Fearing for his life, he and his entourage flee to Medina, where an embryonic Muslim community grows under his tutelage. One might consider the Prophet and his family Islam's first diaspora group.

The term "diaspora," derived from the Greek word *diaspora* or *diaspeirein* (dispersion), has historically been used to refer to the scattering and dispersion of the Jews in the Old Testament and Christians in the New Testament. Contemporary literature uses the word to describe "the phenomenon of people on the move or being moved."[5]

A basic understanding of global people movement trends sheds light on diaspora Muslims and the opportunity the church now has to reach them. The fact of people movements is not new; however, in the twenty-first century the number of people involved in diaspora transition is growing very rapidly.[6] Questions that define specific diaspora study revolve around who the travelers are, when they move, the reasons for their moves, their destinations, and the results of their transitions. Currently, 3 percent of the world's population is leaving their birthplace for new destinations.[7] World cities like Paris, Karachi, Miami, Istanbul, London, Frankfurt, Chicago, Mexico City, and Los Angeles draw immigrants at a rate that will make them home to 61

---

3   Frederick Mathewson Denny, *An Introduction to Islam*, 2nd ed. (New York: Macmillan, 1994), 19.
4   The Qur'an is the "holy book" of Islam. "Qur'an" in Arabic means "recitation," because Muhammad said the angel Gabriel recited God's final, complete, and perfect word to him to give to humankind.
5   Enoch Wan, "Diaspora Missiology," *Occasional Bulletin* (Spring 2007): 3.
6   Nicolas Van Hear, *New Diasporas: The Mass Exodus, Dispersal and Regrouping of Migrant Communities* (Seattle: University of Washington Press, 1998), 2.
7   Wan, "Diaspora Missiology," 3.

percent of the world's population by 2025.[8] The somewhat positive persuasion of urbanization and urbanism[9] supports the global migration trend that is seeing 33 percent of world immigrants going to the seven wealthiest countries in the world where 16 percent of the world's population already lives.[10]

Most people are moving from south to north and east to west.[11] They move for many reasons, either voluntary or involuntary. They might be refugees or exiles forced to leave family, friends, and lands they love. Other people leave homelands voluntarily to join family members who have emigrated before them. Many immigrants seek opportunities for better education, work, and more prosperous living. A growing numbers of Muslim immigrants travel to propagate their faith, but even if they do not intentionally do so, every Muslim immigrant imports his own brand of Islam.

Insights into Diaspora

Diaspora people movements are outwardly imposed or inwardly motivated. Enoch Wan calls these forces "pushes and pulls."[12] Diaspora people move voluntarily or involuntarily. The involuntary push and the voluntary pull come because of the options people have in their respective situations.

Wan illustrates the natural and human causes that push people to leave their homelands. Factors that force people into diaspora are always misery related and caused by elements outside the control of those who flee. Congruently, there are positive forces that "pull" people to immigrate to foreign nations (see table 1).[13]

The voluntary pull gives the immigrant more proactive choices. For example, Murad's cousin has established residency in Ashkhabad, Turkmenistan, and will sponsor him as a student at Eastern Michigan University. Four years in an American school opens doors for Murad to find employment and extend his stay—maybe

---

8   Andrew Davey, *Urban Christianity and Global Order: Theological Resources for an Urban Future* (Peabody, MA: Hendrickson, 2002), 5.
9   Ray Bakke defines "urbanization" and "urbanism" as follows: "By *urbanization* we mean the development of cities as places where size, density and heterogeneity are measured. We might call this the magnet function of cities, drawing humanity into huge metroplexes. By *urbanism* we mean the development of the city as process—that is, the magnifier function of cities, spinning out urban values, products and lifestyles into a world linked by media, even in rural and small-town places." Ray Bakke, *A Theology as Big as the City* (Downers Grove, IL: InterVarsity Press, 1997), 12.
10 Wan, "Diaspora Missiology," 3.
11 Leonore Loeb Adler and Uwe P. Gielen, eds., *Migration: Immigration and Emigration in International Perspective* (Westport, CT: Praeger, 2003), 16.
12 Wan, "Diaspora Missiology," 3.
13 Ibid.

even apply for citizenship and live there permanently. Murad is pulled by factors that improve his quality of life and progressively offer him better choices.

PUSH	PULL
War, political persecution and abuse of power, such as danger of life, exploitation of women and children, and human trafficking	Political freedom and human equality, such as safety, gender equality, and greater opportunity elsewhere including urbanization.
Natural disaster	Quality of life
Man–made disaster; accident, pollution, social isolation, psychological stress	Relief, opportunity The "American dream"
World poverty growth in contrast to health/wealth in countries of desirable destination	Media exposure of "greener pasture" elsewhere
Obligation to improve the state of left–behind group, that is family or community	Success story of or invitation from loved ones abroad, that is family or friends

Table 1: The Push and Pull Forces that Move People

The involuntary push of desperation often leaves the immigrant in a reactive state with little or no voice in the matter of flight or life afterwards. Nazgul, a single woman, is a financial detriment to her family and desperately needs to increase monetary income. The young women and men in her community are moving north and west for employment so they can send back money to their parents to help provide food and shelter. A visa to Europe or the United States is nearly impossible. Turkmen seek a closer nation whose economy holds the potential for employment with much easier access than the United States. Nazgul, pushed from her native land due to a lack of employment, seeks to make her way to the "city of dispersion"—a megacity in Eurasia. She hopes she can help meet her family's needs through gainful employment.

Understanding the roles "push" and "pull" play in diaspora movements greatly enhances the Christian's opportunities for outreach to Muslim immigrants, as it increases one's ability to discern the immigrant's needs and desires as well as to offer venues for genuine relationship and godly witness. It all comes back to the question the angel asked Hagar when she fled Sarai's harsh treatment: "Where have you come from, and where are you going?" (Gen 16:8). The Christian worker who is attune to the details of the diaspora can offer security during very uncertain times, when hearts are receptive to the love Jesus has for them.

Method and Model Used: The Action/Reflection Praxis and the Missional Helix

This essay will employ the action/reflection method of praxis toward ministry and mission.[14] Our initial discussion will focus on efforts by Assemblies of God World Mission (AGWM) workers to engage diaspora Turkmen (women and men) from Turkmenistan with the gospel of Jesus Christ. The action taken to accomplish this will be reflected upon. Therefore this essay will use an action/reflection praxis model to achieve greater guidance and clarity for future missional engagement by the leading of the Holy Spirit and research. The Missional Helix, popularized by Gailyn Van Rheenen, will provide the model for this essay and is described as follows:

> Developing practice of ministry . . . understood as a helix because theology, history, culture, and strategy build on one another as the community of faith collectively develops understandings and a vision of God's will within their cultural context. Like a spring, the spiral grows to new heights as ministry understandings and experiences develop.[15]

Therefore the Missional Helix model components of Theological Reflection (TR), Historical Perspective (HP), Cultural Analysis (CA) and Strategy Formation (SF) will act as the means to reflect upon the action taken thus far in ministry and mission to diaspora Turkmen in the city of dispersion, Eurasia. From this method

---

14   James D. Whitehead and Evelyn Eaton Whitehead, *Method in Ministry: Theological Reflection and Christian Ministry* (Minneapolis: Seabury, 1980), 21–26.
15   Gailyn Van Rheenen, "The Missional Helix: Example of Church Planting," *MR* 26 (January 19, 2011), http://www.missiology.org/?p=157 (accessed March 22, 2014).

and model, a renewed Spirit-driven and researched missiological organic effort will emerge to proclaim the gospel to diaspora Turkmen in the city of dispersion.

Historical Perspective

History and People

According to the government of Turkmenistan, its citizens' ethnic groups are officially 85 percent Turkmen, 7 percent Uzbek, 5 percent Russian, while the remainder are comprised of other groups.[16] In the tenth century Turkmen migrated to what is present-day Turkmenistan.[17] Sometime between the fifteenth and seventeenth centuries, a consolidation of the Turkmen tribes began to occur. Between 1881 and 1885, the Russians conquered the Turkmen.[18] After the Bolshevik Revolution, the Russians formed the Turkmen Soviet Socialist Republic in 1924. This played an important part in the creation of the Turkmen identity, as before this time these ethnic identities were vague.[19]

Turkmenistan reluctantly gained independence in 1991.[20] Although Turkmenistan describes itself as a secular democracy, it is run as an authoritarian state.[21] After independence Turkmenistan began a campaign to create a national identity based on ethnicity.[22] This "Turkmenization" is even reflected in the renaming of cities, particularly those close to the border with Uzbekistan where epitaphs used for the residents belie their second-class status.[23]

Christianity and Islam in Turkmenistan

Within Turkmenistan, one can see the ruins of Nisa of the Parthians and Merv of the Seljuks. Jews from Parthia were in Jerusalem on the Day of Pentecost (Acts 2:8).[24] Meanwhile, Merv, near present-day Mary, served as a base for missionary

---

16 Embassy of Turkmenistan, "Turkmenistan at a Glance," http://turkmenistanembassy.org/turkmenistan-at-a-glance/ (accessed March 26, 2014).
17 Ibid., iv.
18 Ibid., lviii.
19 Ibid., lxxi.
20 Fearing the loss of subsidies, 95 percent of the Turkmen SSR voted for the preservation of the USSR. Paul Brummell, *Turkmenistan: The Bradt Travel Guide* (Guilford, CT: Globe Pequot, 2005), 10.
21 The World Factbook, "Geography: Turkmenistan," https://www.cia.gov/library/publications/the-world-factbook/geos/tx.html (accessed March 26, 2014).
22 Rafis Abazov, *Historical Dictionary of Turkmenistan: Historical Dictionaries of Asia, Oceania, and the Middle East* (Lanham, MD: Scarecrow, 2005), xcvi.
23 Such as two cities bordering Uzbekistan: Dashawuz (The far pool) has been changed to Dashoguz (The far Oghuz) and Charjou (Four channels) to Turkmenabat (Land of the Turkmen).
24 This was before the Turkmen had come to the region.

work and had a Nestorian bishop by the 420s; by 544 it was the metropolitan see of the Eastern Church.[25] In 644, the Nestorian church records a miracle done by the metropolitan of Merv, which impressed a Turkish king, leading to the conversion of him and his subjects.[26] Another large conversion of the Turks occurred in 781–82 and led to the establishment of a Nestorian Central Asian metropolitan to teach the new converts.[27] Again, in the year 1007, as many as 200,000 Turks and Mongols converted to Christianity.[28] This Christian history is now only a very distant memory—if remembered at all.

Islam eventually reached Central Asia. In the seventh century, the Arabs conquered Merv, and the city became an important center for the Abbasid Caliphate. At the peak of the city's development, it was ruled by the Seljuk Turks.[29] The Oghuz Khan,[30] Seljuk, accepted Islam around 985.[31] Islamization steadily increased in the region via the work of Sufi Muslims.[32]

The Turkmen people have experienced the repression of the freedom of religion since the days of Soviet rule. During the mid-1990s, Christian tentmakers could work in Turkmenistan relatively easily. One can trace much of the current Christian presence in Turkmenistan back to those days.[33]

Turkmenistan: A Country and People in Context

Geography and Economy

Turkmenistan is a country in Central Asia with a little more than 5 million people.[34] It shares borders with Iran, Afghanistan, Uzbekistan, and Kazakhstan and hosts giant natural gas reserves.[35] Despite this wealth, the country has a 60 percent unemployment rate, and 30 percent of the people live below the poverty line.[36] The

---

25 Paul Jenkins, *The Lost History of Christianity: The Thousand-year Golden Age of the Church in the Middle East, Africa, and Asia and How It Died* (New York: HarperOne, 2008), Kindle locations 45–46.
26 Richard Foltz, *Religions of the Silk Road: Overland Trade and Cultural Exchange from Antiquity to the Fifteenth Century* (New York: St. Martin's Press, 1999), 67.
27 Ibid.
28 Ibid.
29 Abazov, *Historical Dictionary of Turkmenistan*, 108.
30 A Khan descended from the original Oghuz Khan.
31 Foltz, *Religions*, 100.
32 Ibid., 101.
33 There are probably more than a thousand Turkmen believers inside Turkmenistan.
34 The World Factbook, "Geography: Turkmenistan."
35 U.S. Department of Energy, "Turkmenistan," updated July 2014, http://www.eia.gov/countries/beta/international/country.cfm?iso=TKM.
36 The World Factbook, "Geography: Turkmenistan."

future looks bleak.[37] Turkmenistan has been described as "one of the world's most repressive countries"[38] and the world's fifth most miserable country.[39]

Religion

The Turkmen are traditionally Sunni Muslims. Even so, Turkmen still retain vestiges of the shamanism present before the coming of Islam.[40] The government has used a strictly controlled Islam as a means of creating a Turkmen identity.[41] The first president of Turkmenistan, Saparmurat Niyazov, actually wrote his own holy book, the Ruhnama, to give moral guidance to the nation. This book was used regularly for prayers in mosques throughout Turkmenistan.[42]

Language

The people of Turkmenistan primarily speak the Turkmen language consisting of multiple regional dialects that are not mutually intelligible.[43] A decreasing minority of Turkmen still speak Russian.[44] According to the government of Turkmenistan's statistics, the literacy rate stands at 97 percent,[45] but anecdotal evidence suggests this is inflated. Often Turkmen speakers view their language primarily as a vehicle for communication rather than as a marker of identity. With this in mind, any language that is mutually available between the evangelist and the hearer can potentially serve as a vehicle for communication.[46]

---

37 According to the CIA World Factbook, "[Economic] prospects in the near future are discouraging because of endemic corruption, a poor educational system, government misuse of oil and gas revenues, and Ashgabat's reluctance to adopt market-oriented reforms. The majority of Turkmenistan's economic statistics are state secrets." However, the government uses some of the wealth on the 543 white marble buildings in the capital, Ashgabat, for which it has earned the Guinness World Record for "highest density of buildings made with white marble." The World Factbook, "Geography: Turkmenistan." For photos of the city of Ashgabat, see Radio Free Europe / Radio Liberty, "Turkmenistan's Capital Named World's 'White-marble' City," May 27, 2013, http://www.rferl.org/media/photogallery/turkmenistan-marble-record-architecture/24998685.html (accessed March 26, 2014).
38 Human Rights Watch, "Turkmenistan," http://www.hrw.org/world-report/2013/country-chapters/turkmenistan?page=1 (accessed March 26, 2014).
39 Lisa Mahapatra, "The 25 Most Miserable Places in the World," *Business Insider*, February 22, 2013, http://www.businessinsider.com/most-miserable-countries-in-the-world-2013-2?op=1 (accessed March 26, 2014).
40 Brummell, *Turkmenistan*, 18–19.
41 Ibid.
42 Ibid., 13.
43 Abazov, *Historical Dictionary of Turkmenistan*, xiii.
44 Brummell, *Turkmenistan*, 17.
45 Embassy of Turkmenistan, "Turkmenistan at a Glance."
46 However, the Turkmen language is ideal, as it affords communication with most of the people who come from Turkmenistan even before they learn Turkish. As Turkmen and Turkish are not mutually intelligible, it does also provide a modicum of privacy when speaking on a busy street. Speaking the

Turkmen Diaspora in the City of Dispersion

Despite the wealth of the state,[47] full-time salaries in Turkmenistan are often as low as $150 a month, but may reach $400 a month for low and mid-ranking officials appointed by the president.[48] Meanwhile, wages for illegal workers in the city of dispersion range from $400 to $900 a month, and room and board is often included. The 60 percent unemployment rate,[49] coupled with the more lucrative options in the city of dispersion, is the driving factor in pushing and pulling people from Turkmenistan and to the city of dispersion.[50]

The majority of the Turkmen in the city of dispersion tend to be from the underdeveloped areas bordering Uzbekistan. They can be found in all parts of the city of dispersion, but some areas have greater concentrations than others. Generally, these migrant workers are in their late teens or early twenties. The men typically work in small shops, restaurants, and factories and live together with up to twenty other Turkmen men. Women primarily serve as domestic workers and reside at their place of work, while others are in factories. The vast majority of the laboring Turkmen in the city of dispersion are illegal workers. This makes them easy targets for abuse ranging from not being paid for work to being asked for sexual favors.[51] Still the harsh working conditions offered in the city of dispersion are more rewarding than the alternative options in Turkmenistan. In the end, many immigrants get deported, and most plan to return to Turkmenistan at some point in the future. While missionary efforts in Turkmenistan are restricted, one can acquire direct access to Turkmenistan through the Turkmen in the city of dispersion.

Implications for Fellowship

As Turkmen spread across the city and work irregular schedules, a church located in a specific building at a specific time will immediately disqualify most Turkmen

---

Turkmen language is also valuable in creating solidarity and a point of connection when meeting someone on the street.
47   U.S. Department of Energy, "Turkmenistan."
48   Natallia Moore, "Turkmenistan Domestic Developments," Eurasianet.org, August 2, 2012, http://www.eurasianet.org/node/65742 (accessed March 26, 2014).
49   The World Factbook, "Geography: Turkmenistan."
50   In the first nine months of 2012, an officer in the State Migration Service of Turkmenistan speculated that out of the 150,000 Turkmen that had gone overseas, a full 110,000 most likely would not return. Institute for War and Peace Reporting, "Rising Emigration from Turkmenistan," October 8, 2012, http://iwpr.net/report-news/rising-emigration-turkmenistan (accessed March 26, 2014).
51   One Turkmen woman we know was reported to the police and deported when she refused the advances of a Turkish man.

in the city of dispersion from participation. The transitory nature of the Turkmen in the city of dispersion also creates difficulties, as deportation or relocation can immediately cut off the discipleship or evangelization process.

Action Taken

Our call to work with Turkmen was conceived in prayer and confirmed through unrepeatable events. A variety of practical considerations led to our decision to work among the Turkmen diaspora in the city of dispersion.

Turkic Coworkers

Due to our good relationships with many Turkic Christians in the city of dispersion, a partnership has been forged with two Turkic men and another Central Asian woman to reach Turkmen. Due to their similarity in regards to age and ethnicity to the Turkmen in the city of dispersion, they can gain trust with the people much more quickly than an American could and blend in more easily. Coming from Muslim backgrounds themselves, these near neighbors' witness is immediately more compelling.

Direct Evangelism

We have taken a circumspect but direct evangelistic approach among the Turkmen in the city of dispersion. There is little reason why we, as foreigners, should need to speak with Turkmen and, thus, there is no basis on which to develop relationships without arousing suspicion. Our primary method of evangelism has been Scripture distribution[52] for a variety of practical and theological reasons. Direct evangelism serves as a model for any of the Turkmen who would come to faith and allows us to identify those most open to the gospel. These people will be better equipped to reach their own people. We have little to lose and much to gain.[53]

---

52 Both printed and MP3.
53 In the past several weeks, while seeking out Turkmen, we began a conversation with a Turkic Syrian Turkmen. Having already started a conversation, we offered to teach him about the Bible in Turkish. We were surprised at his responsiveness to the suggestion. We exchanged telephone numbers and called him within the next week and arranged to meet him again—this time with our Turkic coworkers and a Turkmen disciple. In that group of seven people, six ethnic groups and four nationalities were represented. The *lingua franca* was Turkish, which was no one's first or preferred language. As they shared their coming to faith from Islam, this Syrian person was moved and stated that when he heard these things he felt great joy—as if he wanted to cry. Within a few minutes, he made it known that he wanted to believe. After a woman prayed for him, he prayed. He stated that it seemed as if he had been "born again"—words that he had never heard spoken. That same night, he had a dream where a shining man with an unseen face came to him and told him he was on the right path and to continue on. He is growing and is incredibly thirsty for the gospel and is sharing with others.

Contextualization

Beyond employing basic Eastern hospitality and the use of the Turkmen language, we have not made many accommodations in contextualization. So far, this has not seemed problematic—and even may be beneficial.[54]

Discipleship

In discipleship, we have used a Chronological Bible Storying approach.[55] We have emphasized the necessity of passing on what has been learned as well as the responsibility of sharing the gospel with other people. So far, we have effectively helped the new disciples become active proclaimers of their faith. Discipleship meetings typically transpire once a week, but can be a challenge due to the changing nature of the Turkmen work schedule and the size of the city.[56] We hold discipleship meetings at various times and places.

Theological Reflection

Apostolic Function: Proclamation and the Gospel

While Luke's intent was probably not evangelistic and may not have been prescriptive, the Acts narrative describes, in some measure, how the early church preached the gospel. We assume that if one can deduce an apostolic model or pattern here, then

---

54 A year ago we received the telephone number of a Turkmen seeker who had shown up at a local church. Upon calling this seeker, Sunnet, he asked us to come to where he worked as a dishwasher. We sat down for a meal together in this establishment—clearly run by extremely religious Muslims. We had barely sat down for five minutes when Sunnet's first question came: "If Jesus is the Savior, why did God send Mohammad?" Conscious of our surroundings, we said respectfully that, as Christians, we did not believe that God had sent him. This produced a follow-up question, "So, you're saying it's a lie?" This is not the direction we would normally try to lead a conversation with an unknown person, but being asked so clearly, we responded, "Yes." Sunnet later told us that hearing this is what made him decide to follow Christ. God has transformed his life, and he has shared the gospel with dozens of people within the last year.
55 This will be addressed further below.
56 About a year ago an illiterate Turkmen lady, Gul, arrived at our front door with Sunnet and his sister-in-law. They had just met at an employment office, and she wanted to hear the good news, so he brought her to us. We sat and shared for an hour, and she decided that she wanted to follow the Lord, so we prayed with her. She had to be home soon, so she left. We gave her five Gospels of Luke and an MP3 of Luke as well. (That very day, I had bought our first SD cards.) Over the next year, it was very difficult to establish contact with her as she rarely answered her phone and seldom had time off to meet with us. She was, at one point, back in Turkmenistan after being deported for several months. To our surprise, she eventually contacted Sunnet. We learned that, over the last year, her family had put pressure on her to return to Islam, but she would not do so. She refused to renounce her faith in God and Christ, because he had blessed her work and had changed her life. While this is not a model for duplication, it is indicative of the challenge of the situation as well as to the faithfulness of the Holy Spirit when there are no other options.

it can serve as a starting point for developing a strategy that continues in the same trajectory of Acts, not merely imitation.[57]

Spirit-empowered Servants

The Spirit is a crucial part of the apostolic evangelism seen in the book of Acts. The command to remain in Jerusalem until clothed with power (Acts 1:4) and the connection of the power to the apostles' witness (1:8) must be emphasized. Luke seems to emphasize the Spirit's relation to empowerment for mission rather than conversion,[58] although the two concepts are not mutually exclusive.[59] The Spirit's empowerment in Acts is also not seen as merely a one-time experience that one either has or does not have; it is repeatable (Acts 4:31).[60]

The Apostle/Evangelist and Evangelism

Necessity of Proclamation

From a cursory reading of the New Testament, one readily realizes that the gospel must be proclaimed.[61] Ott and Wilson state, "Nothing could be clearer from a reading of the book of Acts than its emphasis on gospel proclamation as the catalyst for church planting."[62] The terms used for evangelism in the New Testament, such as *kerusso* (preaching, proclamation), *kerygma* (announcement; proclamation), *euangelion* (good news), and *martus* (witness, testifier)[63] by their very definitions imply

---

57 Craig Ott and Gene Wilson, *Global Church Planting: Biblical Principles and Best Practices for Multiplication* (Grand Rapids: Baker Academic, 2011), 46.

58 See Roger Stronstad, *The Charismatic Theology of St. Luke: Trajectories from the Old Testament to Luke-Acts* (Grand Rapids: Baker Academic, 2012).

59 "It should be remembered, however, that Luke only rarely focuses explicitly on the Spirit's role in conversion and that he focuses most often on the prophetic-empowerment dimension of the Spirit's activity. Thus Luke allows for a particular dimension of Christian experience subsequent to faith and repentance but is not distinguishing conversion from the latter. The gift, apparently, technically begins at conversion in principle but, in terms of Luke's emphasis on its prophetic-empowerment dimension for mission, may be experienced in this prophetic form subsequent to conversion (and on multiple occasions)." Craig S. Keener, *Acts: An Exegetical Commentary*, vol. 1, *Introduction and 1:1–2:47* (Grand Rapids: Baker Academic, 2012), Kindle locations 23783–88.

60 Both Stephen and Barnabas, among others, are noted as being full of the Spirit (Acts 6:5; 11:24). This is not another way of stating that they had been born again or had been baptized in the Spirit. The Spirit's presence was a defining factor about them in comparison to others who also had the Spirit.

61 In referring to 1 Thessalonians 1:5, I once heard an Indonesian pastor state that the gospel was shared "not only with words, but there were words!"

62 Ott and Wilson, *Global Church Planting*, 47.

63 Frederick William Danker, ed., *A Greek-English Lexicon of the New Testament and Other Early Christian Literature*, ed. (Chicago: University of Chicago Press, 2000), s.vv. *euangelion*, *kerusso*, *kerygma*, *martus*.

proclamation. In the book of Acts people usually shared the gospel with previously unknown people, and a prior relationship was not a prerequisite for proclamation.

The Sword of the Spirit

The Spirit's work is not only to empower witness. C. K. Barrett makes the following suggestion: "The prime agency by which the Spirit extends the sovereignty of Christ is the Word of God."[64] This *logos tou theou* ("word of God," or other uses of *logos*) is not a euphemism for Scripture, but is, in fact, the gospel itself.[65] Paul applies this same usage. *Logos* is often viewed as synonymous with *euangelion* (gospel) and *martyrion* (witness). This connection is made as the gospel is seen as the power of God (Rom 1:16,17), akin to God's powerful and effective word.[66] Paul casts the sword of the Spirit as the word (*rhema* instead of *logos*) of God (Eph 6:17).[67] It seems that the choice of *rhema* in this instance is similar in effect to Romans 10:17 and is accenting the "actual 'speaking forth' of the message, inspired by the Spirit."[68]

This understanding of the gospel as the powerful, creative, generative word of God is what leads us to the conclusion that the *proclamation* of the gospel as the word of God is what invites the Spirit of God to work in a person's heart. Dependence upon the Spirit of God by no means makes the content of the message unimportant; rather it should lead to recognition of the vital importance of the content of the message.[69]

Jesus Is Lord

The gospel is not merely an explanation of how salvation works and an invitation to accept or acknowledge those workings.[70] The resurrection, in particular, is often related to Christ's exaltation as Lord and leads to potentially the first and most

---

64   C. K. Barrett, *Luke the Historian* (London: Epworth, 1970), 63, quoted in Michael Green, *Evangelism in the Early Church* (Grand Rapids: Eerdmans, 2004), Kindle location 210.
65   For example, Acts 4:4,29,31; 6:2,4,7; 8:4; 10:44; 11:19; 12:24; 13:5,7,44,46,48,49; 14:3; 15:7,35,36; 16:6,32; 17:11,13; 18:5,11; 19:10,20; 20:32.
66   A. B. Luter Jr., "Gospel," in *Dictionary of Paul and His Letters*, ed. Gerald F. Hawthorne, Ralph P. Martin, and Daniel G. Reid (Downers Grove, IL: InterVarsity Press, 1993), Kindle locations 4624–52.
67   One should not overlook the connection to prayer in the Spirit in the following verse (v. 18).
68   Gordon D. Fee, *God's Empowering Presence: The Holy Spirit in the Letters of Paul* (Peabody, MA: Hendrickson, 1994), 728–29.
69   Even so, how many times has a testimony been heard that starts with, "I don't remember anything the preacher said, but . . ."?
70   As N. T. Wright is fond of saying, "One is not justified by faith by believing in justification by faith." N. T. Wright, *Pauline Perspectives: Essays on Paul, 1978–2013* (Minneapolis: Fortress, 2013), 218.

important Christian confession, "Jesus is Lord."[71] (While certainly including the idea of authority and rule, it also includes sharing the divine name itself.)[72] The summary of the content of the evangelists' message can often be declaring Jesus to be the Christ (Acts 2:36; 5:42; 8:5; 9:22; 17:3; 18:5,28). Acceptance of this message of Christ as Lord ultimately defines "belief."[73]

By the Spirit

Anyone attempting evangelism among Muslims will immediately recognize the difficulty of the task of evangelism if "Jesus is Lord" is to be the central point of the gospel. Muslims are not the only monotheists who have dealt with this challenge. The evidence in the New Testament renders the idea of an evolutionary model with a slowly developing Christology that entails an incorporation of Greek ideas as historically untenable.[74] Hengel makes the following declaration: "In essentials more happened in christology within these few years [the 18 years between Jesus' resurrection and Paul's writing] than in the whole subsequent seven hundred years of church history."[75] The *experience* of the lordship of the risen Jesus, as mediated by the Holy Spirit, stands as a plausible significant cause of the development of this early astounding confession.[76]

Narrative Context

This confession of Jesus' lordship does not come as merely a statement, but as the culmination of a narrative.[77] Hengel suggests, "From the beginning the proclamation of Jesus Christ and narratives about him were inseparably associated. One could

---

71 W. J. Porter, "Creeds and Hymns," in *Dictionary of New Testament Background*, ed. Craig A. Evans and Stanley E. Porter (Downers Grove, IL: InterVarsity Press, 2000), Accordance electronic ed., version 1.2.

72 Larry W Hurtado, *How on Earth Did Jesus Become a God?: Historical Questions about Earliest Devotion to Jesus* (Grand Rapids: Eerdmans, 2005), Kindle locations 594–95.

73 See Acts 2:44; 4:4,32; 5:14; 8:12,13; 9:26,42; 10:43,45; 11:17,21; 13:39,48; 14:1,23; 15:5,7,11; 16:1,31,34; 17:12,34; 18:8,27; 19:2,4,18; 21:20,25; 22:19.

74 Hurtado, *How on Earth*, Kindle locations 302–3.

75 Martin Hengel, *Between Jesus and Paul: Studies in the Earliest History of Christianity* (London: SCM, 1983), 39–40.

76 Merhdad Fatehi, *The Spirit's Relation to the Risen Lord in Paul: An Examination of Its Christological Implications*, vol. 28, WUNT 2 (Tübingen, Germany: Mohr Siebeck, 2000).
Hurtado further affirms: "The success of earliest Christianity and its appeal and credibility in the eyes of converts seem to have been very heavily connected to its ability to provide religious experiences that corresponded to its rhetoric of being 'gifted,' 'filled,' 'anointed,' and 'empowered' by the Spirit of God." Hurtado, *How on Earth*, Kindle locations 1920–22.

77 Before the Gospels became available in written form, Paul described the tradition of the gospel as was handed down to him; namely, events (1 Cor 15:1–8).

not 'preach' Jesus as the crucified Messiah and Son of God who had been raised and exalted by God without telling his story."[78] Therefore the proclamation of the gospel, Jesus' lordship, is inseparable from the narrative found in the Scripture, and specifically in the Gospels. Pennington continues, "The Gospels are not supplements to the message about Christ (found, for example, in Paul); rather they are the kerygma or proclamation itself. The message of salvation is necessarily a historical narrative."[79] It is, thus, not without reason that the Gospels are so named. The book of Acts continues in using this narrative proclamation.[80]

Conversion, then, from one angle is the acceptance of a new narrative—the biblical narrative. Consequently, one must take into consideration the narrative nature of gospel proclamation when attempting to make the gospel understandable. People build worldviews upon underlying narratives,[81] which they use as a hermeneutical lens through which to interpret events (like the gospel).[82] In addressing conversion, Hiebert indicates that without a change in worldviews, conversion will result in syncretism—a change of beliefs without a corresponding change in behavior, or changed behaviors without an altered belief system.[83] In this way the narrative reconciles the false dichotomy between converts and disciples.[84] Michael Green has gone so far as to say, "Without a coherent eschatology [i.e., a narrative] it is

---

78   Martin Hengel, *The Four Gospels and the One Gospel of Jesus: An Investigation of the Collection and Origin of the Canonical Gospels* (Harrisburg, PA: Trinity Press International, 2000), 86.

79   Jonathan T. Pennington, *Reading the Gospels Wisely: A Narrative and Theological Introduction* (Grand Rapids: Baker Academic, 2012), 34.

80   C. H. Dodd suggests that commonalities in the apostolic preaching, as found in Acts, highlight several key factors: (a) "The age of fulfillment has dawned," (b) "this has taken place through the ministry, death, and resurrection of Jesus" according to the Scriptures, (c) "by virtue of the resurrection, Jesus has been exalted at the right hand of God," (d) "the Holy Spirit in the Church is the sign of Christ's present power and glory," (e) "the Messianic Age will shortly reach its consummation in the return of Christ," and finally, (f) "the kerygma always closes with an appeal for repentance, the offer of forgiveness and of the Holy Spirit, and the promise of 'salvation,' that is, of 'the life of the Age to Come,' to those who enter the elect community." C. H. Dodd, *The Apostolic Preaching and Its Developments: Three Lectures*, 3rd. ed. (London, UK: Hodder & Stoughton, 1963), 21–23.

81   N. T. Wright, *The New Testament and the People of God: Christian Origins and the Question of God* (Minneapolis: Fortress, 1992), Kindle location 3113.

82   Steve Wilkens and Mark L. Sanford, *Hidden Worldviews: Eight Cultural Stories That Shape Our Lives* (Downers Grove, IL: InterVarsity Press Academic, 2009), 20.

83   "Conversion to Christ must encompass all three levels: behavior, beliefs, and the worldview that underlies these . . . Conversion may include a change in beliefs and behavior, but if the worldview is not transformed, in the long run the gospel is subverted and the result is a syncretistic Christo-paganism, which has the form of Christianity but not its essence. Christianity becomes a new magic and a new, subtler form of idolatry." Paul G. Hiebert, *Transforming Worldviews: An Anthropological Understanding of How People Change* (Grand Rapids: Baker Academic, 2008), Kindle locations 205–10.

84   "A people's mythology [used nonpejoratively] serves as a cultural repository of truth, feelings, and morals functioning to validate their belief systems. Myths codify and communicate beliefs, express the deepest feelings, and define and enforce morality. They are not idle tales, but hard-working, active forces.

not possible to do effective evangelism."[85] Without a coherent eschatology, effective discipleship is also not possible.

Spirit Birth

According to the New Testament, coming to Christ can also be described as an experience of the Spirit (John 3:5; Rom 8:9; 2 Cor 11:4; Gal 3:13,14). Of course, this experience is predicated upon Christ's work in history and is accessed by faith in Christ, but the result of such faith is an experience of the Spirit (Gal 3:2–5).[86] Therefore, a "positive" response *alone*, such as a confession or acceptance of the proclaimed message, is not an adequate description or marker of conversion.[87] A worldview change also cannot empower correct behavior. Discipleship, as walking in the Spirit, is only possible by the presence of the Spirit.

Result of Apostolic Evangelism

The results of the apostolic proclamation in the book of Acts were not uniform. While Luke reports a steady increase in numbers of believers (Acts 2:41; 6:7; 12:24; 16:5; 19:20), he also reports various persecutions, martyrdoms, threats, and even misunderstandings (Acts 8:8–18; 17:16–21). Acceptance and rejection, including persecution, serve as valid and even expected results of apostolic preaching.

Strategy Formation

Reliance on the Holy Spirit

As emphasized throughout this chapter, the Holy Spirit plays a key role in regards to proclamation, coming to faith, and in discipleship. Luke, who emphasizes the Spirit in evangelism, also emphasizes prayer—both in Luke and in Acts, and even relates prayer and the Spirit (Luke 11:1–13; Acts 1:14; cf. 2:1–4; 4:23–31). Prayer is

---

They are not intellectual explanations or artistic imagery, but charters of life and moral wisdom." Ibid., Kindle locations 1359–62.

85 Green, *Evangelism*, Kindle location, 382.

86 James D. G. Dunn, *Baptism in the Holy Spirit: A Re-examination of the New Testament Teaching on the Gift of the Spirit in Relation to Pentecostalism Today*, 2nd ed. (London: SCM, 2010).

87 "There exists, in fact, no positive evidence for a movement in the decades after Jesus' death that was not shaped by belief in his resurrection. If there had been such a movement, it was short-lived and has left no traces in the literature, even the earliest of which is marked by the conviction that the one who was crucified is now more powerfully alive. Christianity came to birth because certain people were convinced that they had experienced God's transforming power through the resurrection of Jesus. A scholarship based not on this fact but on its denial may be a study of something or other in antiquity but it certainly is not the study of early Christianity." Luke Timothy Johnson, *Religious Experience in Earliest Christianity: A Missing Dimension in New Testament Studies* (Minneapolis: Fortress, 1998), Kindle locations 1202–6.

an important part of our evangelistic strategy. As a team, we meet corporately twice a week for prayer and emphasize prayer in our discipleship.

Biblical Theology and Culture

Our understandings about conversion and discipleship as a Spirit-driven transformation in worldviews and an altering of a narrative, gives priority of place to biblical theology rather than to anthropology or sociology and limits the scope of any contextualization strategy.[88] Additionally, the threat of persecution or even the complexity of the subject matter[89] is not a determining factor in contextualization.

Language: A Vehicle of Communication

In our situation, the best language to use is the one that affords the clearest communication, which, for Turkmen, is generally the Turkmen language. We will continue to use printed literature when possible, but also audio materials when necessary.

Reproducible Model

We intend to use a reproducible model of house churches for Turkmen. These can easily be reproduced inside Turkmenistan as well. To this end, we plan for our teaching to be simple and thus reproducible. Secondly, we encourage disciples to teach those they lead to Christ and not bring them to a church, but rather to use the new believers' location as a new point of fellowship. We disciple new believers with the intent that every disciple be equipped to disciple others.

Direct Evangelism

We are creating a simplified two-minute narrative summary that announces Jesus as Lord and leads to a call for repentance. This summary presentation will be used with people we meet on the streets. In addition, we are also planning to print a fuller narrative gospel proclamation for distribution with a Gospel. For settings where more time is available, we will create a narrative presentation consisting of

---

88 This approach to contextualization may seem counterintuitive to some people. Interestingly, the eminent French Islamic scholar, Olivier Roy, laments that such a socioculturally divorced approach to religion results in conversions to unrestrained fundamentalism, such as evangelicalism. See Olivier Roy, *Holy Ignorance: When Religion and Culture Part Ways* (New York: Columbia University Press, 2012).

89 There does not seem to be any indication that Paul reinterpreted or minimized the resurrection of the body among Gentiles, despite the unfamiliarity of the thought to Gentiles (see Acts 17:16–21). The very strangeness of this Jewish narrative caused him problems in Corinth as well (1 Cor 15).

five to six stories for incremental sharing with interested seekers who did not make a decision after hearing the gospel for the first time.

Despite the challenges, we provide a local telephone number and email address for follow-up. In exceptional cases, we will ask for their contact details, but normally prefer to respect their anonymity and allow them to make contact with us. Since we frequent certain parts of town, we often run across people with whom we have spoken before.

Narrative Discipleship

We intend to use the same five to six stories used for evangelism (possibly with small modifications) as some of the first lessons in a discipleship curriculum. This reinforces the message used for evangelism and, thus, can serve as both evangelistic training and discipleship. The first discipleship principle will focus on equipping the new believer to share the gospel with other people. We will tie specific topics addressed in further lessons to the narrative. This constant repetition and reinforcement of the narrative should aid in generating the pattern for Christian living.

Mission To, Through, and Beyond the Diaspora

The intent of this organic model is to allow the gospel to spread wherever it goes through relational networks of believers and jumping into new relationship networks and ethnic groups via direct evangelism. An Iranian proverb says, "One foolish man drops a rock into a well that one thousand wise men cannot retrieve." We hope this will be a description of what happens through the Turkmen diaspora in the city of dispersion, and through the Turkmen diaspora in Turkmenistan, and beyond the Turkmen diaspora into the lives of the Uzbeks, Arabs, Afghans, Turks, and Iranians around them in the city of dispersion.

Part Two:

Theory and Models of Diaspora Missiology

Chapter Four
Assessing the Value of Diaspora Community Input in Missiological Research
FRED FARROKH

ABSTRACT

While diaspora missiology has focused on reaching diaspora communities with the gospel, and harnessing the potential of diaspora believers to herald the gospel at home and abroad, my recent PhD dissertation has opened my eyes to the potential value of diaspora community input into missiological research. In this chapter I will assess the strengths and weaknesses regarding diaspora community input in contemporary missiological research. I will show how these factors impacted my field research among Muslim-born persons in metro New York. I conclude that the input of diaspora communities may provide a helpful asset to the global missiological goal of equipping the church for world evangelism.

Ministry to Muslims is arguably the greatest challenge left in the Great Commission. The most controversial missiological issue in ministry to Muslims is appropriate contextualization of the gospel to Muslim audiences. This issue has led directly to the question whether Muslims who come to faith in the Lord Jesus Christ should permanently retain Islamic religious identity and observance. Unfortunately, missiologists have conducted precious little research among Muslim-born persons on this topic of Muslim identity. In my PhD research on this question, I had the opportunity to interview forty Muslim-born persons in metro New York—five were born in the United States, and the others were immigrants who hailed from eighteen different countries. This uniquely diverse group of respondents has provided input that may provide a needed correction in missions to Muslims. I will highlight this input in my paper.

Introduction

This chapter begins with my personal introduction as a Muslim-background Christian and a child of diaspora. Then I will briefly introduce the missiological issue I sought to address in my doctoral research, and describe my choice of conducting field research among diaspora individuals in metro New York (NY). In the context of this research, I assess the strengths and weaknesses of diaspora community input in missiological research. I conclude that diaspora community input can be a significant asset in missiological research. The main thrust of this paper is not identical to that of my PhD dissertation, though I will present those results as an example of the benefits of diaspora communities to missiological research. I note that a significant amount of material in this paper is excerpted from my PhD dissertation, which is not yet in a form from which citations or page numbers can be given.

My PhD research addresses a key missiological question in ministry to Muslims. Most doctoral students will feel their own research has tremendous missiological significance; I am no exception. Since the Muslim world is the largest bloc of peoples unreached by the gospel, and since security concerns in doing research among Muslims have traditionally posed challenges to field research, innovative ways of researching ministry to Muslims must at least arrest the attention of the missiological community. In particular, my research sought to evaluate the appropriateness in the Muslim context of "insider movements," which I will describe below.

Diaspora missiology features many worthy researchable topics in its own right. These include: how to reach diaspora communities with the gospel, and how diaspora Christians may participate in the Great Commission in various contexts. This research focuses on the value of diaspora community input into global missiological research. In particular, I assess strengths and weaknesses of generalizing diaspora data onto other contexts.

Introduction to the Researcher

I share the following material, not as a written "selfie," but merely to provide the necessary context to this paper.

Personal Statement about Being a Diaspora Muslim-background Christian

As a US-born Iranian-American, I was raised in a multicultural setting. My family lived in Iran when I was small, but we returned before I could recall the experience. We attended a Sunni mosque in the United States, since there were no Shi'ite mosques, at that time, where we were living. My upbringing therefore included a significant diaspora community component, which shaped my thought processes and identity. I also developed an appreciation for a country that seemed relaxed enough to be both a melting pot and a mosaic for immigrant groups, even though I experienced times of tension, such as that caused by the Iranian hostage crisis of 1979.

I came to faith in the Lord Jesus Christ when I read through the Bible in my college years. I immediately sensed the call of God to help establish the kingdom of God in the Muslim world, and have pursued this call both in the United States and abroad. I have lived over two years on the island of Cyprus, and thus I can identify with the feeling of being a foreigner in a distant land. I have also undertaken short-term mission trips to Morocco, Egypt, Israel/Palestine, Lebanon, Ukraine, Uzbekistan, Bangladesh, Malaysia, Indonesia, and Philippines.

Personal Statement Regarding My PhD Research

At the time of this writing, March 2014, my PhD dissertation is going through final edits. I undertook the doctoral work through the Assemblies of God Theological Seminary. The dissertation title is "Perceptions of Muslim Identity: A Case Study among Muslim-born Persons in Metro New York." The key missiological question, in lay person's terms, is whether a person can be a Muslim and Christian at the same time. In missiological terms, the question at hand is whether a Muslim who comes to believe the biblical narrative regarding Jesus Christ can and should permanently retain Muslim identity and participate in Islamic corporate worship. This concept of remaining inside Islam, has spawned the concept of insider movements,[1] and has since been applied to other religious contexts.

The development of the insider movement paradigm suffers from a missiological deficiency in that minimal indigenous input has contributed to its development. I realized the immediate need to garner the input of Muslim-born persons on this key subject. These voices should include Muslim-born persons who have come to faith in the Lord Jesus Christ as well as those who have not.

I considered several possible locations for soliciting and recording the input of Muslim-born persons on the missiological topic at hand. Initially I investigated conducting the research in one or more Muslim countries, but time and cost made this impossible for me, since I was simultaneously in full-time ministry in metro NY. A request I made for a multicountry research grant was turned down. (I do, in my research conclusions, recommend that the type of research I conducted be replicated in other contexts and in various Muslim countries.)

---

1   See Kevin Higgins, "Identity, Integrity and Insider Movements: A Brief Paper Inspired by Timothy Tennent's Critique of C-5 Thinking," *International Journal of Frontier Missions* 23, no. 3 (Fall 2006): 117–23; Rebecca Lewis, "Promoting Movements to Christ within Natural Communities," *International Journal of Frontier Missiology* 24, no. 2 (Summer 2007): 75–76.

At that point I began to consider the possibility of doing my dissertation field research among diaspora Muslims in metro NY. For reasons I will describe below, I ultimately decided that the diaspora context would be a good fit for my research design. Since I have been living and ministering in metro NY, I enjoyed an access that I could not easily obtain elsewhere. Needless to say, the prospect of interviewing Muslims and Muslim-background Christians from so many different nations presented a tremendous educational opportunity for a student of intercultural studies.

As a technical matter, I framed the scope of my dissertation in the title, purpose statement, problem statement, and research questions with the delimiter of "metro NY." It was not presented as a global study. However, implications from the study contain global importance because Muslims in metro NY are connected to their coreligionists globally by the religion of Islam, and also since the conclusions of the study were driven by supralocal theological factors.

Personal Statement of Ministry Connection to Metro NY City

I have had direct experiences with diaspora missiology. From 2006 to 2013, I served as executive director of JFM Network (www.jesusformuslims.org), a parachurch ministry that promotes evangelism of Muslim immigrants and discipleship of Muslim-background Christians. I am presently an ambassador-at-large with JFM. I helped start a worshiping group of Iranian Christians, which still presently meets in New Jersey. From 2008 to 2013, I also oversaw a monthly meeting of Muslim-background Christians held in the church where we are meeting today. As a part of JFM Network, I assisted in opening a safe house for Muslim converts to Christ who are suffering persecution or homelessness. These experiences have given me an appreciation for the challenges facing diaspora Muslims and Muslim-background Christians, as well as the opportunities and challenges facing those who minister to them.

Strengths and Weaknesses of Diaspora Community Input into Missiological Research

As mentioned above, diaspora missiology has many researchable facets in its own right, including reaching diaspora communities with the gospel, and the potential for diaspora Christian communities to be a force for evangelism locally and abroad. My own research focused not particularly on reaching diaspora Muslims with the gospel, but enlisting the input of diaspora Muslims and former Muslims in global missional planning. This section reviews both the weaknesses and the strengths of doing so.

To set the context, I have been studying the views of Muslim-born persons on the proposition that a Muslim can permanently retain Muslim identity after coming to saving faith in the biblical Jesus. Western missiologists such as Charles Kraft,[2] John Travis,[3] Joshua Massey,[4] Kevin Higgins,[5] Rebecca Lewis,[6] Rick Brown,[7] and Kevin Greeson[8] are all proponents of this position. While it is beyond the scope of this research to fully address the input of these missiologists, the output of their efforts has been the creation of "insider movements" in the Muslim context, in which Muslims who ostensibly come to saving faith in the biblical Jesus retain Muslim identity and may participate in Muslim corporate worship in the mosque. As a note, experimentation in this type of missiology has occurred initially in Bangladesh, Indonesia, East Africa, and now in many countries where Western missionaries who have been trained in this missiology have encountered Muslims. It is a lesser issue in ministry to diaspora Muslims in the United States, partially because the persecution issue is also lesser here. Nevertheless it is a significant issue in North America in the training of missionaries to Muslims and the financing thereof.

Weaknesses of Metro NY Diaspora Muslim Community Input

In the case of my particular research question, which has a global scope and impact, there are inherent challenges in relying on any one community for research input. The best case scenario in my research would have been to interview Muslims and Muslim-background Christians from throughout the world regarding their perceptions on the missiological issue at hand. I admit this would be ambitious for any individual researcher. I also concede that rarely can a single researcher cultivate all of the field

---

2   Charles Kraft, "Dynamic Equivalence Churches in Muslim Society," in *The Gospel and Islam: A 1978 Compendium*, ed. Don McCurry, 114–24 (Monrovia, CA: MARC, 1979).
3   John Travis, "The C1 to C6 Spectrum: A Practical Tool for Defining Six Types of 'Christ-centered Communities' ('C') Found in the Muslim Context," *Evangelical Missions Quarterly* 34, no. 4 (October 1998): 407–8.
4   Joshua Massey, "God's Amazing Diversity in Drawing Muslims to Christ," *International Journal of Frontier Missions* 17, no. 1 (Spring 2000): 5–14.
5   Higgins, "Identity."
6   Lewis, "Promoting Movements to Christ"; Rebecca Lewis, "Insider Movements: Honoring God-given Identity and Community," *International Journal of Frontier Missiology* 26, no. 1 (Spring 2009): 16–19.
7   Rick Brown, "Biblical Muslims," *International Journal of Frontier Missiology* 24, no. 2 (Summer 2007): 65–74.
8   Kevin Greeson, *Camel Tracks: Discover the Camel's Secret* (Bangalore: WIGTake Resources, n.d.).

research necessary to address the many facets of complicated missiological issues. Worth repeating for its importance is that in my recommendations for future research I encourage research among various Muslim and former Muslim communities in various countries.

The issue hinted at in the previous paragraph is the extent to which the data drawn from a research population can be generalized to a wider population. In hard sciences and social sciences, this is often attained through random sampling. With appropriate ratios in place, random sampling of an entire population is the best methodology from which reliable generalizations can be made. Obviously, obtaining a random sample of the world's Muslims or former Muslims is a daunting challenge.

The perils of making generalizations from a nonrepresentative sample are taught in almost any research methods course. For example, we are here in New York City. If I wanted to find out what proportion of people in the United States were fans of the Boston Red Sox, I would likely not want to interview the first one hundred people I met on the streets of New York! Local antipathy would skew the data in one direction, just as conducting interviews in New England would skew the data in the opposite direction.

In applying this principle to the missiological question at hand, a threat to the validity of the research is posed by the extent to which the diaspora Muslim population is atypical of Muslims at large. In fact, I project the immediate response to my dissertation from those who oppose its contents will be an argument that the diaspora Muslim community in metro NY is nonrepresentative of the global Muslim community, or *umma*. The main rationale that immediately presents itself is the possibility that the diaspora community could have assimilated—become Americanized. This process could obviously render their sentiments as inappropriate for generalizing to a wider population. Clearly this is a significant threat to the validity of generalizing my research findings to the global *umma*.

When considering the assimilation process, several factors must be considered. First, how long has the individual being interviewed been in the country? Second, what age was the person at the time of immigration? Third, to what extent is the person connected to his or her ethnic community? Does he or she live in a neighborhood or pocket of compatriots? Or has he or she been immersed into another, wider population? These questions will be addressed below.

I also concede immediately as naive any proposition that Muslims think as a monolithic group, even within their ethnicities. I understand and appreciate that the sentiments of Muslims on religious, political, and social topics may be as diverse as those of the wider, self-identifying Christian community on similar topics. Furthermore, I understand that many Muslims and Muslim-background Christians in metro NY are refugees, having fled or been expulsed from their home countries by wars, persecutions, and economic catastrophes. These traumas have the potential to influence a person's perspectives on various issues. At this time I turn my attention to the strengths of metro NY Muslim diaspora community input.

Strengths of Metro NY Diaspora Community Input

There are a number of strengths of metro NY diaspora community input into the missiological research I sought to address:
- The Muslim population of metro NY is amazingly diverse.
- Metro NY continues to be an immigration gateway, such that metro NY Muslims are likely to be more recent immigrants, and thus express sentiments that track more closely with Muslims in their home countries.
- Muslims in the West may be freer to speak their minds than those living in Muslim countries, in which repercussions may await those with deviant religious or political views.
- Based on a recent Pew Study,[9] which states that American Muslims are less dogmatic than their global brethren, an *a fortiori* argument can be made that if diaspora Muslims in America will not accept the more flexible definition of the word "Muslim" required by insider movements, then global Muslims likely will not accept it either.

These points will be explained in the order presented above.

The Diversity of the Metro NY Muslim Community

Initially I will set the metro NY Muslim community within the national context. It should be noted that American Muslims remain a research enigma for several reasons. First, there is no general agreement about the number of Muslims residing in the United States. US Census Data does not capture religious affiliation, though inferences can be made through numbering certain ethnic groups, such as Turks, which correlate strongly with Islamic affiliation. Also, some communities where Islam has made inroads, especially the African-American community, witness both a converting into and a falling away process that is hard to quantify. Finally, the

---

9   Pew Research Center, "Muslim Americans: No Signs of Growth in Alienation or Support for Extremism," August 30, 2011, http://www.pewforum.org/2011/08/30/muslim-americans-no-signs-of-growth-in-alienation-or-support-for-extremism/.

reality that the United States' unquantifiable illegal immigrant population includes many Muslims makes the overall Muslim population an elusive figure. The Pew 2011 Survey counts 2.75 million Muslim Americans.[10] Though this number is up by 200,000 from their 2007 survey, it nevertheless remains much lower than Muslim community estimates. President Obama, in his famous 2009 Cairo speech, referenced "nearly seven million American Muslims in our country today."[11]

The Pew 2011 study finds that "a 63% majority of Muslim Americans are first generation immigrants to the U.S., with 45% having arrived in the U.S. since 1990. More than a third of Muslim Americans (37%) were born in the U.S., including 15% who had at least one immigrant parent."[12] Notably, my research focuses on Muslim-born persons only, not those who have converted into Islam. This would therefore exclude about one-fifth of American Muslims who are converts. I approximated this figure by subtracting from the 37 percent American-born population the 15 percent who had at least one immigrant parent—and were therefore likely to have been born Muslim. Similar statistics for the breakdown of the Muslim population in metro NY are unavailable. The national chart could be depicted as follows:

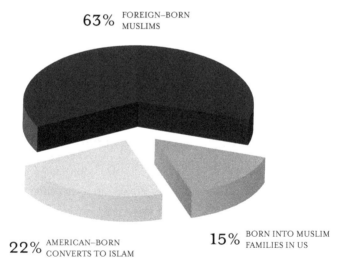

Figure 1: Muslim Americans

---

10   Ibid., 20.
11   Barack Obama, "Remarks by the President on a New Beginning" (speech, Cairo University, Cairo, Egypt, June 4, 2009), http://www.whitehouse.gov/the_press_office/Remarks-by-the-President-at-Cairo-University-6-04-09/ (accessed December 1, 2013).
12   Pew Research Center, "Muslim Americans," 8.

Regarding ethnic mix, the Pew Survey states:

> First-generation Muslim Americans come from a wide range of countries around the world. About four-in-ten (41%) are immigrants from the Middle East or North Africa, while about a quarter (26%) come from South Asian nations including Pakistan (14%), Bangladesh (5%) and India (3%). Others came to the U.S. from sub-Saharan Africa (11%), various countries in Europe (7%), Iran (5%), or other countries (9%).[13]

All of these communities are represented in metro NY.

I am indebted to Chris Clayman and Meredith Lee, who recently undertook a monumental project locating, describing, and numbering unreached diaspora people groups in metro NY. That research was published in 2010 under the title *ethNYcity*. It covers many Muslim people groups in metro NY, but it does not cover all of them.

This *ethNYcity* research includes American Community Survey (ACS) data from the United States Census Bureau (2008 figures). ACS "total ancestry" number is based on self-identification. The ACS "foreign born" reflects first-generation immigrants. Clayman and Lee also include community estimates based on discussions with community leaders. The community estimates are higher due to the tendency of leaders to include undocumented community members and possibly even to round up. In the case of Iranians, Clayman and Lee present Persian Jews as a separate people group. With the exception of the Indonesian and Egyptian count, which include perhaps a majority of Christians in those respective counts, the data listed in table 2 approximates Muslim populations in metro NY:

---

13 Ibid., 8

PEOPLE GROUP	ACS TOTAL ANCESTRY	ACS FOREIGN-BORN	COMMUNITY ESTIMATE
Pakistanis	65,171	66,933	120,000
Egyptians	47,728	35,344	110,000
Bangladeshis	NA	69,968	100,000
Turks	48,977	32,110	70,000
Iranians	30,989	19,219	60,000–70,000
Afghans	11,888	8,204	20,000
Palestinians	10,805	NA	30,000
Senegalese	4,553	NA	30,000
Indoesians	NA	6,677	8,000–15,000

Table 2: Muslim Population in NY

Because of the large numbers of Muslim immigrants in metro NY, it is possible to obtain a diverse sample of Muslims for missiological research. Furthermore, there are Muslim-background Christians living and worshiping in metro NY who hail from many different nations and ethnic groups. These factors of diversity present in metro NY could scarcely be replicated in any given Muslim country. I sought to replicate this diversity in my research design.

Positive Attributes of Metro NY as an Immigration Gateway

I would accept as reasonable the proposition that the longer an immigrant community has lived in diaspora, the more likely their collective worldview is likely to drift away from that of their compatriots back home. This issue of assimilation is further complicated since many of the Muslim communities continue to receive significant infusions of new immigrants. These new waves of immigrants bring with them their own perceptions and thought processes, no doubt reflecting the current polarization of thinking now taking place in the Muslim world regarding the Islamic renaissance as manifested in *shari'a*-oriented ideologies.

In this vein, American Muslims constitute a fascinating subject of research because of the dynamic changes within the community. Abu-Laban describes the successive waves of Muslim immigrants to North America, in chronological order, as "pioneers," "transitional," and, most recently, "differentiated." The first two waves were interested in maintaining their Muslim identity yet tended to be more assimilative, while the "differentiated cohort" exhibits an "offensive-activist" mentality.[14] Hausfeld notes that the more recent "offensive-activist" cohort sense the spiritual vacuum in America and feel Islam is a viable answer to it.[15] Having been born into and raised in the transitional cohort, and as I now observe the differentiated cohort, my sense is that Hausfeld's assessment is accurate.

Metro NY as a gateway city reflects Muslims of all these cohorts. Furthermore, it is likely that the Muslim immigrants in metro NY tend to be more recent immigrants. In fact, of my fourteen interviews with local Muslims that were of the chance, "street-intercept" variety (defined below), only one was US-born. Of the twenty Muslims I interviewed, they averaged forty years of age, with their length of time in the United States at just over twelve years. I will discuss the demographics of my study at length below; the point here is that metro NY Muslims reflect the gateway distinctive of recent immigrants with vivid memories of their home countries.

Freedom of Thought and Conscience as a Research Asset

As I walked the streets of Uzbekistan in 2011, reflecting on the suppression and persecution of political and religious deviants, I pondered how difficult it might be to obtain honest answers to missiological research in such a country. Even indigenous research assistants would have a hard time ascertaining the genuine sentiments of local individuals, especially on a topic as controversial as someone straying from Islam. For that reason, a diaspora setting may provide a much more open situation, especially where the research participants are recent immigrants.

My own experience in the field research I conducted between August and October 2013 confirmed this. The majority of the Muslim persons I encountered randomly on the streets of metro NY were willing to talk about "Muslim identity." One negative experience occurred as I interviewed a Palestinian-American young

---

14   Sharon M. Abu-Laban, Regula B. Qureshi, and Earle H. Waugh, *Muslim Families in North America* (Edmonton: University of Alberta Press, 1991), 13.
15   Mark Hausfeld, *Islam in America: Understanding and Engaging Diaspora Muslims through the Local Church* (Springfield, MO: Assemblies of God Theological Seminary, 2009).

man. A friend rode by and yelled to him, "Don't talk to him. He's with the FBI." On the other hand, a Bangladeshi man seemed to relish the opportunity to set the record straight regarding the views of people in his home country: "Muslims in Bangladesh don't have the way of thinking you see on CNN."

In my own doctoral research, I asked forty Muslim-born persons a series of eleven questions, based on an identical vignette. This generated 440 responses, which I recorded by dictation. I included 180 of those verbatim responses in the text of my dissertation. This is the type of firsthand research that has been sorely lacking in missiology related to ministry to Muslims.

A Fortiori Argument Regarding Generalizing of My Research

My research focused on Muslim identity, or, in indigenous thought forms, Muslim-ness, or, the essence of being a Muslim. This is a religious topic, so a bit of background on the religious practices of American Muslims is helpful. The Pew 2011 study notes: "69% say that religion is very important in their lives, and about half (47%) report at least weekly attendance at a mosque for prayer. Similarly, about half (48%) say they make all five *salah* prayers daily, and another 18% report making at least some *salah* daily."[16]

The most significant statement in the 2011 Pew Study, as it affects this research, is found on page 11:

> Yet the survey finds that most reject a dogmatic approach to religion. Most Muslim Americans (57%) say there is more than one true way to interpret the teachings of Islam; far fewer (37%) say that there is only one true interpretation of Islam. Similarly, 56% of Muslim Americans say that many different religions can lead to eternal life; just 35% say that Islam is the one true faith that leads to eternal life.

Pew concludes: "In this respect, Muslim Americans differ from many of their counterparts in the Muslim world and are similar to U.S. Christians."[17] Pew does not provide statistics about the tolerance or fluidity of beliefs of Muslims in other countries. Nevertheless Pew's analogy is that just as American Christians tend to be less dogmatic than their brethren globally, so Muslim Americans are less dogmatic

---

16   Pew Research Center, "Muslim Americans," 11.
17   Ibid., 11.

than the global *umma*. Even prior to doing any interviews, Pew's survey suggests that if Muslim Americans will not accept the broader, more fluid definition of Muslim that is required by retentionism, then it will not likely be accepted by the wider Muslim community. In other words, if Muslim Americans will not accept within their perception of Muslim identity a person who believes in the Bible and Jesus as Lord and God, then the global *umma* is not likely to accept it either, on the basis of an *a fortiori* argument.

Example of an Application of Diaspora Community Input in Missological Research

Field Work among Metro NY Muslims

For my PhD dissertation field research I interviewed 40 Muslim-born persons in metro NY. Twenty-eight were men and 12 were women. Half of them were Muslims and the other 20 were Muslim-background Christians. For the Muslims, I interviewed 15 Muslim laypersons and 5 Muslim scholars.

Before discussing the diversity of this research sample, I will address my methodology in obtaining the interviews. Four of the interviews with the scholars/imams were prearranged by local contacts or myself. For the interviews with lay Muslims, 13 of the 15 interviews were of the variety labeled by Russell Bernard as "street-intercept.[18] I simply walked up to people on the streets in Muslim neighborhoods and greeted the potential interviewee, "*Salaamu alaikum*" ("Peace be upon you"). Their responses almost invariably indicated to me whether they were Muslims. If affirmative, I brandished my seminary ID card and said, "I am a Christian seminary student studying Muslim identity. Would you have time for me to ask you questions about this?"

In a number of cases the person did not have time to talk, and in other cases the person did not speak enough English to participate. I did not seek to conduct interviews in other languages, though I concede that this excluded a segment of potential interviewees whom I met. I also had personal contacts seeking to arrange interviews with other scholars, such as local imams hailing from Indonesia, Bangladesh, and Turkey, but I was unsuccessful in obtaining those interviews in a reasonable amount of time. Nevertheless I am confident the diversity of the

---

18   H. Russell Bernard, *Research Methods in Anthropology: Qualitative and Quantitative Approaches*, 3rd ed. (Walnut Creek, CA: AltaMira, 2002), 243.

Muslim interviewees, who were born in 13 different countries, is a great asset to this dissertation.

I did two of the interviews on the courtyard of a mosque after Friday prayers. I also did several street-intercept interviews on a Friday afternoon at the time observant Muslim men would typically be at mosque. This enabled me to capture the responses of several less observant Muslims. In every case, I tried to conduct the interviews absent from the presence of others who might overhear and thus influence the interviewee's responses. In several cases this was not possible and an onlooker or friend was present.

Though it is not culturally appropriate for a man to approach Muslim women on the streets, I was able to interview one Muslim woman in a public area at a local university, and another Muslim woman through an arranged and chaperoned interview. Otherwise I was limited to interviewing men in the Muslim segment of the interviews. For the Muslim-background Christians, I was able to interview ten women and ten men.

There was at least one interviewee whose English was just above the borderline to participate in a survey that featured hypothetical and philosophical questions. I only repeated or rephrased questions that it appeared the interviewee was struggling to understand. In every case I took dictation as the person spoke. I have represented their verbatim comments in the words they themselves used. Each participant signed a consent form that stated the purpose of the interview. The consent form confirmed the interviewee's identity would be confidential.

In summary, the 20 Muslims I interviewed for my PhD dissertation hailed from 14 different birth countries and 10 different ethnic groups. Only one was US-born, even though the Pew Study has 37 percent of American Muslims being US-born. This suggests that NY-area Muslim immigrants are more likely to be first-generation immigrants than is the case for Muslims nationwide. The average age of the Muslim interviewees is 40.6 years. The age range is 23 to 84 years. The average time spent in the United States is 12.3 years.

The one American-born interviewee had visited his ancestral homeland. Five interviewees stated they visit their home country frequently. Only three stated they had not visited since moving to the United States. Of these three, none had immigrated to the United States at an age younger than 28; their length of time living in the United States was 5, 6, and 13 years, respectively. So, even those who haven't visited their home country since immigrating are well positioned to describe a vignette taking place in that country.

Sixteen of the 19 foreign-born interviewees had lived in their home countries as adults. Of the three that hadn't, one came to this country when he was 9 years old, another when he was 12, and the third when he was 14. Two of these three had visited their home countries after immigrating to the United States. I met one interviewee, who had emigrated from Pakistan when he was 12, at the Pakistan Day Parade in Manhattan. Though I did not ask him whether he had visited Pakistan since he immigrated, his presence at this event suggests he remains connected to his community. All in all, this group of 20 Muslims seems well positioned and informed to comment on the sentiments of Muslims in their respective home countries.

All of the Muslim interviewees said they came from families where both their parents were Muslims. Regarding sectarian identification, all but one said they were Sunni Muslims. One young Pakistani proudly volunteered that he was a Sufi. I did not probe the Sunnis to see if they had other leanings, such as Sufi, Salafist, etc.

Field Work among Metro NY Muslim-background Christians

Regarding the Muslim-background Christians, I interviewed 20 adult individuals—10 men and 10 women. The mean age of the interviewees is 48.4 years. The range of ages is 25 to 73. Three of the interviewees are from Shi'ite family background; the other 17 are from Sunni background. The average length of time this cohort have been believers in the Lord Jesus Christ is 19.3 years. The newest believer had trusted Christ 2 years ago, while the longest-serving believer had been in Christ 35 years. All of these believers, except one, were raised in homes where both parents were Muslims.

Four of the 20 interviewees (20 percent) were US-born. One foreign-born interviewee immigrated to the United States with his family when he was one year old. All of the 20 interviewees were born into Muslim families and were raised Muslims; none were converts from other religions. All of the US-born interviewees have visited their respective ancestral homelands as adults. One had lived in that country as an adult. Fifteen of the 16 foreign-born interviewees have lived in their birth countries as adults (past 18+ years of age). Five of the 16 foreign-born interviewees came to faith in Christ in their respective countries, and can therefore add the perspectives of having lived as Muslim-background Christians in Muslim countries. The average length of time lived in the United States by this cohort is 24.9 years, just over half of the 48-year mean age. These factors make it reasonable that this cohort of interviewees could respond to a vignette set in their respective countries. As such, this diaspora research features a diverse sample and is not disconnected to the global picture.

Field Work Results

While I have described my research methodology at some length above, I would like to include the results to provide an example of diaspora community input into missiological research. As noted above, I interviewed forty Muslim-born persons in metro NY to garner their perceptions on whether they felt a Muslim who came to believe in the biblical narrative regarding the Lord Jesus Christ was in fact still a Muslim. I did this in interviews that employed a third-person vignette of a Muslim who became interested in the Bible and Jesus through the Internet. That individual then came to believe that God visited the earth in the form of Jesus, who died on the Cross and rose from the dead. However, this individual continued to identify himself or herself as a Muslim on a permanent basis thereafter.

Though the interviews featured eleven questions, one question in particular probed the interviewees' perspectives on the central question of whether a Muslim who comes to believe the biblical narrative regarding Jesus Christ is still a Muslim. Thirty-eight of the forty interviewees stated such a person is no longer a Muslim. Only one stated the person was still a Muslim; one other was unsure. The Muslim-background Christians were unanimous in stating a Muslim who comes to believe in the biblical narrative regarding the Lord Jesus Christ is no longer a Muslim.

Their primary reasoning was theological. They felt a belief in the divine Jesus was a repudiation of the central Islamic doctrine of divine unity, known as *tawhid*. This constitutes a repudiation of the prophetic veracity of Muhammad. Since affirmation of the prophethood of Muhammad is the indispensible ingredient for obtaining and retaining Muslim identity, individuals who continue to affirm the prophethood of Muhammad will never be able to fully find their identity in Christ.

In summary of the field research, I interviewed 40 Muslim-born persons from the United States, Burkina Faso, Sierra Leone, Morocco, Egypt, Lebanon, Palestine, Jordan, Saudi Arabia, Turkey, Iran, Kazakhstan, Uzbekistan, Pakistan, India, Bangladesh, Guyana, and Trinidad. They range in age from their 20s to their 80s. Twenty of the 40 are Muslim-background Christians. Ninety-five percent of the interviewees reject the concept of insider movements—that permanently retaining Muslim identity is compatible with biblical faith in the Lord Jesus Christ. Once again, I recommend this type of research on insider movements be conducted among indigenous persons in nondiaspora settings.

Conclusions

Diaspora missiology has significant merits. Perhaps one overlooked merit is the relationship of research among diaspora communities to global missiological questions. This paper assessed the strengths and weaknesses of diaspora community input into missological research in general.

A caveat exists in generalizing diaspora community input to wider, nondiaspora contexts. The threat to the validity of such applications increases to the extent the diaspora community may be found atypical of their nondiaspora compatriots. Where significant time or even generations have passed, this threat will increase.

Nevertheless diaspora community input has significant value in missiological research for several reasons. First, in a diaspora setting like metro NY, it is possible to gain access simultaneously to a tremendous diversity of diaspora communities. Second, diaspora settings that are global gateways, such as metro NY, may allow closer connectivity of thought processes and relationships between the diaspora communities and their ancestral homelands. Third, when seeking to conduct research among peoples from nations where freedom of speech is curtailed, diaspora communities can provide voices that are subject to the same level of intimidation. Fourth, where other research has previously established relationships between a diaspora population and an abroad population—such as was provided by the Pew 2011 Survey of American Muslims—field research findings among the diaspora group may be able to be generalized to the wide, nondiaspora population. All of these reasons suggest that well-conceived research among diaspora groups can be an asset to missiological research in general.

Chapter Five
Mission by and beyond the Diaspora: Partnering with Diaspora Believers to Reach Other Immigrants and the Local People

STAN DOWNES

ABSTRACT

We live in an age of massive movements of people around the earth, and God is using these movements to create many new opportunities for Christian witness. This chapter explores the potential for and experience of diaspora Christians participating in cross-cultural ministry in their new host countries. Rather than just planting and maintaining church fellowships only for their own ethnic and cultural groups, migrating Christians can have a major spiritual impact on the peoples of other cultures among whom they live. The experience of Romanian Christians living in Western Europe is used as a case study.

Introduction

Ours is an age of massive movements of people around the earth. Patrick Johnstone estimates that there are 191 million migrants currently and that that number may grow by another 170 million by 2050.[1] People are on the move for a variety of reasons. Some move voluntarily; others move because it is not safe or possible to live where they were. As believers we believe that God uses movements of this type for his purposes. Professor Craig Ott writes, "This sovereign working of God in human history and the movement of peoples we find to be a means of God spreading His glory among all people and preparing people to receive that message."[2] Diaspora missiology is based on the desire to understand what God is doing through these movements and to take advantage of the opportunities presented to us.

Enoch Wan in his book *Diaspora Missiology: Theory, Methodology, and Practice* identifies three types of diaspora missions:

---

[1] Patrick Johnstone, *Future of the Global Church* (Colorado Springs: Biblica, 2011), 4.
[2] Craig Ott, "Diaspora and Relocation as Divine Impetus for Witness in the Early Church," in *Diaspora Missiology: Theory, Methodology, and Practice*, ed. Enoch Wan (Portland, OR: Institute of Diaspora Studies, 2011), 75.

1. Missions to the diaspora: reaching the diaspora groups themselves.
2. Missions through the diaspora: diaspora Christians reaching out to their kinsmen wherever they are.
3. Missions by and beyond the diaspora: motivating and mobilizing diaspora Christians for cross-cultural missions.[3]

Much of the focus of diaspora missiology is on the first category—missions to the diaspora. We have great opportunities for ministry when people move from countries where there is little freedom to present the gospel to other countries that have no such limitations. For example, there is greater freedom to evangelize Moroccans in Spain, Turks in Germany, and Chinese in South Africa than in their home countries. I attended the Consultation on the Diaspora Peoples of Europe in September of 2013, and the majority of the presentations and the bulk of the discussion were on missions *to* the diaspora peoples in Europe. It is appropriate to focus on this ministry as it gives us the unique opportunity to reach people who are unlikely to be reached in their home countries. It is legal and less dangerous to approach them in open countries, and they also tend to be more receptive to spiritual matters in a new environment.[4] In addition, ministry to diaspora peoples can and often does lead to the second type of diaspora ministry—Christians in those groups ministering to their people in other locations.

This chapter goes a step further and deals with the third category—mission by and beyond the diaspora. In it I explore the potential for and experience of diaspora Christians in impacting people of other ethnic groups for Christ. For this purpose I draw on my studies, on my experience as a missionary in Romania from 1996 to 2008 with OC International, and my role as OC's Europe area director since that time.

Thesis Statement

It is my belief that diaspora believers and diaspora churches can and should be a major force in world missions by reaching not only the populations among whom they live but also reaching other immigrant people groups in the same locality. A Lausanne publication on diaspora ministry boldly states, "Christian believers in diaspora ... are one of the most strategic 'missionary' forces in the history of missions ... evangelizing members of the host society and other ethnic groups in

---

3 Wan, introduction to *Diaspora Missiology* (2011), 5.
4 Enoch Wan, "The Phenomenon of Diaspora," in *Diaspora Missiology* (2011), 13.

their context."⁵ Ed Silvoso adds, "According to the Bible, every time that God chose to bless and transform a powerful nation, He used foreigners and immigrants—Joseph, Daniel, Esther, Paul, etc."⁶ My hope is that diaspora believers around the world will come to realize that their new homes are mission fields and that they have an opportunity and the responsibility to make a difference there—and will do so.

The General Pattern of Church Planting among Diaspora Groups

In many diaspora groups there are very few believers—for example, migrants from the Middle East and from the Buddhist and Hindu lands of Asia. By contrast, other diaspora groups contain a significant number of believers. Examples are diasporas from Latin America, sub-Saharan Africa, Eastern Europe, and parts of Asia such as the Philippines and China. When these believers settle in their new locations, they typically gather together for mutual support and fellowship. Often they form churches that cater to members of their specific groups, using the language and worship styles from their home countries. In some cases the rejection or lack of welcome by the existing local churches has also motivated them to start their own churches.⁷ In large cities there can be large numbers of diaspora churches. Samuel Cueva wrote in 2010 that there were at least seventy registered Latin American churches in Barcelona!⁸ The planting of diaspora churches can also result in a dizzying variety of churches in an area. A Baptist study in Germany in 2005 found 210 international Baptist churches formed in very diverse communities including Russian, Ghanaian, Congolese, Tamil, Vietnamese, and Iranian.⁹ Hans Lund estimates that there are seven thousand immigrant churches just in Europe.¹⁰ There are, of course, thousands of ethnic churches in the United States—Hispanic, Korean,

---

5   Lausanne Committee for World Evangelization, *Scattered to Gather: Embracing the Global Trend of Diaspora* (Manila: LifeChange, 2010), http://www.jdpayne.org/wp-content/uploads/2010/10/Scattered-to-Gather.pdf, 27.
6   Testimonial in Samuel Lee, *Blessed Migrants: God's Strategy for Global Revival* (Bloomington, IN: iUniverse, 2008), ix.
7   Mark Sturge, *Look What the Lord Has Done: An Exploration of Black Christian Faith in Britain* (Queensway, England: Scripture Union, 2005), 42.
8   Samuel Cueva, "Mission, Missionaries and the Evangelization of Europe," *Evangelical Review of Theology* 34, no. 4 (October 2010): 9, http://www.back2europe.org/getattachment/7af255e3-a83b-4e38-8098-c2ba12978547/Resource-2.aspx (accessed April 4, 2014).
9   Michael Kisskalt, "Immigrant Churches in the German Baptist Union," in *Ethnic Churches in Europe: A Baptist Response*, ed. Peter F. Penner (Prague: International Baptist Theological Seminary, 2006), 189.
10 Hans Lund, "Migrant Churches in Europe" (presentation at the Diaspora Consultation, Amsterdam, September 24–25, 2013).

Chinese, and Romanian, to name a few. Whether they know it or not, these churches form part of the harvest force where they are.

Challenges to Cross-cultural Impact

The problem is that these churches are often ineffective in impacting people from other cultures. Writing about Korean churches in their diaspora, Minho Song says, "In most diaspora Korean churches, the *apostolic* dimension of the church is either weak or missing."[11] Similarly, Kim-Kong Chan, writing of the Chinese diaspora, states, "The current growth in the Chinese diaspora communities seems to be more of a target for mission to the diaspora and mission through the diaspora but has not reached the potential of 'mission by and beyond the diaspora.'"[12] This is true of many diaspora churches. There are several reasons why these diaspora churches may have little impact on other local populations.

The cultural factors that bind the diaspora group together often separate them from the local people. Song continues,

> Finding themselves aliens and sojourners in a new setting, diaspora Christians have the natural tendency to stay amongst themselves because they find comfort and a sense of belonging to their kind. This homogeneous pull brings and binds them together, but ultimately bans them from meaningfully participating in the lives of those who are outside of the group.[13]

Believers in a diaspora group tend to focus on evangelizing and discipling the people within their cultural group. They feel an obligation to do so, and relating to their own group is much easier than relating cross-culturally to other people groups.

Another major reason is unfamiliarity with the local language. Most people hesitate to express themselves when they know that they cannot speak a language well. And the local speakers of the language may have little tolerance for those who speak it poorly. When diaspora believers have a group or church in which they use

---

[11] Minho Song, "The Diaspora Experience of the Korean Church and Its Implications for World Missions," in *Korean Diaspora and Christian Mission*, ed. S. Hun Kim and Wonsuk Ma (Eugene, OR: Wipf & Stock, 2011), 125.

[12] Kim-Kong Chan, "Missiological Implications of Chinese Christians in Diaspora," in Wan, *Diaspora Missiology* (2011), 193.

[13] Song, "Diaspora Experience," 125–26.

their native language extensively, it actually slows down their progress with the language of the host culture.

Since most diaspora churches use only their native language for their worship services, it is unlikely that local people would attend and participate in those services.

Unfamiliarity with the local culture is another barrier. The newcomers lack the social cues to know when and how it is appropriate to enter into a conversation about spiritual things. I once read a book about British culture that stated strongly that bringing up religion in conversation is a major social mistake there. People who are used to sharing their faith openly in their home culture would not necessarily know this.

Often the cultural gap between the local people and the diaspora people results in prejudice of one by the other. An example is the case for Romanians living in Western Europe. Professor Christina Ilie writes, "Unfortunately the Spanish public perception of Romanian immigrants is not [a] very good one, as they are seen as the most disagreeable group of [immigrants]."[14] It is a challenge for people with a lower social standing to influence those of higher standing, but it is not impossible. Paul rejoices (1 Cor 1:27,28) over the fact that God chooses humble people and uses them mightily. There are many stories, for example, of how Filipina housemaids have led whole households to the Lord in various countries.

The style of worship used in diaspora churches may be considered strange to the local people. Many diaspora groups are used to enthusiastic worship and to lengthy services. It is hard for people who are used to formal and shorter services to adjust to different worship patterns.

Often the local believers and their churches do little to connect with or encourage the churches of diaspora believers. This is largely due to cultural and linguistic differences, but often the people in the host culture simply don't "see" the other churches and believers.

Even when the diaspora group and the host society use the same language, the connection is not always easy. For example, the evangelical churches in the Basque area of Spain often have a majority of members from Latin America rather than from Spain. As a result, the services resemble those in Latin America. Spaniards

---

14   Cristina Ilie, "Criminality among Romanian Emigrants in Spain," *International Journal of Academic Research in Business and Social Sciences* 4, no. 3 (March 2014): 509, http://hrmars.com/hrmars_papers/Criminality_among_Romanian_Emigrants_in_Spain.pdf (accessed April 3, 2014).

visiting the service can understand the language but may determine that those churches are not for them.

Potential for Impact

In spite of these difficulties, Christian diaspora communities have a great potential to impact members of their host society as well as members of other diaspora groups. *Scattered to Gather*, a publication of the Lausanne Committee for World Evangelization, points out four advantages that believing diaspora communities have over traditional missionaries: they require no missionary visas, need no expensive international travel (since they are already there), face no political restrictions, and face few closed doors.[15] Samuel Lee adds, "Once the migrant understands the purpose of God in his or her life, then God releases authority and power to that person to act in that land . . . Migrants in their nation are potential blessings and the key to revival in the hosting land."[16]

In addition to large numbers of people immigrating to other countries, another major world trend is the growth of the missions movement in the Majority World (Global South). As churches in Africa, Asia, and Latin America grow in their vision and heart for cross-cultural missions, so do their communities in the diaspora. Often pastors are called from the home country to lead churches in the diaspora. Sometimes missionaries are also sent to work with and within the diaspora communities.

Positive Signs and Examples

In spite of the difficulties, there are good examples in which the diaspora church has had an impact on the local population.
- Samuel Lee reports effective ministries by Indonesians and Surinamese among the Dutch in Holland, Nigerians with British people, and Koreans with the local people of Japan and Germany.[17]
- Kingsway International Christian Centre in England is a black-majority megachurch with a Nigerian pastor. It is the vision of KICC "to share the Good News of Jesus Christ with the 11 million people resident in London."[18]
- Overseas Filipino workers are well known for their zeal and effectiveness in communicating Christ wherever they are. The goal of the Philippines Missions

---
15 Lausanne Committee for World Evangelization, *Scattered to Gather*, 10.
16 Lee, *Blessed Migrants*, 11.
17 Ibid., 24–25, 69.
18 Kingsway International Christian Centre, "The KICC Vision," http://www.kicc.org.uk/Church/Vision/tabid/45/Default.aspx (accessed April 3, 2014).

Association and the Philippine Council of Evangelical Churches was to have 200,000 tentmaking missionaries by 2010 as part of their diaspora.[19]
- A Romanian Pentecostal church in Barcelona has a missions committee tasked to find ways to reach Spanish people.
- A Romanian believer in Spain opened a youth club as a ministry to Spanish young people.
- The Youngnak Korean Presbyterian Church of Toronto has helped Thai and Myanmar leaders plant churches for believers in their own immigrant groups.
- A Chinese church in Bucharest supports a local orphanage.

A Wonderful Opportunity: Mission to Other Diaspora Groups

Diaspora believers and their churches have a wonderful opportunity to reach out to other groups of immigrants. Pastor Cody Lorance borrows descriptors from anthropologist Miriam Adeney,[20] saying, "These 'liminal, hyphenated, polycentric, multilingual Christians' are the natural 'bridge-builders' who can effectively lead in cross-cultural mission endeavors to other diaspora communities."[21] They share the experience of struggling to adjust to a new situation and culture. They share the burdens of learning languages and of not being fully accepted by the host society. The diaspora believers can assist the non-Christian immigrants in a host of practical ways, showing them what they have done to "make it" in their new homes. The diaspora believers also have the opportunity to show the non-Christians immigrants what a true, vibrant Christianity looks like. In many countries of Europe, non-Christian immigrants are more likely to meet a believer from another part of the world than from the country where they are living! Local churches often do not have the energy or passion to reach the non-Christian immigrants, so it is important that the believing immigrants attempt to do so.

What Should Diaspora Believers and Their Churches Do?

1. Realize that they are on a mission field. Every country is a mission field in the sense that there are always people who need the Lord and places that need

---

19   Robert F. K. Lopez, "The Philippine Missions Association (PMA) Tentmaking Agenda: Raising an Army of Outstanding Filipino Witnesses," in Pantoja, Tira, and Wan, *Scattered*, 197.
20   Miriam Adeney, "Colorful Initiatives: North American Diasporas in Mission," *Missiology: An International Review* 39, no. 1 (January 2011): 7, http://mis.sagepub.com/content/39/1/5.full.pdf (accessed April 3, 2014).
21   Cody C. Lorance, "Reflections of a Church Planter among Diaspora Groups in Metro-Chicago: Pursuing Cruciformity in Diaspora Missions," in Wan, *Diaspora Missiology* (2011), 275.

churches. However, diaspora believers often find themselves in countries where the spiritual condition is worse than the countries from which they come. This can motivate the migrants to active and effective ministry.

2. To the extent that the diaspora group has been oppressed by the host culture either at home or in the host country, the diaspora believers need to forgive those offenses and love their new neighbors for the sake of the gospel.
3. Pray for the people and churches of the host society. God told the Jewish diaspora through Jeremiah, "Also, seek the peace and prosperity of the city to which I have carried you into exile. Pray to the Lord for it, because if it prospers, you too will prosper" (Jer 29:7). If diaspora believers pray fervently and consistently for the country, those prayers will have a significant impact.
4. Prepare the people to interact well with the people of the local culture and encourage them to do so. Part of this process is to encourage people to work hard to learn the local language.
5. Engage in community activities, including (but not limited to) church-sponsored events and fellowships of Christian leaders.
6. Consider offering a bilingual service or planting a church using the local language.
7. Partner with churches within other diaspora communities.

What Can the Indigenous Churches Do to Assist the Diaspora People and Churches?

Quoting an article from Orientdienst, a German mission agency, Jimmy Martin outlines four options churches have for engaging with immigrant believers. Those are: integrating immigrants fully into existing churches, sharing facilities with immigrant congregations, assisting immigrant believers to form their own independent churches, and lastly developing multicultural churches that can integrate people from many cultures.[22] In addition to those options, indigenous churches can do the following:

- Offer practical support to the immigrant population—for example, assisting in language learning, finding jobs, finding housing, and helping with justice issues.
- Fellowship with people from diaspora churches and hold joint worship services.
- Include the newcomers in social and evangelistic projects.
- Connect with and encourage their leaders.

---

22 Jimmy Martin, "International and Multiethnic Churches," in *Ethnic Churches in Europe: A Baptist Response*, ed. Peter F. Penner (Prague: International Baptist Theological Seminary, 2006), 156–57.

- Seek to learn from them.
- Assist in planting ethnic and multiethnic churches. For example, the Rocky Mountain District of the Evangelical Free Church recently hired a director of ethnic church planting and development to assist diaspora groups in this way.

What Can the Churches in the Diaspora Group's Homeland Do?

It is often discouraging for church leaders to see their people emigrate. Pastors don't like to lose their members and especially their leaders. Rather than resent the departure of their people, church leaders can inspire and equip them to be tentmaking missionaries in the places to which they are going. In the Philippines, the Philippine Missions Mobilization Movement encourages believers who are emigrating to be prepared to be effective witnesses in their new environment. They have developed a number of training materials,[23] and a website (www.farfromhome.info) has been established to provide additional training materials.

Greater Opportunities with Later Generations

The first generation to move to a new place will always have the hardest time adjusting and may have a harder time having a spiritual impact on the local people. The situation is quite different for later generations. As children grow up in the new environment and go to school, they become proficient in the local language and much more in tune with the host society. They are then better equipped to minister to the people around them. Michael Kisskalt writes, "They are an important group in the process of integration and can help by being a bridge not only in the society but also between local and immigrant churches."[24] It is important for church leaders to help young people maintain their religious fervor and desire to evangelize the people around them. The people in these later generations may choose to join the churches of the host culture. That can be a challenge to the diaspora churches in which they were raised, but it can be a great blessing to the local churches.

Ministry Through and Beyond the Diaspora vs. Reverse Missions

People groups are on the move for many reasons. Increasingly believers are moving to new places with ministry as part of their motivation. As a result, the dividing

---

23 Jojo Manzano and Joy C. Solina, eds., *Worker to Witness: Becoming an OFW Tentmaker* (Makati City, Philippines: Church Strengthening Ministry, 2007).
24 Michael Kisskalt, "Cross-cultural Learning: Issues of the Second Generation of Immigrant Churches," in *Ethnic Churches in Europe: A Baptist Response*, ed. Peter F. Penner (Prague: International Baptist Theological Seminary, 2006), 120

line between "missionary" and "migrant" is becoming blurred. "Reverse missions" is defined as "those from the former mission fields such as Africa, the Caribbean, Asia and South America sending missionaries and engaging in cross-cultural mission to the Western world."[25] The people engaged in reverse missions are often part of diaspora groups, and they can lead those groups in effective cross-cultural ministry.

Consider these examples:

- Ike Nwaobasi, a Nigerian missionary with the Deeper Life Christian Church, learned German and planted three churches in Austria in which most of the worshipers were Austrian. Ike talks enthusiastically about his "piano strategy." He says it takes the black keys and the white keys on a piano to make beautiful music, and it takes white and black people together to make a beautiful church. His goal was to plant churches for the Austrians, and to a large extent he succeeded.
- Rev. Israel Olofinjana is a Nigerian pastor serving in a Baptist church in London. He has become well known for his advocacy of "reverse mission." In *Turning the Tables on Mission* Rev. Olofinjana includes the stories of eleven key people who have come from the Global South to minister in the UK. These people can be considered members of diaspora groups, but their primary motive for immigrating to the UK is to do mission. He has recently established the Centre for Missionaries from the Majority World (www.cmmw.org) to offer training and encouragement to cross-cultural workers.
- Rev. Jesus Londono has a similar vision which he calls Back to Europe. The main purposes of Back to Europe are to raise awareness of Europe as a mission field and to mobilize the church around the world toward Europe.[26] The concept of Back to Europe is that the countries that once received missionaries *from* Europe are now capable of sending missionaries *to* Europe. Those are the same countries that have significant diaspora groups in Europe already.

Case Study: Romania Diaspora Ministry

During the time that my wife and I served as missionaries with OC International in Romania, we heard more and more about the flight of Romanians to Western Europe. Even though communism had fallen several years before, economic conditions in Romania were still tough for many people. Romania's links with the European Union created the possibility for many Romanians to emigrate to Western Europe

---

25   Israel Olofinjana, ed., *Turning the Tables on Mission* (Watford, UK: Instant Apostle, 2013), 25.
26   Back to Europe, "Main Purposes of B2E," http://www.back2europe.org/About-Us/Additional-information.aspx (accessed April 3, 2014).

in search of financial gain. Many worked as laborers, doing work that Spaniards no longer wanted to do.

In places where the Romanians gathered, they often started churches. Those churches became centers for social interaction as well as religious expression. Often trained pastors emigrated to lead these churches. Over time several of these Romanian language churches grew to become the largest evangelical churches in the cities in which they were located! Training organizations based in Romania sent teachers to equip the believers in these congregations. The Romanian Pentecostal Church opened a seminary near Madrid, Spain, and at one time it had 120 students,[27] nearly as many students as the seminary in Bucharest!

We received reports that Spanish pastors were delighted that Romanians were planting churches and even that some saw the Romanian churches as the fulfillment of prophecy. In some cases Spanish people have attended Romanian worship services. Some small groups were formed with Romanians and Spanish people together. At least one Romanian church in Spain had a committee tasked with finding ways to impact the Spanish people.

During the same period, interest in cross-cultural missions was growing rapidly in Romania. Romanian missionaries were being sent out to places like China, India, North Africa, and Peru. The Kairos missions course (www.kairoscourse.org) was being used widely to introduce churches and individuals to missions, and some short-term missions efforts were organized. Kairos courses have also been taught in Romanian churches in Spain and Italy.

These developments generated a significant potential for Romanian believers to impact societies in Western Europe. Through extensive nationwide research our team determined that evangelicals comprised approximately 2 percent of the Romanian population,[28] significantly exceeding the percentage in most Western European countries. At the time it was estimated that there were a million Romanians living in Spain. Using the 2 percent figure, we can then estimate that there were twenty thousand evangelical Romanian believers in Spain. The 2001 edition of *Operation World* estimated the evangelical population of Spain to be 174,000.[29] Therefore the

---

27   Costel Grămadă, "Festivitate la Seminarul Biblic 'Emmanuel' din Arganda del Rey, Spania," *Cuvântul Adevărului* (January 2006).
28   OC International and Misiunea Mondială Unită, *God's Heart for Romania* (Bucharest, Romania: OC International and Misiunea Mondială Unită , 2001), 3, http://ocresearch.info/sites/default/files/Romania%20National%20Church%20Census%20Report%202001.pdf.
29   Patrick Johnstone and Jason Mandryk, eds. *Operation World* (Milton Keynes, UK: Authentic Media, 2001), 583.

Romanian evangelicals may have comprised 11 percent of the country's total. C. Peter Wagner has estimated that 10 percent of believers have the gift of evangelism.[30] If even 5 percent of the Romanian believers in Spain had that gift, that meant that there were one thousand gifted Romanian evangelists in Spain—a significant addition to the harvest force already there!

Need for More Study

As we have seen, it can be quite a challenge for diaspora believers to make a spiritual impact on the local people among whom they live. Good examples are few. Rev. Israel Olofinjana's book *Turning the Tables on Mission* tells the stories of eleven leaders from the Global South who are ministering in the United Kingdom. While those individuals have had some impact on some British people, they are primarily working in multiethnic churches or in churches of their own culture. Enoch Wan includes eight case studies in his book *Diaspora Missiology*, but all of them deal primarily with missions to or through the diaspora. More examples of mission by and beyond the diaspora need to be found and publicized as an encouragement to the thousands of diaspora churches around the world.

Conclusion

It is clear that there is great potential in mission by and beyond the diaspora. However, the potential is largely waiting to be realized. Those people in diaspora communities need to seek ways to impact their host cultures and other immigrant communities. Those of us in host societies can minister to diaspora groups and seek to instill in them a vision for missions through, by, and beyond their communities.

---

30 C. Peter Wagner, *Your Spiritual Gifts Can Help Your Church Grow* (Venture, CA: Regal Books, 1980), 177.

Part Three:

Biblical and Theological Guidelines

Chapter Six

Diaspora Ministry in the Book of Acts: Insights from Two Speeches of the Apostle Paul to Help Guide Diaspora Ministry Today

LARRY W. CALDWELL

ABSTRACT

Most Christians do not read the book of Acts from the perspective of diaspora missiology. However, the majority of Acts shows us diaspora ministers of the gospel (like the Apostle Paul) ministering to diaspora and nondiaspora peoples in both diaspora and nondiaspora contexts. Paul is an especially good example of how a diaspora person does ministry that is sensitive to ministry context (who is the audience and where are they located) but also with sensitivity in terms of message context (what is actually said to the audience). This paper will specifically address the message context of diaspora ministry by looking at two examples from Paul's diaspora ministry: first, his message to the Jews and God fearers of Pisidian Antioch (Acts 13) and, second, his message to the Athenians in the Aeropogus (Acts 17). Implications for diaspora ministry today will conclude the paper.

Introduction

Who was the Apostle Paul, diasporically speaking? Recent biblical studies of diaspora, viewed from the perspective of missiology, are noting the biculturalism of Paul that grew out of his diaspora roots. They note that Paul's biculturalism made him the ideal person to bring the gospel to both Jew and Gentile.[1] Craig Ott, for example, has identified Paul in relationship to diaspora:

> Diaspora is one way by which people become bicultural and through which people are prepared for cross-cultural mission. Paul himself . . . is an extraordinary example of a diaspora Jew who, after being exposed to both Jewish and

---

[1] See, for example, Wan, *Diaspora Missiology* (2014). For an excellent overview of the various understandings of Paul and his premissionary life, see Eckard J. Schnabel, *Early Christian Mission: Paul and the Early Church* (Downers Grove, IL: InterVarsity Press, 2004), 923–27.

Greek cultures, was positioned to serve as a bridge for the gospel from the Jewish world to the Gentile world.[2]

So, again, who was Paul, this Jew of the diaspora?

We know from the book of Acts that Paul was born in Tarsus (Acts 22:3). As a result, like hundreds of thousands of other Jews scattered throughout the known world of that day,[3] Paul, because of the location of his birth outside of the Promised Land, was by default a diasporic Jew. Consequently Paul was able to navigate both the Jewish world of his physical lineage and the Gentile world where he spent at least the formative years of his life. He was a citizen of both Tarsus (Acts 21:39) and, especially, of Rome (Acts 16:37,38; 22:25–29; 23:27; cf. 25:10,11; 28:19). He was born a Roman citizen and, unlike many others, did not have to win or purchase his citizenship (Acts 22:28). Because Paul was from a devout, conservative Jewish diaspora family (his father was a Pharisee, Acts 23:6), his heart language used in his family home was most likely Hebrew (and some Aramaic?), for at root he was still a Jew.[4] Nevertheless, as a bicultural person Paul undoubtedly was also fluent in Greek, the language used by the majority non-Jewish urban population of Tarsus, where Paul spent his early years.

While we know that Paul was born in Tarsus, we do not know whether or not he was a second-generation diasporic person (in other words, his Jewish father/mother? moved to Tarsus and Paul and any siblings were subsequently born there) or whether he was third generation or later (the son of a father/mother who also was born in Tarsus?). We do know that Paul left Tarsus and went to Jerusalem to study under Gamaliel (Acts 22:3), but, again, at what age that happened we do not know. A likely guess is around the time that he was twelve, the age at which Jewish boys began their formal religious training.[5] Though his Jerusalem years formed him religiously, Paul was still influenced by his Tarsus roots; there was always a bicultural interplay between the Tarsus Paul and the Jerusalem Paul. As Andries B. Du Toit notes, "Tarsus was Paul's main sociological and cultural home, although he

---

2   Ott, "Diaspora and Relocation," 89.
3   See Acts 2:5–11, where Luke gives a hint of the multicultural complexity of the diaspora Jews who were in Jerusalem that first Pentecost morning.
4   See Romans 11:1; 2 Corinthians 11:22,23; Galatians 1:13,14; and Philippians 3:5,6.
5   See the story of Jesus in the temple at age twelve (Luke 2:42).

also received his first religious impressions there. Jerusalem was his religious and theological home, although he also socialized there."[6]

The fact that Paul was able to study in Jerusalem indicates that his parents were wealthy.[7] Paul, like his father, was a Pharisee (Acts 23:6; 26:5) who, as a diasporic Jew was sometimes considered "second-class" in the eyes of those Jews born in Jerusalem and Judea,[8] and thus was often needing to prove himself to the Jewish establishment in Jerusalem. This is perhaps why he was so zealous "for the traditions of my fathers" (Gal 1:14), why he was instrumental in Stephen's death (Acts 7:58; 8:1), and why he wanted to persecute the early followers of the Way in Antioch (Acts 9:1–3; 22:5; 26:12).[9]

Even Paul's name reflected two different cultures: Saul/Paul. Luke, in writing about him while he was persecuting the early church, refers to him by his Jewish name, Saul (Acts 8:1–3); likewise during his conversion and its immediate aftermath (Acts 9). Later, during the first missionary journey of this "chosen instrument to proclaim my name to the Gentiles" (Acts 9:15), Luke refers to him by his Roman/Greek name, Paul (Acts 13:9), and does so throughout the remainder of the book of Acts. The dual nature of his very name again illustrates Paul's biculturalism and the role that such biculturalism played in his ministry to both Jews and Gentiles.[10]

So what does all of the above have to do with the topic of this paper? I think that it is important from the outset to see that Paul, as a diasporic person, was also a bicultural person. He was at home in two cultures: Jewish and Greek. We must see this fact in light of all of the speeches of Paul as found in the book of Acts. As a bicultural person, Paul could and did express his speeches in ways that were

---

6   Andries B. Du Toit, "A Tale of Two Cities: Tarsus or Jerusalem Revisited," *New Testament Studies* 46, no. 3 (2000): 401, quoted in Ott, "Diaspora and Relocation," 90.

7   Schnabel, *Early Christian Mission*, 926

8   Though all Jews were equal with one another in light of the Torah, there was still a hierarchy of social status and class. We get a clue of this in the Gospel accounts where the disciples are seen as "different" by the Jews of Jerusalem because of their strange accents, different clothing, and lack of education; see Matthew 26:73 and Acts 2:7; 4:13.

9   This sense of class inferiority is perhaps also why Paul felt that he had to show that he was equal with the twelve apostles who remained in Jerusalem, his fellow Jews who, though born in Galilee, were still born in the Promised Land and thus, at least unconsciously considered themselves superior to diaspora Jews (see Gal 2:1–10).

10   Schnabel, *Early Christian Mission*, 925, gives us some keen insights into the dual nature of his name: "As a 'Hebrew born of Hebrews' (Phil 3:5), as a full Jew whose family maintained the Jewish customs, his (Hebrew) name was Saul (Heb., *Sha'ul*; Gk., *Saulos*). His Roman (or Greek) name was *Paulos*: this was either (1) the *cognomen*, an official element of the *tria nomina* that his family received after manumission from the Roman owner who had released an ancestor (his father?) from slavery, or (2) the *signum* or *supernomen*, the Roman, Latin-sounding surname that the family used. Many exegetes regard the second option as more likely."

remarkably appropriate for his specific audiences, whether they were Jew or Gentile. As a bicultural person he was sensitive both to his exegesis of the biblical text (in his case, the Old Testament), as well as to his exegesis of the audience to whom he was speaking. In this way Paul was sensitive both to ministry context (who is the audience and where are they located) as well as sensitive to message context (what is actually said to that audience).

This brief paper will specifically address both the ministry context and message context of diaspora ministry by looking at two examples from the bicultural Paul's ministry: first, his message to the Jews and God fearers of Pisidian Antioch (Acts 13) and, second, his message to the Athenians in the Aeropagus (Acts 17). Both speeches give good evidence of the sermonic dexterity that the bicultural Paul displayed and how his biculturalism influenced the content of his sermons. The paper will conclude with some implications of this for those who are bicultural diasporic followers of Jesus doing diaspora ministry today.

Paul's Speech in Pisidian Antioch

Paul's speech in Pisidian Antioch is the first recorded speech of his missionary career. Luke describes it in its context as follows (Acts 13:13–43):

> From Paphos, Paul and his companions sailed to Perga in Pamphylia, where John left them to return to Jerusalem. From Perga they went on to Pisidian Antioch. On the Sabbath they entered the synagogue and sat down. After the reading from the Law and the Prophets, the leaders of the synagogue sent word to them, saying, "Brothers, if you have a word of exhortation for the people, please speak."

> Standing up, Paul motioned with his hand and said: "Fellow Israelites and you Gentiles who worship God, listen to me! The God of the people of Israel chose our ancestors; he made the people prosper during their stay in Egypt; with mighty power he led them out of that country; for about forty years he endured their conduct in the wilderness; and he overthrew seven nations in Canaan, giving their land to his people as their inheritance. All this took about 450 years.

"After this, God gave them judges until the time of Samuel the prophet. Then the people asked for a king, and he gave them Saul son of Kish, of the tribe of Benjamin, who ruled forty years. After removing Saul, he made David their king. God testified concerning him: 'I have found David son of Jesse, a man after my own heart; he will do everything I want him to do.'

"From this man's descendants God has brought to Israel the Savior Jesus, as he promised. Before the coming of Jesus, John preached repentance and baptism to all the people of Israel. As John was completing his work, he said: 'Who do you suppose I am? I am not the one you are looking for. But there is one coming after me whose sandals I am not worthy to untie.'

"Fellow children of Abraham and you God-fearing Gentiles, it is to us that this message of salvation has been sent. The people of Jerusalem and their rulers did not recognize Jesus, yet in condemning him they fulfilled the words of the prophets that are read every Sabbath. Though they found no proper ground for a death sentence, they asked Pilate to have him executed. When they had carried out all that was written about him, they took him down from the cross and laid him in a tomb. But God raised him from the dead, and for many days he was seen by those who had traveled with him from Galilee to Jerusalem. They are now his witnesses to our people.

"We tell you the good news: What God promised our ancestors he has fulfilled for us, their children, by raising up Jesus. As it is written in the second Psalm:

"'You are my son; today I have become your father.'

"God raised him from the dead so that he will never be subject to decay. As God has said,

"'I will give you the holy and sure blessings promised to David.'

"So it is also stated elsewhere:

"'You will not let your holy one see decay.'

"Now when David had served God's purpose in his own generation, he fell asleep; he was buried with his ancestors and his body decayed. But the one whom God raised from the dead did not see decay.

"Therefore, my friends, I want you to know that through Jesus the forgiveness of sins is proclaimed to you. Through him everyone who believes is set free from every sin, a justification you were not able to obtain under the law of Moses. Take care that what the prophets have said does not happen to you:

"'Look, you scoffers, wonder and perish, for I am going to do something in your days that you would never believe, even if someone told you.'"

As Paul and Barnabas were leaving the synagogue, the people invited them to speak further about these things on the next Sabbath. When the congregation was dismissed, many of the Jews and devout converts to Judaism followed Paul and Barnabas, who talked with them and urged them to continue in the grace of God.

Several items can be noted from Paul's speech to these "Israelites and you Gentiles who worship God."

First, Paul exegeted his ministry context, making sure that the content of his message fit the context of his audience. The audience was made up of diasporic Jews (vv. 16,26,43) like Paul, as well as non-Jewish Gentiles (most likely natives from Pisidian Antioch?) (vv. 16,26,43). Since both groups were undoubtedly knowledgeable about the Hebrew Scriptures, Paul freely alludes to events in the Law (Exodus) and in the Writings (Joshua, Judges, and Samuel), as well as quoting directly from the

Writings (Ps 2:7; 16:10) and the Prophets (Is 55:3; Hab 1:5). It is significant to note that Paul quotes from the three major sections of the Old Testament canon (Law, Writings, and Prophets) as he attempts to prove to his audience the good news: "What God promised our ancestors he has fulfilled for us, their children, by raising up Jesus" (vv. 32,33). Paul reasoned correctly that many Pisidian Antiochan Jews, and those Gentiles there who also worshiped the true God, would be convinced of this fulfillment in the person and work of Jesus since it was seen throughout the major parts of the Old Testament. The fact that "many of the Jews and devout converts to Judaism" who heard Paul's message talked further with Paul and Barnabas concerning what Paul had spoken, and since these "many" were "urged . . . to continue in the grace of God" (v. 43), we can no doubt conclude that they became believers as a result of Paul's audience-appropriate message.

Second, Paul used hermeneutical methods that were well known by his Jewish and God-fearing audience. When Paul quotes the Old Testament passages in this sermon, he is using a common first-century hermeneutical technique known as *midrash*, where the truth of what has been said is verified by the use of an Old Tesament quotation that supports it. *Midrash* uses Old Testament scripture in a "that is this" type formula, where "that Old Testament passage" is truly understood or is relevant for today in the "this of the gospel message of our present situaton." How does *midrash* work in Acts 13? In verses 32 and 33 Paul midrashes Psalm 2:7, "You are my son; today I have become your father," in light of the good news that what God "promised our ancestors he has fulfilled for us, their children, by raising up Jesus." In other words, "that" excerpt from Psalm 2:7 is the "this" of the raised Jesus. Likewise, in verse 34 the "that" paraphrase from Isaiah 55:3—"I will give you the holy and sure blessings promised to David"—is again the "this" of the risen Jesus whom "God raised . . . from the dead so that he will never be subject to decay." The "this" of the never decaying Jesus is further confirmed in verse 35 by the "that" of the second half of Psalm 16:10, "You will not let your holy one see decay." Paul finishes his speech by charging his audience to believe the "this" truth of his message of Jesus by quoting the "that" from Habakkuk 1:5, which refers to scoffing and perishing and not believing the wonderful things that God is now doing in their days. Though modern audiences may be confused by the hermeneutics used by Paul here (for example, what about the original context of these quoted Old Testament passages?), Paul's original audience had no such concerns. They understood the hermeneutical methodology that Paul was employing.[11]

Third, Paul displayed his knowledge of his audience (obtained by his observations from his arrival in Pisidian Antioch to the day of the Sabbath [Acts 13:14]?). Paul did this by referring to them in different ways. He refers to the diasporic Jews gathered there as "Israelites" (v. 16) and "children of Abraham" (v. 26) (note that Luke merely refers to them as "Jews" [v. 43]). Paul refers to the Gentiles gathered there as "you Gentiles who worship God" (v. 16) and "you God-fearing Gentiles" (v. 26) (note that Luke also refers to them as "devout converts to Judaism" [v. 43]). This knowledge of his audience seems to have been used by Paul for the purpose of helping to gain a better rapport with them, as evidenced by his use of the more intimate word, "friends," a word he applied to both groups (v. 38).

Fourth, Paul did not hesitate to clearly speak of the gospel. Thus, while understanding the context of his audience, as well as displaying his knowledge of them, Paul does not hesitate to clearly point out what the good news is all about: Jesus was raised from the dead (vv. 30,32,37), and through this raised Jesus they can have forgiveness from their sins (v. 38) if they believe (vv. 39,41). Audience sensitivity never took precedence over Paul's desire to clearly proclaim the truth of the gospel.

Paul obviously struck a positive chord with his speech, since the people of the synagogue invited Barnabas and himself "to speak further about these things on the next Sabbath" (v. 42). Unfortunately, this did not happen, as the events in Acts 13:44–52 make clear.[12]

Paul's Speech in Athens

Paul's speech in the Areopagus in Athens (Acts 17:22–31) must be seen in the entire context of Acts 17:16–34, with verses 16–21 being Luke's introduction to the actual speech event:

---

11   For a more in-depth analysis of the Apostle Paul's hermeneutical methods, particularly *midrash*, see Larry W. Caldwell, "Reconsidering Our Biblical Roots: Bible Interpretation, the Apostle Paul and Mission Today," parts 1 and 2, *International Journal of Frontier Missiology* 29, no. 2 (April–June 2012): 91–100; vol. 29, no. 3 (July–September 2012): 113–21.

12   The events subsequent to Paul's speech on the following Sabbath—namely, the jealousy of the Jews at the large crowds that had gathered, the turning of Paul and Barnabas to the fully pagan Gentiles (and their *midrash* of the Isaiah 49:6 text to justify their actions), the acceptance of the message by many of these Gentiles, and the persecution and expelling of Paul and Barnabas from the region—do not negate the positive response that Paul's first speech initially had on some of the audience.

While Paul was waiting for them in Athens, he was greatly distressed to see that the city was full of idols. So he reasoned in the synagogue with both Jews and God-fearing Greeks, as well as in the marketplace day by day with those who happened to be there. A group of Epicurean and Stoic philosophers began to dispute with him. Some of them asked, "What is this babbler trying to say?" Others remarked, "He seems to be advocating foreign gods." They said this because Paul was preaching the good news about Jesus and the resurrection. Then they took him and brought him to a meeting of the Areopagus, where they said to him, "May we know what this new teaching is that you are presenting? You are bringing some strange ideas to our ears, and we would like to know what they mean." (All the Athenians and the foreigners who lived there spent their time doing nothing but talking about and listening to the latest ideas.)

Paul then stood up in the meeting of the Areopagus and said: "People of Athens! I see that in every way you are very religious. For as I walked around and looked carefully at your objects of worship, I even found an altar with this inscription: to an unknown god. So you are ignorant of the very thing you worship—and this is what I am going to proclaim to you.

"The God who made the world and everything in it is the Lord of heaven and earth and does not live in temples built by human hands. And he is not served by human hands, as if he needed anything. Rather, he himself gives everyone life and breath and everything else. From one man he made all the nations, that they should inhabit the whole earth; and he marked out their appointed times in history and the boundaries of their lands. God did this so that they would seek him and perhaps reach out for him and find him, though he is not far from any one of us. 'For in him we live and move and have our being.' As some of your own poets have said, 'We are his offspring.'

"Therefore since we are God's offspring, we should not think that the divine being is like gold or silver or stone—an image made by human design and skill. In the past God overlooked such ignorance, but now he commands all people everywhere to repent. For he has set a day when he will judge the world with justice by the man he has appointed. He has given proof of this to everyone by raising him from the dead."

When they heard about the resurrection of the dead, some of them sneered, but others said, "We want to hear you again on this subject." At that, Paul left the Council. Some of the people became followers of Paul and believed. Among them was Dionysius, a member of the Areopagus, also a woman named Damaris, and a number of others.

Like he did in Pisidian Antioch, while waiting in Athens, Paul was a keen observer of his surroundings (v. 16). Likewise, as in Pisidian Antioch, Paul first went to the synagogue and reasoned with the "Jews and the God-fearing Greeks" (v. 17); however, he did not limit himself to the synagogue, for he also talked daily in the marketplace "with those who happened to be there" (v. 17). We can safely assume that "those who happened to be there" included Jews, God-fearing Gentiles, and pagan Gentiles like the group of Epicurean and Stoic philosophers that Luke specifically mentions. Paul communicated so well that his pagan Gentile audience invited him to speak at the prestigious Areopagus, because they were intrigued by his "strange ideas" and they wanted "to know what they mean" (v. 20). Clearly by now this diaspora Jew is comfortable in both Jewish and Gentile contexts. As Ott says,

Paul's experience as a diaspora Jew in Tarsus may well have prepared him for engaging an environment of religious pluralism, competing worldviews, and value systems. This skill is seen in his Areopagus speech and his ability to dialogue with both Jewish and Gentile audiences.[13]

Once again, several items can be noted from Paul's speech in the Areopagus to these "people of Athens." First, Paul took the time to exegete his audience. Like

---

13 Ott, "Diaspora and Relocation," 91.

he did in Pisidian Antioch, here in the Areopagus Paul made sure that the content of his message fit the context of his audience. Even though Paul was "greatly distressed" because of all of the idols that he had previously observed in Athens (v. 16), nevertheless he carefully noted these idolatrous objects of worship, so much so that he even found an altar with the inscription: "to an unknown god" (v. 23). Surprisingly, rather than condemning them for their idolatry, Paul instead commends them: "I see that in every way you are very religious" (v. 22). He then goes on to sympathize with their religious strivings and to help them understand that "you are ignorant of the very thing you worship—and this is what I am going to proclaim to you" (v. 23). No doubt the Athenians were impressed by Paul's cultural sensitivity and positive response to their religiosity. They were ready to listen to his ensuing message.

Second, Paul was not afraid to use sources outside of the Old Testament. His Athenian audience most likely knew little about the particulars of the Old Testament. Thus Paul, in his speech, only alludes to the Old Testament, he does not directly quote from it. Instead, Paul displayed his knowledge of his audience by referring to their own poets. The first quote, "For in him we live and move and have our being" (v. 28), comes from the fourth line of a poem attributed to Epimenides the Cretan from around 600 BC. It speaks of Zeus:

> They fashioned a tomb for you, O holy and high one—The Cretans, always liars, evil beasts, idle bellies![14]—But you are not dead; you live and abide for ever, For in you we live and move and have our being.

The second quote, "We are his offspring" (v. 28), comes from the fifth line of the opening of the work known as the *Phainomena*, written by Paul's fellow Cilician, Aratus (born 310 BC):

> Let us begin with Zeus. Never, O men, let us leave him unmentioned. All the ways are full of Zeus, and all the market-places of human beings. The sea is full of him; so are

---

14 Note that the second line of this poem is also referred to by Paul in Titus 1:12, "One of Crete's own prophets has said . . . 'Cretans are always liars, evil brutes, lazy gluttons.'" Paul goes on to agree with Epimenides: "This saying is true" (Titus 1:13). Titus had been left by Paul on the island of Crete to continue the work they had apparently started there (Titus 1:5). Titus was now facing difficulties from Cretans both outside and inside the church. Paul used Epimenides, a Cretan, to make a point against these Cretans.

the harbors. In every way we have all to do with Zeus, for we are truly his offspring.[15]

Of course Paul is quick to reinterpret (*midrash*?) what their poets are saying about Zeus to what he, Paul, is saying about God in relationship to God making himself known, not as "an image made by human design and skill" (v. 29) but as a God who "is not far from any one of us," and who can be found by those who seek him (v. 27). Paul is using their own poets to show that this unknown God can indeed be known.

Third, as at Pisidian Antioch, so too here in the Areopagus, Paul did not hesitate to speak of the gospel. He speaks of the need to repent (v. 30) and of a day of judgment by the man God appointed and raised from the dead (v. 31). Interestingly, Paul had already had a mixed response to his message of Jesus and the resurrection when he had previously spoken to the Greeks in the marketplace (v. 18). One might think that by now Paul would have learned his lesson about the possibility of a negative response to his message of the resurrection, which indeed did happen as "some of them sneered" (v. 32). To the contrary, even though Paul knew that speaking of the resurrection in the Areopagus would be for some a stumbling block to accepting the gospel, it had to be talked about since the fact of the resurrection of Jesus is so crucial to everything that the gospel is. So rather than compromise, Paul—after doing his best to understand the context of his audience and to communicate in ways that they would best understand—speaks clearly about a key component of the gospel, namely the resurrection of Jesus. As a result of his lack of compromise, Paul did see some success: "Some of the people . . . believed," even a member of the Areopagus, Dionysius, as well as "a woman named Damaris, and a number of others" (v. 34). This positive response to Paul's message, though seemingly small, was significant given the possibly cynical nature of the Areopagus crowd (cf. Luke's disparaging comment about them in v. 21).[16]

---

15 Both the poem attributed to Epimenides and the lines from the *Phainomena* are taken from F. F. Bruce, *The Book of Acts*, The International Commentary on the New Testament (Grand Rapids: Eerdmans, 1988), 338–39.

16 Some might argue that the seemingly underwhelming response to Paul's message in the Areopagus denotes failure, that Luke specifically includes the Athens speech to show the early church what *not* to do when presenting the gospel. This argument, however, is without merit. The amount of space that Luke gives to Paul's speech in Athens—five paragraphs in total, with quotes from the two poems, as well as the mentioning of the names of two prominent people who did believe, and speaking also of "a number of others" (v. 34)—offers clear evidence that Luke considers this speech to be an important example of the progression of the gospel "to the ends of the earth" (Acts 1:8).

Implications for Diaspora Ministry Today

Diaspora Christians today are playing a key role in the ministry of the church worldwide.[17] This is seen both in their evangelizing efforts among their own diaspora people group, as well as in their crossing cultural barriers and becoming missionaries to other diaspora people groups, many of whom are unreached peoples. Diaspora Christians in ministry today, like the Apostle Paul, need to: (1) embrace the fact that they are bicultural people; and (2) use their biculturalism to powerful effect in their various ministries, especially as they pay attention to both the context of their audience as well to the actual message that they convey to that audience.

There are many implications for bicultural diaspora Christians today that can be drawn from the examination of these two speeches of Paul in the book of Acts. These implications are especially pertinent for those who are diaspora Christians and who are, or who want to be, cross-cultural missionaries. I will here mention five implications and will do so by speaking directly to those who are diaspora Christians.

1. *Accentuate the positive.* Recognize the many positive attributes of being a person of the diaspora. While there are certainly many negative aspects to being a diasporic person, let the positives outweigh the negatives. The greatest positive is the fact that, whether or not you like it, you are now a bicultural person: a person of your native home culture as well as a person of your adopted foreign culture. Like the Apostle Paul, as a bicultural person you have many strengths that you bring to ministry, especially ministry in cross-cultural situations. Disaporic bicultural followers of Jesus make good missionaries, if they are aware of, and allowed to use, the bicultural gifts that they have gathered in the midst of their diasporic adventures. This fact is especially true for those of you who are second-generation diaspora individuals.

2. *Exegete your audience.* Diasporic ministers of the gospel need to be able to communicate the truths of the gospel in light of the particular audience that they are addressing, being aware of both ministry context and message context. As we have seen, Paul did this all the time. While he was an expert at exegeting the Old Testament, as a bicultural diasporic man, Paul was also well equipped to exegete the specific audience to whom he was trying to bring the results of his Old Testament exegesis. If you are preparing to become a missionary, make sure that you take courses in how to better exegete the Bible (courses in Bible interpretation, Old

---

17   In a theological sense all Christians are diasporic Christians since Jesus has called all of his followers to "not belong to the world" (John 15:19). That being said, there are unique implications for those Christians who are truly bicultural because they have lived for a significant time in at least two different cultures.

Testament, New Testament, and so on) as well as courses that will help you better exegete the culture (courses in anthropology, sociology, communication, and so on). Along with this, like Paul did with the pagan poets, don't be afraid to use the media of your audience (music, movies, books, YouTube, Twitter, and so on) to help communicate the truths of the gospel message.

3. *Don't be too quick to condemn.* Diaspora missionaries indeed need to be distressed about the things they see in their own culture, and in other cultures, that are sinful. Paul, too, was deeply upset by the paganism of the Athenians. But, like Paul, try to find the underlying positive aspects that ultimately find their expression in sin. And like Paul did, attempt to put a positive spin on it. Anybody can be quick to condemn. It's harder to do your homework, understand why the sin is occuring, and use that understanding for gospel purposes.

4. *To the Jew, first.* Like was true for Paul, it's natural to go to your own people first with the gospel. After all, they need to hear about Jesus too. But don't leave it at that. As diaspora missionaries you are best prepared to take the gospel to people who are different from yourself. Take advantage of your unique biculturalism for the building up of the kingdom among all peoples.

5. *Be aware of possible prejudice.* As was true for Paul, diaspora missionaries face possible prejudice both from their own people living in their country of origin as well as from the native people of their adopted country. Diaspoa missionaries of the gospel need to be aware of this prejudice if it occurs and to persevere in spite of it.

Conclusion

There is no better way to end this brief paper on diaspora ministry—as seen through an examination of two speeches of Paul in the book of Acts—than with the very words of the Apostle Paul himself in describing his own unique bicultural ministry. This is seen in the powerful paragraph that Paul wrote in 1 Corinthians chapter 9, verses 19–23:

> Though I am free and belong to no one, I have made myself a slave to everyone, to win as many as possible. To the Jews I became like a Jew, to win the Jews. To those under the law I became like one under the law (though I myself am not under the law), so as to win those under the law. To those not having the law I became like one not having the law (though I am not free from God's law but am under Christ's

law), so as to win those not having the law. To the weak I became weak, to win the weak. I have become all things to all people so that by all possible means I might save some. I do all this for the sake of the gospel, that I may share in its blessings.

May all of us—bicultural diaspora people or not—take these words to heart, for the sake of the gospel and its continuing expansion among all the people groups of the world.

Chapter Seven

God's New Humanity in Diaspora:
A Church *of* the Nations and *for* the Nations[18]

DAVID STEVENS

ABSTRACT

This chapter develops the biblical theology of the church as God's "New Humanity," but with a special emphasis on being a church of the nations and for the nations. The identity of God's multiethnic people is traced from creation and fall to recreation and renewal in Christ. Throughout, particular emphasis is placed on the crucial importance of shaping our corporate identity as God's multiethnic people. When our identity is reframed, our relationships are reoriented. Finally, the article explores several implications of viewing the church as God's New Humanity for mission endeavors among the diaspora.

Situated in southern France stands a unique church building. It is located in the heart of the region most favorable to the Protestant Reformation. While many Protestant structures throughout the country were decimated during the awful days of the Counter-Reformation, some still remain in the region of the Rhone River valley. The uniqueness of this particular church building is that it is *both* Protestant and Catholic. However, the two congregations do not share the same sanctuary, for a massive dividing wall separates one from the other.

I'll never forget speaking in that church (the Protestant side) one evening during a regional prayer gathering. The memory remains indelibly etched in my mind. Our prayers echoed Jesus' prayer that his followers might be one "so that the world may believe" (John 17:21). How ironic that behind me stood the very wall that symbolized a seemingly irreconcilable division between Protestant and Catholic dating to the sixteenth century. As I inquired about the history of the wall, I learned that since the two congregations could never decide who was to have final ownership of the building, they split it right down the middle by building an impenetrable barrier. We, too, have built our walls. They come in different sizes and shapes. Their color and building materials may vary, as well as the way in which they are constructed. Some are denominational, others are socioeconomic. Still others are generational or determined by gender. Our particular focus is on the walls built by ethnicity.

Our walls, like that literal wall made of stone and mortar that for generations has divided two congregations, are massive and seemingly indestructible. Furthermore, such walls constructed by ethnic segregation keep the church from being a church *of* the nations and *for* the nations in this age of diaspora.

Dancing with Diaspora

To become a church *of* the nations and *for* the nations, we must first recognize that we are a church *among* the nations. Consider these facts:

- Racial and ethnic minorities accounted for roughly 85 percent of the US population growth of 27.3 million people over the past decade (2000–2010).[1]
- In the year 2010, the United States had well over 30 million *more* people considered racial and ethnic minorities than it did in 2000.[2]
- As of 2010, 36.7 million of the nation's population were foreign-born, up from 19.8 million in 1990 and 31.1 million in 2000.[3]
- Today we have more Jews in the United States than in Israel; we have more blacks than in any country apart from Nigeria, Africa; and we are the third largest Spanish-speaking country in the world. One out of four people is a minority.[4]

What is projected over the next fifty years?

- By the year 2050, minorities will become the majority, comprising approximately 54 percent of the US population.[5]
- The Hispanic population will nearly triple, from 46.7 million to 132.8 million during the 2008–50 period, growing from 15 percent to 29 percent of the American population.[6]
- The Asian population is projected to climb from 15.5 million to 40.6 million. Its share of the nation's population is expected to rise from 5.1 percent to 9.2 percent.[7]

---

1   Hope Yen, "Census Estimates Show Big Gains for U.S. Minorities," *The Oregonian*, February 4, 2011, A10; Karen R. Humes et al., "Overview of Race and Hispanic Origin: 2010," 2010 Census Briefs, http://www.census.gov/prod/cen2010/briefs/c2010br-02.pdf.
2   Humes et al., "Overview of Race," 4–5.
3   U.S. Census Bureau, "Nation's Foreign-born Population Nears 37 Million," http://www.census.gov/newsroom/releases/archives/foreignborn_population/cb10-159.html.
4   Rod Cooper, "People Just Like Me: Does the Bible Give Us Freedom to Build Deliberately Homogeneous Churches?"in *Building Unity in the Church of the New Millennium*, ed. Dwight Perry (Chicago: Moody, 2002), 156.
5   CNN-US, "Minorities Expected to Be Majority in 2050," http://articles.cnn.com/2008-08-13/us/census.minorities_1_hispanic-population-census-bureau-white-population?_s=PM:US.
6   Haya El Nasser, "U.S. Hispanic Population to Triple by 2050," *USA Today*, February 12, 2008, http://www.usatoday.com/news/nation/2008-02-11-population-study_N.htm#11.
7   Ibid.; cf. Humes et al., "Overview of Race," 4–5.

- New immigrants along with their children and grandchildren (born in the United States) will account for 82 percent of the projected population increase from 2005 to 2050. By 2050, 19 percent of the population will be foreign-born, up from 12 percent in 2005.[8]
- Also by 2050, African, Asian, and Latin American Christians will comprise 71 percent of the world's Christian population.[9]

In light of these momentous demographic changes, Philip Jenkins reminds us there will be some surprising developments for the church at large: "Soon the phrase 'a white Christian' may sound like a curious oxymoron, as mildly surprising as 'a Swedish Buddhist.' Such people can exist, but a slight eccentricity is implied."[10] Truly the American society has rapidly become a "stew pot" of multiple ethnicities and the cultures they represent.

How well is the church learning to "dance with the diaspora"? The most recent research demonstrates that:

- Churches today are more segregated than they were prior to the abolition of slavery.[11]
- Churches are ten times more segregated than the neighborhoods in which they are located and twenty times more segregated than nearby public schools.[12]
- If a racially mixed congregation is one in which no racial group comprises 80 percent or more of the congregation, then according to the latest research 92.5 percent of churches in the United States are racially segregated.[13]

Evidently our dance with the diaspora is somewhat out of step. While the surrounding culture is becoming more and more ethnically diverse, eleven o'clock on Sunday morning continues to be, as Martin Luther King once described it, "the most segregated hour of Christian America."[14]

---

8 Nasser, "U.S. Hispanic Population."
9 Soong-Chan Rah, *The Next Evangelicalism* (Downers Grove, IL: InterVarsity Press, 2009), 13.
10 Philip Jenkins, *The Next Christendom* (New York: Oxford University Press, 2002), 3.
11 Rodney M. Woo, *The Color of Church: A Biblical and Practical Paradigm for Multiracial Churches* (Nashville: B&H Academic, 2009), 23.
12 Lucky Severson, "Interview with Michael Emerson," in *Religion and Ethics Newsweekly*, December 19, 2008, http://www.pbs.org/wnet/religion and ethics/episodes/december-19-2008/interview-with-michael-emerson/1736/.
13 Curtiss Paul DeYoung et al., *United by Faith: The Multiracial Congregation as the Answer to the Problem of Race* (Oxford: Oxford University Press, 2003), 2. Approximately 12 percent of Catholic churches, just less than 5 percent of evangelical churches, and about 2.5 percent of mainline churches can be described currently as multiethnic.
14 Martin Luther King Jr., *A Knock at Midnight*, ed. Clayborne Carson and Peter Holloran. (New York: Warner Books, 1998), 30–31.

What is the solution? I will argue that in order to become a church *of* the nations and *for* the nations—effectively reaching the diaspora at our doorstep—we must first understand and live into our identity as God's "New Humanity." In other words, the biblical response to the present crisis of dividing walls that fragment the body of Christ is *to understand and be who we are*. But to achieve this, we must go back to the very beginning.

The Creation of Humanity

All that precedes the grand finale of God's creation of humankind, though receiving the divine affirmation as "good," is clearly distinguished from humanity that alone exists as the very image of God. The inspired wording is unmistakable:

> Then God said, "Let us make mankind in our image, in our likeness, so they may rule over the fish in the sea and the birds in the sky, over the livestock and all the wild animals, and over all the creatures that move along the ground." So God created mankind in his own image, in the image of God he created them; male and female he created them. (Gen 1:26,27)

The doctrine of the *imago Dei* in Genesis 1 stands as a reminder of our true humanity with all of its privileges and responsibilities. It tells us who we are and who we are to become. As F. R. Barry has noted, "God created man in his own image. All the rest of the Bible is a commentary on that phrase."[15] While in the history of interpretation scholarship has reached somewhat of an impasse over the meaning of the *imago Dei*, I believe the passage itself yields several clear indications that point us in the right direction. Furthermore, as we take our findings concerning the image and view them in relation to the New Testament passages that speak of the creation and renewal of the New Humanity (Eph 2:15; 4:22–24; Col 3:9–11), the full nature of the image as well as implications for the church in and for the diaspora begin to take shape.

The basic meaning of the Hebrew term translated "image" in Genesis 1 is "something cut out, likeness, semblance" or a "statue, copy, drawing."[16] The emphasis

---
15   F. R. Barry, *Recovery of Man* (New York: Charles Scribner's Sons, 1949), 61.
16   Francis Brown, S. R. Driver, and Charles A. Briggs, *A Hebrew and English Lexicon of the Old Testament* (Oxford: Clarendon, 1970), 853; Ludwig Koehler and Walter Baumgartner, *Lexicon in Veteris*

of the word is on *physical shape* or *form*. It seems most natural, then, to understand the term "image" in Genesis 1:26–27 (cf. 5:1; 9:6) in a very concrete sense referring to a fashioned image or a representative figure.

This concrete, tangible understanding of "image" cannot be disassociated from a further question: Is humanity created "in" or "as" the image of God? The exegetical evidence clearly points towards the latter.[17] Mankind does not *have* the image, nor was he created *in* the image, but he himself *is* the image and as such functions in a representative capacity. This is crucial for understanding the development of this concept throughout the rest of Scripture.

It was not uncommon in the Ancient Near East for a king to set up an image of himself in a remote province for the one purpose of extending his authority and rule. In many cases, the image (statue) itself represented the king's occupation of the conquered land. In fact, such a close correlation existed between image and king that to revile the image was to dishonor the king. Similarly, man *as* image is God's authoritative representative on earth with the unique role of exercising dominion. That this is true is evident from the structure of Genesis 1:26, "Let us make mankind *in* our image . . . so that they may rule," which is best translated, "Let us make man *as* our image . . . *in order that* they might rule" (italics mine). Even as a pagan king would establish his statue on foreign soil to signify his presence and ownership, so the transcendent Creator of Genesis 1 has become tangibly immanent through his authoritatively established vice-regent, humanity.

Humanity as image effectively represents God, not only to the degree that he rules over creation, but also to the degree that he resembles his Creator. That is why in Genesis 1 man is further described as the "likeness" of God. But in what ways does humanity as the image of God resemble God? Genesis 1:26 reads, "Then God said, 'Let *us* make mankind in *our* image'" (italics mine). Hidden away in the unexplained "us" and "our" of this verse is the veiled allusion to the most intimate of relationships between Father, Son, and Holy Spirit. The relational oneness of the great Three-in-One is the template expressing God's most cherished intentions for all of humanity—relational diversity in unity. God intended man to experience the ecstasy of community and in this way to resemble his Creator. This is emphasized by the intentional vocabulary of Genesis 1:26. The author could have depicted God

---

Testamenti Libros (Grand Rapids: Eerdmans, 1953), 2:804; James B. Pritchard, ed. *Ancient Near Eastern Texts Relating to the Old Testament*, 3rd ed. (Princeton: Princeton University Press, 1969), 93.

17 See Stevens, *God's New Humanity*, ch. 2.

as saying, "Let us make *a man* as our image," using vocabulary that views man *as an individual*.[18] On the other hand, the vocabulary of Genesis 1:26—*ādām*—most often describes humans or humankind in a generic sense; that is, collective humanity.[19] After all, God could have chosen to create each new individual directly from the dust, but he chose to do otherwise. Each human being is inextricably connected to all of humanity and carries both the privileges and responsibilities of that relationship of solidarity. Given such solidarity of the human race, it follows that no one individual or group of individuals manifests the fullness of the image of God. Rather, "The image of God is, as it were, parceled out among the peoples of the earth. By looking at different individuals and groups we get glimpses of different aspects of the full image of God."[20]

In summary, humanity as the image of God exists as God's authoritatively mandated vice-regent on planet earth. From the beginning, humanity was entrusted with the dignified vocation of *ruling* over creation, *resembling* his Creator, and experiencing the *relational* community that characterizes the nonhomogeneous Three-in-One—Father, Son, and Holy Spirit.

The Fall of Humanity

What happened to humanity as God's image as a result of sin? In what specific ways did humanity's fall into sin damage his roles of rule, resemblance, and relationship? More positively, what hope does the Bible offer concerning humanity's renewal to the image of his Creator? And how do these questions relate to the role of the church *in* and *for* the diaspora?

Separation lies at the very heart of sin's impact upon the three expressions of man as the *imago Dei*: *rule, resemblance,* and *relationship*. The tragic results of self-assertive sin profoundly marred humanity's privileged role as God's image, bringing alienation to man's relationship vis-à-vis God, fellow man, and all of creation.

First, sin struck at humanity's mandate to rule. Though mankind was created to have dominion as God's vice-regent over all the earth, a creature—the very embodiment of Satan—exerted dominion over man and thus disrupted creation order. "Thorns and thistles" and "painful toil" became part and parcel of man's

---

18   It is commonly translated "husband" (Gen 3:16; Ruth 1:3) and often describes the general distinction between male and female (Lev 15:16; Isa 4:1).
19   Cf. Genesis 6:7; 7:23; 9:6; Exodus 9:25; Numbers 8:17; 1 Samuel 16:7; 1 Chronicles 29:1; Job 20:4; Psalm 8:4.
20   Richard Mouw, *When the Kings Come Marching In* (Grand Rapids: Eerdmans, 1983), 47.

struggle to fulfill his role as God's image over an alienated world. Evil was now crouching at humanity's door (Gen 3:17,18; 4:7).

Second, sin struck at man's resemblance to his Creator. Humanity's essence and role as the "likeness-image" of God was severely compromised: "Then the eyes of both of them were opened, and they realized they were naked" (Gen 3:7). Consequently, corporate humanity became disabled in its capacity for self-awareness, its openness to divine address, and its spiritual responsiveness. Though man ever remains the image of God, he nevertheless must now contend with both physical and spiritual disease, deformity, and ultimate death.

Finally—and most important for our purposes—sin dealt a death blow to man's relational capacity. With the intrusion of sin came also consequent alienation, both between man and God and between man and fellow man (Gen 3:9; 11:7,8). Explicit trust and transparency—illustrated by man's nakedness—vanished, leaving only insecurity and fear. Humanity was fractured at its core.

As man attempts to become more than he is, he becomes less than he is. Not only is this true in the garden of Eden but also in the plains of Shinar. Through a series of literary chiasms, antithetical parallelism, and subtle word plays, the author highlights in Genesis 10–11 the puzzling paradox of sin. Man never finds in sin that which he enters sin to find. What all the earth attempted to avoid actually happened: *diaspora*.

Genesis chapters 10 and 11 are inseparable. The latter explains the former. The Table of the Nations in chapter 10 is unexplainable apart from the interpretive insight of the Tower of Babel in chapter 11. The primary purpose of Genesis 10 detailing the Table of the Nations is to demonstrate that the human race, though originally united in origin, now becomes divided by language, territory, and politics. The literary bookends surrounding this table are found in Genesis 9:19 and 11:9:

> These were the three sons of Noah, and from them came the people who were *scattered* over the whole earth. (Gen 9:19, italics mine) From there the Lord *scattered* them over the face of the whole earth. (Gen 11:9, italics mine)

These chapters highlight the fact that mankind's determination to gather in one place and build was in direct disobedience to God's command to replenish and have dominion over the earth (Gen 1:26,27; 9:1–3). God's original design for humanity was the systematic colonization and nurture of the entire earth, with each people group and consequent culture having a form of local government (Gen 1:28; 9:1). Man chose, however, to establish a strongly centralized government that would eventually result in the oppression of others, if not the entire world. Could it be that mankind innately sensed the sociological axiom that social separation causes cultural differentiation and consequently rebelled against it? We do not know. What seems clear is that apart from the alienating influence of sin, diversity of culture would not *in itself* prove to be a dividing wall among the peoples of the earth.

Given the intrusion of sin, a multiplicity of nations carrying out their divinely given mandate to protect humanity as the image of God would be more viable and less destructive than collective humanity gathered in one place and intent on one prideful purpose. Mankind, however, pursued uniformity for the purpose of power and oppression. Consequently (and quite paradoxically), man's common language (Gen 11:1) became a multiplicity of confused languages (Gen 11:9), and man's place of unity ("there" Gen 11:2) became his place of disunity "from there" Gen 11:8).[21] The people arrogantly intended to "make a name" for themselves (Gen 11:4; cf. Ps 14:1). In doing so, they failed to realize that Yahweh is the only one who can make one's name great (Gen 12:2,3)!

God's purposes, however, will not be thwarted. In the confusion and scattering of the nations, God chooses a seed that will ultimately bring blessing to the peoples of the earth now in diaspora. This is the story of Terah and his son, Abraham (11:27–15:11). Out of the Old Humanity scattered at Babel, a New Humanity will be gathered at Pentecost. In some ways, Abraham as the father of many nations becomes himself a type of "second Adam" in whom all the peoples will be blessed. Thus the arrangement of Genesis 11 and 12 is not accidental. The problem (Gen 11) and the solution (Gen 12) are brought into immediate juxtaposition. God chose Abraham as the microcosm to bring blessing to all of humanity as the macrocosm.[22]

The Creation of the New Humanity

The blessing of the Abrahamic covenant is ultimately realized in the person and work of the second man, the last Adam, Jesus Christ. As the *very* image of God (Col 1:15), he is the head of a new progeny, the New Humanity, composed of all

---

21 Allen P. Ross, *Creation and Blessing: A Guide to the Study and Exposition of Genesis* (Grand Rapids: Baker, 1988), 247.
22 See Gordon J. Wenham, ed. "Genesis 1–15," in *Word Biblical Commentary* (Waco, TX: Word, 1987), 213.

who believe. What the first man, Adam, erased, the second man, Christ, *more than* replaced. This is what Paul describes in Ephesians chapter 2.

> For he himself is our peace, who has made the two groups one and has destroyed the barrier, the dividing wall of hostility . . . His purpose was to create in himself *one new humanity* out of the two, thus making peace, and in one body to reconcile both of them to God through the cross, by which he put to death their hostility. (Eph 2:14–16; italics mine)

Paul is very selective in his choice of words to describe the new man of Ephesians 2:15. His use of the word "create" presupposes the Old Testament doctrine of creation, strongly suggesting that the creation account of Genesis 1:26,27 is the interpretive link to understanding the creation of the one new man. Beyond this, Paul chooses the term "humanity" (*anthrōpos*) in describing this new entity. Just as for the Hebrew term *ādām*, the basic underlying concept of *anthrōpos* is "generic man," the "human race," or "mankind."[23] His emphasis is upon a "new man" viewed *collectively*, not individually. As such, the one new man—the New Humanity—is the sphere in which reconciliation of Jew and Gentile takes place and in which both together are reconciled to God. It is in the New Humanity that diversity in unity replaces diversity in alienation.

It is this diversity in alienation that Paul describes in Ephesians 2:11–13. Because of satanically inspired sin, collective mankind as God's likeness-image was marred, his representative role on earth was perverted, and he became alienated in his relationship with God and fellow man. This schism between peoples experienced at Babel came to manifest itself especially in the chasm between God's covenant nation Israel and non-Israelites. The epitome of this growing hostility was seen in the temple, constructed by Herod the Great. The temple itself was made up of three courts: the Court of the Priests, the Court of Israel, and the Court of the Women. Beyond this, however, was the Court of the Gentiles. To get to this court, one had to descend five steps from the temple itself to a wall. Then on the other side of the wall one would descend fourteen more steps to another wall. Beyond that was the Court of the Gentiles. From here, Gentiles could look up and see the temple but

---

23 Aristotle brings out the corporate meaning of the term when he speaks of a multitude of citizens coming together to form "one man," and later Arrianus can term humanity "the ideal man." Aristotle, *Politica*, 3.6.4; Arrianus, *Epictetus*. 2.9.3.

were not allowed to approach it. They were separated by a one-and-a-half-meter stone barricade. Along this barricade were various notices that read in Greek and Latin: "Trespassers will be executed." Two of these notices have been discovered by archaeologists in the last hundred years. On one of these the exact wording is: "Let no foreigner enter within the partition and enclosure surrounding the temple. Whoever is arrested will himself be responsible for his death which will follow."[24] The "dividing wall" in the temple that separated Jew and Gentile was not historically broken down until the Roman legions under Titus destroyed the temple in AD 70. At the time that Paul wrote this epistle, the wall was still standing—literally, *but not spiritually*.

The alienation between Israel and the Gentiles is merely in microcosm a reflection of the relational estrangement that perpetuates humanity's Babel experience to this very day. It rarely takes the form of literal concrete walls such as the balustrade of Herod's Temple or the impenetrable wall that divided the church building I visited in southern France. *Our dividing walls are much more subtle and intangible.* It is precisely their subtle, intangible character that makes them so powerful. We allow color, culture, and class, as well as a whole array of human sociological determinants—individualism and religious consumerism—to regulate the definition of "our kind of people." We certainly never put up a sign stating that trespassers will be executed. We don't need to. In far too many churches, our homogeneity of ethnicity already speaks clearly and loudly of who is "in" and who is "out." What other explanation can account for the fact that today a mere 7.5 percent of Christian churches can be classified as ethnically mixed?

Throughout this epistle Paul argues profoundly and passionately that the reason we as believers are to live together in unity—inclusive of differences of ethnicity, background, and culture—is because God has graciously, through the sacrificial death of his Son, made Jew and Gentile "one new humanity" (Eph 2:15). As Jesus' Jewish body hung on the cross, he grasped believing Jews with one hand and believing Gentiles (i.e., the nations in diaspora) with the other and brought them together as one body. In other words, *in reality* the dividing walls of ethnicity have been once and for all deconstructed (Eph 1–3). Therefore, *in our experience* we must deconstruct the walls, never allowing them to be reconstructed (Eph 4–6).

---

24 Adolf Deissmann, *Light from the Ancient East*, trans. Lionel R. M. Strachan, 4th ed. (Grand Rapids: Baker, 1978), 80; cf. Josephus, *Jewish Antiquities*, 15:417.

Meditate on this mystery. At creation, God breathed into the first man's nostrils and he became a living soul. God then caused a deep sleep to fall upon Adam, during which time God opened his side, took one of his ribs, and fashioned a woman who was to be his bride and partner. Eve was the only woman in the history of mankind taken from her husband's body before being his bride. She was bone of his bone and flesh of his flesh. In a similar way, the second man, Christ, was led to the Cross and into the sleep of death. His side was pierced, and the blood that flowed from his wound gave birth to the New Humanity—"bone of his bone and flesh of his flesh." Then once again the great Three-in-One breathed and the New Humanity became a living organism.

The New Humanity, even as Eve, is both body and bride—one flesh with the Head and bride of the Head. As Eve had no existence apart from Adam, so the church, the New Humanity, has no existence apart from Christ. The Old Humanity with Adam as its head has now been superseded by the New Humanity with Christ as its Head. Both at the Cross and Pentecost, Jesus more than replaced what Adam erased. The ecstasy of community has been restored, and the Trinity rejoices!

The Birth of the New Humanity

Conception and birth go hand in hand. If the Cross brought about the conception of the New Humanity, Pentecost brought about the birth of the New Humanity. The Cross is God's remedy to the Fall; Pentecost is God's remedy to Babel. At Pentecost, the *mystery* of the New Humanity became the *reality* of the New Humanity.

Pentecost is nothing less than a reversal of the experience of the Tower of Babel (Gen 11), a truth noted by commentators since the early church fathers. Think of it. At Babel, humanity arrogantly ascends toward heaven, attempting to restore on its own terms relationship with God and fellow man. The initiative proves disastrous. At Pentecost, heaven humbly yet powerfully descends to humanity in the third Person of the Trinity, reconciling the irreconcilable. At Babel, the languages are confused and the people dispersed. At Pentecost, the languages are understood and the people unified. At Babel, the people are scattered as an act of judgment. Following Pentecost, the people are also eventually scattered, preaching not judgment but God's blessing upon the nations (Acts 8:4). While Babel depicts earth's divided nations, Pentecost is God's "United Nations."

To drive this point home, Luke goes out of his way to note that those witnessing this phenomenon were "from every nation under heaven" (Acts 2:5). Luke, of course, is speaking from his own worldview, referring specifically to the Greco-Roman world around the Mediterranean basin. He describes five major people groups, apparently moving from east to west. Interestingly, the cosmopolitan character of the crowd included representatives of all three of the principal divisions of humanity mentioned in Genesis 10: Shem, Ham, and Japheth. Those previously divided by language were now hearing the gospel of reconciliation *in their own language* as the incontestable sign of the dramatic reversal of Babel.

From all indications, the early church strived to live out this diversity in unity so characteristic of Pentecost in their own local churches (Acts 2:42–47). One of the most notable churches in the New Testament world was the church of Antioch. Antioch was the third-largest city in the then-known world, boasting a population of nearly half a million people. Its cultural and ethnic diversity was also noteworthy. Antioch was the home to Syrians, Romans, Greeks, Arabs, Persians, Armenians, Parthians, Cappadocians, and Jews.[25] It is not surprising, then, that the leadership of the church at Antioch was just as diverse as its surrounding community. Luke writes in Acts 13:1, "In the church at Antioch there were prophets and teachers: Barnabas, Simeon called Niger, Lucius of Cyrene, Manaen (who had been brought up with Herod the tetrarch) and Saul." Of those mentioned by Luke, two were from Africa, one from the Mediterranean, one from the Middle East, and one from Asia Minor. The church at Antioch was truly a church *of* the nations and *for* the nations, sending out the first missionary team to reach the diaspora with the gospel (Acts 13:2,3).

Such diversity was not without its problems. In Acts 6, we see the Grecian Jews began to complain against the Hebraic Jews because their widows were being overlooked in the daily distribution of food. The pragmatic solution in this case—and the one likely preferred by the majority of homogeneous church growth advocates today—would have been to create two distinct denominations rather than deal with the difficulties of working across ethnic and socioeconomic lines.[26] It would have been quite natural for these Grecian Jews to have reasoned, "It's too difficult trying to live in community with these Hebraic Jews. If we form our own homogeneous group, the gospel might grow even faster!" That might appear to be the wisest thing

---

25 Ibid., 27; Rodney Stark, *The Rise of Christianity: How the Obscure, Marginal Jesus Movement Became the Dominant Religious Force in the Western World in a Few Centuries* (San Francisco: Harper, 1997), 156–58.
26 This had been their experience as Jews *before* their conversion. The Hellenists would attend synagogues where their worship was expressed in their own language and culture. In fact, one of those is mentioned in this very context—the Synagogue of the Freedmen (Acts 6:9). On the other hand, Hebraic Jews maintained their own synagogues where the Scriptures were read and worship was conducted in Hebrew (or Aramaic). See F. F. Bruce, *The Acts of the Apostles: The Greek Text with Introduction and Commentary* (Grand Rapids: Eerdmans, 1990), 181.

to do from a merely human perspective. God, however, had other plans. His desire is for the unity of the New Humanity across ethnic lines. He wants his church to be one, not just *theologically*, but *experientially*; not just *universally*, but *locally*. The leadership of the early church wisely recognized that too much was at stake. God's purposes of spiritual diversity in unity must become a tangible reality. The prayer of Jesus for oneness would be answered even in the more mundane aspects of the life of the local church. Rather than opt for pragmatic solutions, the Jerusalem congregation "faced head-on the challenges posed by diversity with action that was prayerful, immediate, empowering, and that further implemented Jesus' vision of a house of prayer for all the nations."[27] Anything less than this would have been a return to Babel rather than an expression of Pentecost.

The Renewal of the New Humanity

To the degree that the church lives out its conception and birth as the New Humanity, she is renewed according to the image of her Creator. This is the teaching of Colossians 3:9–11 (cf. Eph 4:22–24).

> Do not lie to one another, since you have put off the *old man* with his deeds, and have put on the *new man* who is renewed in knowledge according to the image of Him who *created* him, where there is neither Greek nor Jew, circumcised nor uncircumcised, barbarian, Scythian, slave nor free, but Christ is all and in all. (Col 3:9–11 NKJV, italics mine)

It is my conviction that the collective nuance of the New Humanity in Ephesians 2:15 must govern our understanding of the old/new man as described in Ephesians 4 and Colossians 3. Furthermore, the creation motif in these verses links all three passages to the creation of mankind in Genesis 1. For far too long the "old/new man" terminology has been read through the individualized lenses of Western culture. As a result, we have missed not only the intended meaning of Paul's precise terminology in these passages, but also the relevance of these texts for the dividing walls that piecemeal the landscape of the contemporary church. This interpretation is confirmed by Paul's description of the new man in Colossians 3:11. Here the new man is described as the *place* or *sphere* in which there is neither "Greek nor Jew, circumcised nor uncircumcised, barbarian, Scythian, slave nor free, but Christ is all

---

27 DeYoung et al., *United by Faith*, 24.

and in all." To reduce Paul's understanding of the old/new man to an individualistic "old/new nature" renders this affirmation in verse 11 nonsensical. No, the relational affirmations of this verse are a reality *in* the new man as a *collective* entity for whom Christ is all and in all (cf. Gal 3:28)!

For all who are part of the New Humanity, a renewal takes place that is *in accordance with*[28] the image of our Creator. While touching each individual member of the New Humanity, this renewal has in view the church as a corporate entity. Just as Adam *alone* was not the full image of God apart from Eve, so in the New Humanity no one individual *alone* (or one local church alone) stands as the full image of God apart from others. We all—red, yellow, black, or white—desperately need one another for this renewal to take place. As the New Humanity experiences this collective renewal, which crowds out the divisiveness of the past and pushes us toward the complete diversity in unity of the future, the three characteristics intrinsic to humanity's representative role as image are restored.

First, the New Humanity is being renewed to *rule*. Our identity as the New Humanity reminds us that we were originally created (Gen 1) and then recreated (Eph 2) as God's official representatives, entrusted with the vocation of being God's vice-regent in this otherwise alienated world (Ps 8; Heb 2:5–9). As the scriptural story of humanity unfolds, we see that our mandate to rule extends far beyond our relationship to this earth and its culture. We rule by putting off the old and putting on the new. We also rule by exercising our authority over the demonic powers that seek to reconstruct the divisive walls that have been torn down through Christ's cross work.

Second, the New Humanity is being renewed to *resemble* its Creator. Just as the original humanity was created as the likeness-image of God (Gen 1:26), so the New Humanity is being renewed into the likeness of its Creator, Jesus Christ. While we were never created *as* gods, we were designed to be *like* God—to individually and collectively share in his communicable attributes such as justice, love, peace, and mercy.

This points us to the third aspect of our renewal as the New Humanity—*relationship*. As the New Humanity, we faithfully resemble our Creator to the degree that we reflect in our relationships the unity of Father, Son, and Holy Spirit, who together provide the template for the renewal of redeemed humanity. When we

---

28 Paul intentionally chooses his vocabulary to convey the distinction between all humanity *as* the image of God and the New Humanity, which is now being renewed *according to* (*kata*) the image.

clothe ourselves with the New Humanity, we clothe ourselves with the reality that "there is neither Greek nor Jew, circumcised nor uncircumcised, barbarian, Scythian, slave nor free, but Christ is all and in all" (Col 3:11; cf. Gal 3:28).

What could Paul possibly mean when he states that in the New Humanity these religious, cultural, and social distinctions no longer exist? Does the renewal of the New Humanity result in a leveling of ethnic and cultural identity? It is helpful to distinguish between the concept of "distinctions" and "boundaries." Distinctions are those factors—whether ethnic, cultural, or otherwise—that contribute to determining individual or group identity. Paul is obviously not arguing for a leveling of *distinctions*. Greeks remain Greeks and Jews remain Jews. Such distinctions exist intrinsically and are invariable.

Boundaries, on the other hand, are created when distinctions begin to have primary defining force in the life of a person or group. Boundaries are symbolic and variable; they help a group distinguish itself from other groups. In some spheres of life, ethnic boundaries may be acceptable and needed. Paul is arguing, however, that in the New Humanity, ethnic (Greek/Jew), social (slave/free), and religious (circumcised/uncircumcised) distinctions *must no longer have primary defining force*. When they do, they become boundary markers that fragment the larger whole—the body of Christ. They keep us from being a church *of* the nations and *for* the nations.

From this perspective, Christ calls us *past* our ethnicity, but not *out of* our ethnicity. Furthermore, the renewal of the New Humanity is not *irrespective* of differences of ethnicity and culture, but *inclusive* of such differences. The unity of the New Humanity is not "color blind." We are not collectively renewed as the New Humanity by superficially ignoring our differences of color and culture, but by profoundly appreciating our differences. Distinctions still exist within the body of Christ, but evaluations based on those distinctions must be deconstructed. Distinctions still exist, but they no longer have primary defining force. Paul is saying that in the nonhomogeneous New Humanity such distinctions must *never* be the basis of defining our primary identity or determining our unity. Such boundary markers have been replaced by Christ, who "is all and in all" (Col 3:11).

The diversity in unity that characterizes the Trinity as well as the New Humanity will certainly not be obliterated in heaven. The diversity and universal inclusivism of the heavenly New Humanity is explicitly described in the words of the new song vocalized by the heavenly choir in Revelation 5:9,10:

And they sang a new song, saying: 'You are worthy to take the scroll and to open its seals, because you were slain, and with your blood you purchased for God persons *from every tribe and language and people and nation.* You have made them to be a kingdom and priests to serve our God, and they will reign on the earth.'" (italics mine)

This scene of such exultant, multiethnic worship must be interpreted against the backdrop of Babel in Genesis 11. There the nations were all of one "lip" and one "vocabulary" as they arrogantly conspired to unite earth with heaven. Though confused at Babel, these same lips will be purified to worship the Lord. Zephaniah 3:9, states: "Then will I purify the *lips* of the peoples, that all of them may call on the name of the Lord and serve him shoulder to shoulder" (italics mine). The worship of the New Humanity in Revelation 5:9,10 (cf. 7:9,10) is in direct fulfillment of Zephaniah's prophecy. The babble of Babel has become the beauty and purity of multiethnic worship before the Lamb of God.

The New Humanity and the Diaspora

When Jesus taught his disciples to pray, he requested of the Father that the realities of heaven become realities on earth—"Your will be done, *on earth* as it is *in heaven*" (Matt 6:10, italics mine). Randy Alcorn correctly observes, "We tend to start with Earth and reason up toward Heaven, when instead we should start with Heaven and reason down toward Earth."[29] The perennial question must be asked—*If the kingdom of heaven is not segregated, why on earth is the church?*

The answer is clear: rather than living into our identity as God's New Humanity, the church has become sociologically predictable. As the image of God we each have an innate longing for belonging that can only be satisfied by understanding and experiencing we are together in Christ. All too often, however, cultural norms conform us more to the patterns of the Old Humanity rather than those of the New Humanity.

What are these cultural norms that make the life of the church so predictable? The first is a pervasive individualism so characteristic of American society. Such individualism has nurtured a society marked by personal choice, consumerism, and competition, resulting in an ever-increasing homogeneity of groups well defined by symbolic boundaries and social solidarity. It is precisely this predictable sociological process that constructs the dividing walls of ethnicity, socioeconomic class, and affinity groups within the church today. This is illustrated in figure 2:

---

29 Randy Alcorn, *Heaven* (Wheaton, IL: Tyndale, 2004), 54.

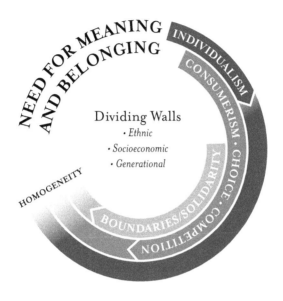

Figure 2: Predictable Sociological Process

What then is the biblical response to the sociological dynamics that inevitably lead to the construction of dividing walls in the church today? How can the church of the twenty-first century become more and more a church *of* the diaspora and *for* the diaspora?

The answer to those questions begins with *knowing* who we really are and *considering* it to be true (cf. Rom 6:1–14). The present-day phenomenon of widespread segregation in the church along lines of color, culture, and class is at its very core a problem of identity. *We must understand and help others understand who we are as the New Humanity and the implications of our collective identity for the life of the church.* This is "identity formation."[30] Identity formation focuses on shaping

---

30 Several recent works on identity formation in the church that are noteworthy include William S. Campbell, *Paul and the Creation of Christian Identity* (London: T & T Clark, 2008); Klyne R. Snodgrass, "Introduction to a Hermeneutics of Identity," *Bibliotheca Sacra* 168 (January–March 2011), 3–19; "Jesus and Identity," *Bibliotheca Sacra* 168 (April–June 2011), 131–45; "Paul's Focus on Identity," *Bibliotheca Sacra* 168 (July–September 2011), 259–73; "Pauline Perspectives on the Identity of a Pastor," *Bibliotheca Sacra* 168 (October–December 2011), 387–401. See also Mikael Tellbe, *Christ-believers in Ephesus: A*

perspectives rather than offering pragmatic solutions. The goal of identity formation is to establish a biblical-theological foundation from which believers can learn to decipher their lives in the mirror of the text. It is teaching someone to fish rather than handing someone a fish. Such an approach is far better than pragmatic solutions.

When our identity is reframed, our relationships are reoriented. Distinctions are acknowledged and valued, but boundaries of color, culture, and class are obliterated. Far too often, however, this is not the case. As figure 3 illustrates, when we attribute primary defining force to such distinctions as color, culture, and class—all of which make up the diversity of the body of Christ and can potentially enrich our experience of community—these distinctions subtly (and often unconsciously) become boundary markers determining group identity.

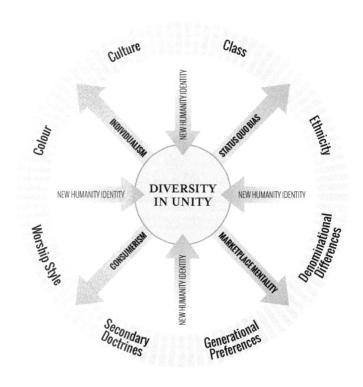

Figure 3: Determinants of Group Identity

Textual Analysis of Early Christian Identity Formation in a Local Perspective (Tübingen, Germany: Mohr-Siebeck, 2009).

This movement toward fragmentation is often fueled by sociocultural factors such as individualism, religious consumerism, and marketplace mentality. Simply put, color, culture, and class (as well as all the other distinctions that begin to have defining force in our lives) become the determinants of local church identity rather than Christ. The result is segregation in and among local churches—thus blacks tend to worship with blacks, whites with whites, Korean Americans with Korean Americans, baby boomers with baby boomers, millennials with millennials, *ad infinitum*. From a sociological perspective, we have become very predictable.

On the other hand, when believers experience a renewal of their New Humanity identity with its radical inclusivism, they begin to boldly move into environments marked by diversity in unity. Here such distinctions as color, culture, and class are appreciated, *but no longer have primary defining force in determining group identity*. Rather, such distinctions are made subservient to our collective core identity as the New Humanity where "Christ is all and in all."

In light of what the New Testament both describes and prescribes, I am convinced that to plant and nurture independent, homogeneous, ethnic-specific churches in an increasingly multiethnic environment will inevitably compromise the process of renewal of which Paul speaks in Colossians 3:11. What then is the solution? At Central Bible Church, where I previously served as senior pastor, we have moved toward an approach that Mark DeYmaz terms "graduated inclusion."[31] There are about fifteen ethnicities represented in the Central Bible Church family. Of these, two in particular—a group of Oromo-speaking believers (mainly from Kenya and Ethiopia) and a group of Romanian-speaking believers—also gather each week as a language-specific group. We recognize that some—particularly first-generation internationals—find it difficult to immediately integrate into and worship with the larger church family that is so immersed in North American culture. We nevertheless view these specific language groups as integral to Central Bible Church and as an evangelistic outreach to other Romanian and Oromo-speaking people in our city. The shepherd-elder (a Kenyan) responsible for the Oromo believers is also part of our larger elder team. Though the Romanian believers are relatively new to our church family, we are working together on the same process of graduated inclusion.

---

31 Mark DeYmaz and Harry Li, *Ethnic Blends: Mixing Diversity into Your Local Church* (Grand Rapids: Zondervan, 2010), 100–11. See also his recent e-book *Should Pastors Accept or Reject the Homogenous Unit Principle?* (Little Rock, AR: Mosaix Global Network, 2011), http://www.mosaix.info.

Furthermore, we encourage regular joint worship services that help facilitate the process of inclusion into the larger church family. Even all of this, however, is not a matter of *assimilation* (adopting our culture or norms) or of *accommodation* (superficially adjusting to their culture or norms), but of *inclusion* (all adopting the biblical norms of diversity in unity) as we strive by God's grace to become a church *of* the nations and *for* the nations.

Several years ago I had the opportunity to once again visit the church building in southern France that I mentioned at the beginning of this article. Happily, that massive dividing wall is no longer there. Originally built in 1806, it was deconstructed in 2008 as a sign of unity between the Catholic and Protestant congregations occupying the building. Unfortunately, however, throughout America and around the world, dividing walls of color, culture, and class continue to fragment the body of Christ, compromising our witness to the world of the reality of the gospel. As believers of all ethnicities, let us reaffirm our New Humanity identity and be in this generation the living, tangible answer to the fervent intercession of Jesus Christ. Each time we recognize and repent of ways in which we contribute to the present-day dividing walls in Christ's church, each time we reaffirm our New Humanity identity, and each time we enlarge our boundaries to include the different "other," we are bringing the realities of heaven down to earth, and the Trinity rejoices.

Part Four:

Strategy and Models

Chapter Eight
Three Models of Acculturation: Applications for Developing a Church Planting Strategy among Diaspora Populations

DAVID R. DUNAETZ

ABSTRACT

Cross-cultural church planters often work with individuals from several cultures or with immigrants from one specific culture. These church planters can develop a more effective church planting strategy by understanding three models of acculturation, the process by which individuals respond and change when coming into contact with a new culture. These three models can be used to help choose an appropriate church planting strategy according to the context.

Cross-cultural church planters in urban settings may find choosing a target audience to be far more complex than they had foreseen. They may imagine themselves planting a church that will reach the unreached indigenous population. But the majority of large cities in the world are multicultural, filled with peoples having different languages, behaviors, and values. It is quite possible that when these church planting missionaries come into contact with members of these diverse cultures, they find them to be just as needy as the majority culture and without a viable church in their city or region. It is also possible that these immigrants will be more open to developing friendships and to studying the Bible with the missionaries than are members of the host culture.

If immigrants are part of the initial group that the missionary hopes will eventually become a self-supporting church, there are several paths that such a group may take on its way to maturity. One option would be for the missionaries to focus on using the national culture, taking care to avoid introducing any cultural elements into the programs that would be more characteristic of the immigrant cultures than the national culture. Alternately, the missionaries could decide to focus on the culture that is the most open to the gospel, creating a diaspora church that will be attractive primarily to members of the new target culture. Yet another option would be trying to plant a multicultural church, rather than a monocultural one, where church members find their unity not in their culture of origin, but in the gospel, in their common experiences of life in the city, and perhaps in a similar socioeconomic level. Such a church may remain multicultural indefinitely, but the missionaries might find that growth is fastest among members of one of the cultures, resulting in a multicultural church dominated by one culture, or even in a monocultural church if members of other cultures leave because they no longer feel comfortable in the community.

The missionaries' strategy will be greatly influenced by their goal. Is their goal to plant a church among a specific people, essentially ignoring members of other cultures? Or is their goal to reach the most people for Christ possible in the given context? The purpose of this study is to help pioneer church planters understand how diaspora populations acculturate to their host culture. This will then allow church planters to more effectively design and implement a church planting strategy appropriate to their situation.

Acculturation

When members of one culture move into another culture, many changes occur. On the individual level, members of both cultures are influenced by members of the other culture. On the group level, both cultures adapt to the presence of the other culture. This process of change is known as *acculturation*.[1] This is an important concept for the cross-cultural church planter working with diaspora communities. To minister effectively, the church planter must not only understand the culture of the diaspora community, the culture of the host country, and the values of the individuals with whom he or she works, but also how both of the cultures have mutually influenced and continue to mutually influence each other and, even more importantly, how the individual members of the nascent church are changing because of their interaction with the host culture.

Acculturation must be distinguished from both *enculturation*, the process by which people learn their first culture, and *assimilation*, the process of adopting a

---

[1] J. W. Berry, "Acculturation: Living Successfully in Two Cultures," *International Journal of Intercultural Relations* 29 (2005), 697–712; J. W. Berry et al., *Cross-cultural Psychology: Research and Applications* (Cambridge: Cambridge University Press, 2002); R. Y. Bourhis, L. C. Moise, S. Perreault, and S. Senecal, "Towards an Interactive Acculturation Model: A Social Psychological Approach," *International Journal of Psychology* 32 (1997): 369–86; A. M. Padilla, and W. Perez, "Acculturation, Social Identity, and Social Cognition: A New Perspective," *Hispanic Journal of Behavioral Sciences* 25 (2003): 35–55; R. Redfield, R. Linton, and M. J. Herskovits, "Memorandum for the Study of Acculturation," *American Anthropologist* 38 (1936): 149–52.

new culture as one's own while losing the beliefs and behaviors associated with one's original culture.[2] Whereas enculturation occurs primarily in a familial context, acculturation occurs whenever a person has regular contact with members of another culture. One possible outcome of acculturation is assimilation, but, as we will see, there are other possible outcomes as well.

The effects of acculturation can be observed at both the group and individual levels. Because cross-cultural church planters are typically more concerned about influencing individuals than cultures, the focus in this study is on acculturation that occurs at the individual level, also known as *psychological acculturation*.[3] Psychological acculturation occurs both in members of the immigrant or minority culture and in members of the host or majority culture. However, the effects are usually far stronger in the members of the immigrant or minority culture. Although some cross-cultural church planting missionaries may work with minority peoples who are not immigrants (e.g., Amerindians or other indigenous peoples), cross-cultural church planters working with diaspora populations will more commonly be working with people who have immigrated to their country of residence sometime after World War II. The psychological acculturation of immigrants will thus be the focus of this study.

Many factors influence what the acculturation of immigrants will look like. The common beliefs and social norms of the home culture are initial factors that influence acculturation. The beliefs and norms of the host culture will interact with those of the home culture to be another major source of influence. Of special importance are the host culture's beliefs about how immigrants should acculturate. On the individual level, the reasons for immigration will exert an influence on how each person acculturates. Those who willingly immigrated for economic reasons will choose an approach to acculturation that is different from those who are refugees, even if both come from the same home culture into the same host culture. Those who immigrate as adults will acculturate differently than those who immigrate as children or those who are born in the host country to parents of first- or second-generation immigrants. We will examine three models of acculturation (the one-dimensional melting pot model, the two-dimensional acculturation strategies model, and the social identity model) to better understand the factors that influence

---

2   Berry et al., *Cross-cultural Psychology*.
3   T. D. Graves, "Psychological Acculturation in a Tri-ethnic Community," *Southwestern Journal of Anthropology* 23 (1967): 337–50.

the behavior, the emotional well-being, and the relationships of members of a diaspora community. Models are simplified generalizations of what behaviors can be expected under various conditions. They do not describe what should happen; they simply describe what actually happens, due to human nature, personal choice, or environmental factors. The models examined here have been tested with empirical data; the evidence indicates that to a large degree they all successfully predict the behaviors described.

Although these models will be applied to the immigrants with whom cross-cultural church planters work, it can be noted that these models also describe what these church planters themselves may experience on a personal level. Acculturation occurs for missionaries as well as for immigrants. Although the painful experiences of adapting to a new culture may be seen as a necessary evil to become an effective cross-cultural worker, they are the same difficulties that immigrants experience. These common experiences can serve as bonds to build deeper relationships with members of the immigrant community, enabling the missionary to be a more effective minister of the gospel.

The Melting Pot One-dimensional Model

In the melting pot model, immigrants enter a new culture with relatively little knowledge of it. Gradually, over a period of years or generations, they master the new culture and eventually assimilate into it, no longer identifiable as foreigners. An early version of this model was used by University of Chicago sociologists in the first half of the twentieth century that included three stages that immigrants experience[4]: contact with the new culture, accommodation to the new culture, and assimilation into the new culture. Contact with the new culture occurs when the immigrant arrives in the new country and begins to interact with members of the host culture. This results in the possibility of conflict because of differing expectations of appropriate behavior. To reduce the likelihood of conflict, members of the immigrant community make accommodations to the host culture, slowly accepting the social norms of the host culture. This eventually leads to assimilation, where the behavior and attitudes of the immigrant community become indistinguishable from those of the host culture.

---

4   Padilla and Perez, "Acculturation"; S. Persons, *Ethnic Studies at Chicago, 1905–45* (Urbana: University of Illinois Press), 1987.

Applications for Church Planting

This simple, straightforward model of assimilation described the nineteenth-century assimilation of European immigrants into American culture very well, and continues to be useful to describe the experiences of many immigrants living in Western countries today.[5] The assimilation of immigrants often takes three or four generations.[6] The implications of this model for church planting are clear. The first generation of immigrants will be much more at ease in their home culture; the establishment of an ethnic church will be especially attractive to the first generation. The second generation tends to be bicultural and capable of fully functioning in both cultures; they will feel less need for a church that maintains the culture of their parents, and may even prefer a church that is more in touch with the dominant culture. By the third generation, there are few traces of the original culture, and churches using this original culture will not be attractive. This means that each generation of a diaspora culture can be best reached by a different type of church. It also means that churches that are planted among first-generation immigrants using their home culture need to be prepared to change as the church matures and leadership passes onto the second and third generation. A church planter should prepare a young diaspora church for this change long before the change is necessary, incorporating the expectation of cultural metamorphosis into the church's fundamental values and vision. This can reduce the likelihood of the older generation eventually refusing to let go of the cultural elements that are important to them but which are no longer meaningful to the younger generation.

Building upon this simple model, Redfield and colleagues[7] added the idea that it's not only the immigrant community that changes when coming into contact with the host community, but the host community also changes as it adopts elements of the immigrants' culture (e.g., food, music, or literature). So, just as young diaspora churches need to be prepared to face cultural change as the church matures, young churches of the dominant culture need to be prepared to change as well, especially if they successfully reach out to and evangelize an immigrant community. These

---

5 A. G. Ryder, L. E. Alden, and D. L. Paulhus, "Is Acculturation Unidimensional or Bidimensional? A Head-to-head Comparison in the Prediction of Personality, Self-identity, and Adjustment," *Journal of Personality and Social Psychology* 79 (2000): 49–65.
6 G. McIntosh, and A. McMahan, *Being the Church in a Multi-ethnic Community: Why It Matters and How It Works* (Indianapolis: Wesleyan Publishing House, 2012); J. S. Phinney, "Ethnic Identity in Adolescents and Adults: Review of Research," *Psychological Bulletin* 108 (1990): 499–514.
7 Redfield, Linton, and Herskovits, "Study of Acculturation."

changes will come from both outside the church (from the dominant culture as it adapts to the immigrant culture) and from within the church as immigrants bring elements of their own culture into it. Thus all young churches in multicultural contexts need to be prepared for change, regardless of the initial culture that defines the church's identity when it is first planted.

Factors Influencing Assimilation

"It takes three generations for immigrants to assimilate" is a simplistic but convenient rule of thumb. However, there is much variation in the time necessary to assimilate (if, in fact, the immigrants assimilate, which, as we will see later, is not always the case) due to differences in individuals and cultures. Schermerhorn has argued that the movement toward assimilation into the host culture depends on the centripetal and centrifugal tendencies of both the immigrant culture and the host culture.[8] The immigrants' centripetal tendencies push them to assimilation. These centripetal tendencies may be part of the immigrants' culture, such as valuing the music and literature of the host culture more than those of their home culture or a strong belief that immigrants should adapt to the host culture. In contrast, the immigrants' centrifugal tendencies motivate them to preserve their lifestyle and culture, such as a belief that their language or religion is superior to the host culture's. Similarly, the host culture has unique centripetal tendencies (that encourage assimilation of the immigrants) and centrifugal tendencies (that resist assimilation of immigrants) for immigrants of each culture depending on the host culture's attitude toward the immigrant culture.

This means that church planters need to be aware of the centripetal and centrifugal tendencies of both the immigrant and host culture. If in both cultures the centripetal forces are dominant, the need for an ethnically homogenous church with a strong commitment to the immigrant culture will be lower than if the centrifugal forces are dominant. For example, a church planter in Europe might want to start a church that reaches the Arab Muslim diaspora community. However, the core group of the nascent church might be more concerned about integrating into European culture than preserving their own culture; in addition, the Europeans of the dominant culture may also want them to integrate. In a case like this, a young

---

[8] R. A. Schermerhorn, *Comparative Ethnic Relations: A Framework for Theory and Research* (Chicago: University of Chicago Press, 1978).

church might be more attractive to the Arab Muslim community if it adopts the host culture in Europe as its reference point rather than trying to preserve Arab culture. In this one-dimensional model of acculturation, the acculturation of an individual may be measured by asking them about their preferences for cultural elements from their host culture relative to those from the culture of origin.[9] These cultural elements may include ethnicity of friends, the language(s) they use, the foods they eat, their ethnic identity, their knowledge of history, and their culturally based beliefs and values. Ryder and colleagues from the University of British Columbia studied the characteristics of immigrants who have the highest level of acculturation (which implies assimilation into Western cultures in this one-dimensional model).[10] Unsurprisingly, the amount of time and the percentage of one's life spent in Western culture both predicted higher levels of acculturation. Those who have been in the West longer and those who came to the West at a younger age tend to adopt more Western cultural elements than those who came more recently or at an older age. Ryder also found that the time spent in the Western educational system also predicts acculturation beyond the amount of time spent in the West and the age at which one immigrated. In addition, immigrants who were more extraverted, who were more open minded and open to new experiences, or who suffered from fewer psychological problems (e.g., anxiety or depression) experienced higher levels of acculturation.

Church planters should note that the common characteristics of potential leaders in a young diaspora church (education, extraversion, open-mindedness, and emotional stability) might push these leaders to acculturate more quickly than the majority of members of the diaspora community. This can be a source of tension that the church planter must handle carefully. The church planter might want to focus on developing leadership from among the young, dynamic, Westernized youth. However, the majority of the diaspora community may be more comfortable with the more traditional leadership of the older generation. A balance must be found with representatives of both ends of the spectrum playing a role in church leadership.

Although this simple one-dimensional model of acculturation is quite useful, a more sophisticated, two-dimensional model will be able to better account for the variety of acculturation experiences that members of diaspora communities encounter.

---

9   Ryder, Alden, and Paulhus, "Unidimensional or Bidimensional?"; R. M. Suinn et al., "The Suinn-Lew Asian Self-identity Acculturation Scale: An Initial Report," *Educational and Psychological Measurement* 47 (1987): 401–7.
10   Ryder, Alden, and Paulhus, "Unidimensional or Bidimensional?"

The Two-dimensional Model of Acculturation Strategies

John Berry of Queen's University, Ontario, observed that assimilation is not the goal of all immigrants who are experiencing acculturation.[11] Some prefer to be bicultural, having the ability to fully function in both their home and host cultures. Others prefer to live separately from their host culture, remaining in their own cultural enclave. Berry observed that the strategies chosen by an immigrant depend on two independent preferences. The first preference is the immigrant's desire to maintain his or her home culture. Some are strongly attached to their home culture and have no intention of abandoning it; others are far less committed to their home culture and willingly abandon the behaviors, beliefs, and attitudes associated with it. A second, independent preference concerns the immigrant's desire to have relationships with members of the host culture. Some immigrants want to have frequent contact or close relationships with members of the host culture, so they make efforts to understand and, when necessary, adopt the behaviors, attitudes, and beliefs that make better communication and closer relationships possible; others have little interest in developing such relationships and feel little need to learn about the host culture.

The various combinations of these two preferences (see figure 4) result in the use of four different acculturation strategies. Twelve immigrants who arrive in a host culture and who want to maintain their culture while having few interactions or relations with members of the host culture use a strategy that can be called separation. Seeking to minimize the influence of the host culture on their lives, immigrants who choose this strategy tend to live close together in relatively homogenous communities and participate in activities that are typical of the home culture rather than the host culture. Immigrants with the opposite of these preferences tend to use a second acculturation strategy, assimilation. This strategy is used when immigrants move to a new culture and seek to develop relationships with people of the host culture, but do not have a strong desire to maintain their own culture (traditions, values, language, etc.); their goal is typically assimilation into the host culture. A third strategy, *integration*, is used by immigrants who seek both to have relationships with members of the host culture (requiring them to adopt at least the basic elements of the host culture) and to maintain their own cultural identity, especially when in the presence of members of their own culture. The integration strategy is valued in multicultural societies and has generally been found to produce

---

11   J. W. Berry, "A Psychology of Immigration," *Journal of Social Issues* 57 (2001): 615–31; Berry, "Acculturation," Berry et al., *Cross-cultural Psychology*.

the best psychological outcomes for immigrants (e.g., lower levels of depression and anxiety). A fourth strategy, *marginalization*, is characterized by a low desire for relationships with members of the host culture and a rejection of one's home culture. This strategy may be chosen by social deviants or delinquents ostracized from their own community and unable (or unwilling) to adopt the basic elements of the host culture; this strategy is most strongly associated with negative psychological outcomes, such as depression or anxiety.[12]

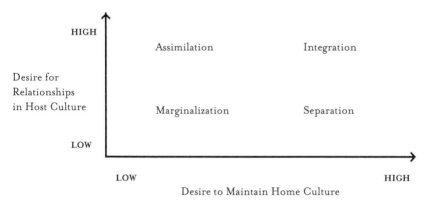

Figure 4: Four Acculturation Strategies[13]

Church Planting Strategies

These four acculturation strategies (separation, assimilation, integration, and marginalization), based on two dimensions (figure 3), can also describe church planting strategies that can be applied to diaspora communities. The church planter, along with the initial core group, will be responsible for the strategy that the church adopts and its implementation. The strategy chosen will define major aspects of the church's ministry for many years, if not the entire life of the church. Neither young, inexperienced church planters nor veterans of multiple church plants may be aware that a choice of strategies exists. Church planters may simply adopt the strategy that they have seen modeled in other churches without considering the possibility of

---

12 Ryder, Alden, and Paulhus, "Unidimensional or Bidimensional?"; E. Shiraev and D. Levy, *Cross-cultural Psychology*, 4th ed. (Boston: Pearson Education, 2009).
13 Berry, "Immigration"; Berry, "A Psychology of Immigration."

using a different strategy. However, the choice of strategy can significantly influence the impact that a church can have on its surrounding community.

Separation

A church planting strategy that focuses on maintaining the culture of the diaspora community with minimal attempts to reach the dominant culture can be considered a strategy of separation. This strategy would be typical of a church plant that focuses exclusively on immigrants of a specific culture and uses the language of this group for all its ministries. This strategy makes it easier to attract new immigrants to church activities because the church community provides a safe haven where recently arrived immigrants can meet people of their own culture who have at least some experience navigating the host culture. Diaspora members can freely express themselves in their own language and in ways appropriate to their home culture. This permits the Christian community to meet the felt needs of those who have recently arrived and demonstrate Christ's love in concrete ways. The gospel can be communicated in the heart language of the immigrants, accompanied by food and community activities that are meaningful to them, making the gospel even more attractive.

Yet there are certain drawbacks to a strategy of separation. For example, it is difficult, if not impossible, to reach anyone outside of the specific immigrant community due to language and cultural barriers. This strategy may also hinder assimilation or integration of the members into the host culture; this can be costly on both a psychological and economic level. If immigrants do not develop the ability to communicate with members of the host culture, they may face economic hardships, exclusion, and the inability to understand the worldview that their children will develop. Furthermore, this strategy may not appeal to the more forward and innovative members of a diaspora community, those who may likely become the next generation of leaders. Such individuals may see a strategy of separation as a sort of ghettoization of the diaspora community, creating an isolated body that cannot meet their needs or benefit from their skills and gifts.

Assimilation

A church planting strategy that assumes that the diaspora church members will gradually assimilate into the national culture will try to have programs and styles that correspond to how Christians from the national culture express themselves. For example, a church planter in Portugal who has found openness to the gospel among Angolan immigrants may try to develop a church with a Portuguese style of worship rather than an Angolan style of worship, especially if the Angolans have a desire to assimilate into Portuguese culture.

There are a number of advantages to using a church planting strategy focused on assimilation. First, it allows for multiethnic churches composed of members with diverse cultural backgrounds. Rather than having to learn and understand the culture of each immigrant group in a church in order to communicate, everyone agrees to use the national culture as the means of self-expression. For example, if a church plant is primarily composed of native Portuguese, Cape Verdeans, and Angolans, everyone can agree to do things the Portuguese way. Such a church can be attractive to immigrants because it provides them with a safe environment to practice expressing themselves in a language and culture that they want to master. Another advantage of this strategy is that it enables the church to better reach members of the host culture. Rather than remaining an ethnic enclave, a church plant using the national culture can reach nationals, especially if exposure to and association with other cultures is valued within the national culture, or at least within a significant subgroup of the national culture. However, this *multicultural ideology*[14] is more common in the English-speaking world than elsewhere[15] and might not be as appreciated as missionaries from North America might expect.

So although there are certain advantages, there are also certain drawbacks to using an assimilation strategy in church planting. Young churches that express themselves in the national culture are not accessible to all immigrants. The language, the worship style, and the food may all be incomprehensible to some members of a diaspora community, even if other members are present and partaking. Such experiences may be too stressful for them and may not communicate the gospel. In order to reach such immigrants, churches that use another strategy must be planted.

Integration

A church planting strategy that aims for integration seeks to form a community where both cultures are present. Perhaps both the diaspora community's language and the host culture's language are used in worship. Elements from both cultures determine how the programs are integrated. This is a very attractive approach to individuals who are bicultural, especially members of the diaspora who were

---

14   Berry, "Psychology of Immigration."
15   R. Y. Bourhis et al., "Acculturation in Multiple Host Community Settings," *Journal of Social Issues* 66 (2010): 780–802.

born in the host country and who feel completely at ease with both cultures. Like the assimilation strategy, the integration strategy can be attractive to immigrants because it provides a safe haven for learning and interacting with elements of the host culture. Like the separation strategy, this strategy also makes it relatively easy to reach out to new immigrants.

However, an integration strategy can be upsetting to members of diaspora cultures who want to preserve all aspects of their own culture. Seeing the second generation become completely bicultural can indicate that the third generation will have little understanding of the original diaspora culture and may be more likely to leave the church. Another limitation is that an integration strategy requires everyone, except those who are already bicultural, to learn a second culture (whether they be members of the diaspora culture or the host culture) in order to fully participate and understand all that is happening in the church. This means that the church plant will have great difficulty reaching members of the dominant culture or immigrants from other cultures.

Marginalization

A church planting strategy that aims for marginalization does not seem like it would have much potential for success. However, Bourhis and colleagues have sought to better understand how Berry's quadrant defined by a low desire to maintain one's home culture and a low desire for relationships with members of the host culture plays out. They reconceptualized Berry's two dimensions as a desire to maintain cultural identity of one's original culture and a desire to adopt the cultural identity of the host country.[16] Immigrants who have little desire to have either cultural identity (Berry's marginalization) tend to go in one of two directions. The immigrants who feel rejected by both cultures, or who choose to reject both cultures, may experience *anomie*, a cultural alienation that may be characterized by delinquency, marginalization, isolation, and extreme maladaptation to the host culture. However, other immigrants, those who choose to identify themselves as individuals more than as members of one culture or another and who wish to relate to others as individuals rather than members of ethnic groups or cultures, choose an *individualist* approach to acculturation. These immigrants are likely to form relationships or join groups based on their own needs and values rather than the norms of either culture. Such immigrants are more likely to come from countries

---

16 Ibid.; Bourhis et al., "Interactive Acculturation Model."

that tend to be highly individualistic such as Anglo and European countries,[17] but in all cultures there are some members who are more individualistic than others and are more likely to adopt an individualist approach.

In high-density, multiethnic urban areas in individualistic countries, the individualist approach might seem the most natural, especially to people who have grown up in such a context. Many urban church planters have used this strategy.[18] Members of these churches might find their identity more in their own freely chosen relationships than in the culture that they were raised in or currently live in. They might also find a natural camaraderie with those who have grown up in the same multiethnic urban situation and have experienced many of the same things they have.

A church planting strategy based on an individualist approach has the advantage of encouraging the development of a Christ-centered community with minimal interference from cultural commitments that might run contrary to the gospel. Such a strategy would emphasize that "our citizenship is in heaven" (Phil 3:20) and that we are "foreigners and strangers on earth" (Heb 11:13). This strategy is also able to welcome everyone, even individuals who may be disdained by their own or host cultures. Becoming a member of a Christian community is likely to counteract the negative psychological effects associated with marginalization.[19] Yet the individualist approach also has significant disadvantages. A young church planted with this strategy will develop its own unique culture. New (or not yet) Christians who begin attending will need to learn a new culture in order to fully enter into its community. A church that has rejected outside cultures may also suffer from an inability to attract non-Christians, especially those who have good social connections and may be the most apt to lead others to Christ. Such a church can come across as cultlike and dangerous.

There is no one church planting strategy that fits all diaspora church planting contexts. The church planter needs to prayerfully consider the needs of the community, the cultural contexts, and the expectations of the core group before proceeding through any door that the Lord may open.

---

17   G. Hofstede, G. J. Hofstede, and M. Minkov, *Cultures and Organizations: Software of the Mind*, 3rd ed. (New York: McGraw-Hill, 2010).
18   McIntosh and McMahan, *Being the Church*.
19   M. R. Leary, "Responses to Social Exclusion: Social Anxiety, Jealousy, Loneliness, Depression, and Low Self-esteem," *Journal of Social and Clinical Psychology* 9 (1990): 221–29; K. D. Williams, "Ostracism," *Annual Review of Psychology* 58 (2007): 425–52.

The Social Identity Model of Acculturation

A third model of acculturation is based on research in the field of social psychology focusing on how individuals develop a sense of identity. Social identity theory[20] begins with the idea that people need a strong sense of group identity for their well-being.[21] Moreover, people are motivated to have a positive view of themselves.[22] So individuals are motivated to not only belong to groups but to think and act in such a way that they feel good about themselves because of their group memberships. The social identity model of acculturation predicts that immigrant behavior will be motivated by this desire to enhance self-esteem via their social identity; that is, their group memberships.[23]

Social identity is a crucial issue for immigrants. Before leaving their home country, they may have had a high social standing, or at least a well-defined place in their country of origin's social structure. However, as immigrants, they may be viewed as outsiders with a low standing and no clear role to play in their host culture. If they are members of a negatively viewed ethnic group, their visible and difficult-to-change attributes (e.g., skin color, physiognomy, or accent) may lead to stigma and to a negative social identity[24] regardless of their actual contributions to the host culture. Immigrants, therefore, may be highly motivated to build a positive social identity through various strategies. One strategy is to try to become members of the dominant group through assimilation. Sometimes this is not possible because of visible characteristics or an inability to fully adopt the host culture. The assimilation approach is costly, because it means shedding one's home culture and identity. A second strategy is to develop pride in one's own group, by placing a greater value on activities that the group excels in (e.g., education, cuisine, sports, music) and downplaying what the dominant culture excels in (e.g., education, technology, entertainment). A third strategy involves limiting the comparisons that one makes to

---

20 M. A. Hogg, "Social Identity Theory," in *Contemporary Social Psychological Theories*, ed. P. J. Burke (Stanford, CA: Stanford University Press, 2006), 111–36; M. A. Hogg, and D. I. Terry, "Social Identity and Self-categorization Processes in Organizational Contexts," *Academy of Management Review* 25 (2000): 121–40; H. Tajfel, and J. C. Turner, "The Social Identity Theory of Intergroup Behavior," in *Psychology of Intergroup Relations*, 2nd ed., ed. S. Worchel and W. G. Austin (Chicago: Nelson-Hall, 1986), 7–24.

21 K. Lewin, *Resolving Social Conflicts* (New York: Harper & Row, 1948).

22 C. M. Steele, "The Psychology of Self-affirmation: Sustaining the Integrity of the Self," in *Advances in Experimental Social Psychology*, vol. 21, ed. L. Berkowitz (San Diego: Academic Press, 1988), 261–302.

23 Berry et al., *Cross-cultural Psychology*; Padilla and Perez, "Acculturation"; Phinney, "Ethnic Identity."

24 Padilla and Perez, "Acculturation"; Phinney, "Ethnic Identity."

only members of one's own culture. For example, rather than comparing themselves to Germans, relatively high-standing Turkish immigrants might choose to compare themselves to other Turks in Germany who are lower in some measure of status in order to boost their own social identity. A fourth strategy, and the one that is most important from a church planting perspective, is to join a new group that gives status, and hence change one's social identity, in order to enhance one's self esteem.

Churches, Status, and Self-Esteem

Immigrants will be attracted to a young church if joining such a church is perceived to raise their status and increase their self-esteem. Several factors will influence their decision. First, they will evaluate the social status of the people in the church. Are they people whom the potential member can respect? Are they people whom the potential member would like to have as friends? Would friendships with the church members increase the potential member's status in the eyes of his or her present friends and family? If his or her social status would go up by joining the church, the potential member will be more motivated to join the group. If not, a barrier will arise, providing motivation for the person to avoid the church.

Secondly, potential church members will evaluate how they are judged by people in the church. If potential church members feel accepted, valued, and desired by the present church members, their self-esteem will go up and they will be motivated to join. If they receive the message that they have little to offer to the group, their self-esteem will go down and they will be motivated to avoid the group.

This means that church planters have to deal with a very strong tension. A young church filled with bright, sociable, fun-loving, attractive people will appeal to more people than will a church with foolish, awkward, unattractive people. Yet Christ loves everyone equally and calls us to do the same. We are to avoid any form of favoritism towards high-status people (Jas 2:1–13). If a church planter follows this principle, young churches will be most attractive to people of low status because they will be valued there, whereas elsewhere they are not valued. But if the church is primarily composed of low-status people, it becomes less attractive to outsiders. This apparently was the situation in at least some of the churches that the Apostle Paul planted (1 Cor 1:26–31). Paul argues that God calls the lowly and weak to be his people to shame the strong and arrogant, demonstrating that any true righteousness and holiness that a person has comes through Christ.

This leaves the church planter with the question, "Is it possible to remain faithful to the gospel, yet start a church that will be attractive to anyone other than those of low social status?" A possible response comes with the church planter's approach to leadership selection. Research has demonstrated that the leaders of an organization are responsible for an inordinate amount of the increase or decrease in status that a person receives when joining a group.[25] The leader or leaders become the *prototype* of what the members of the group aspire to be. If the leader is seen as highly respectable, upright, socially skilled, and living in a manner consistent with the espoused values, a potential church member's social identity will get a boost in self-esteem by joining such a group. However, if the leader is seen as incompetent, untrustworthy, awkward, or hypocritical, joining such a group would hurt one's social identity, and the potential member would be motivated to avoid the church because of its leadership. Although this is not the vocabulary that the Apostle Paul used in describing why he set high standards for leadership in churches (1 Tim 3:1–13; Titus 1:6–9), his desire to see people who excel at living out the gospel appointed to leadership is perfectly consistent with what social identity theory would predict is the best way to help a young church grow.

For church planters working among diaspora communities, this means that leadership must not be appointed too quickly. Near the end of his ministry, the Apostle Paul said, "Do not be hasty in the laying on of hands, and do not share in the sins of others" (1 Tim 5:22). Rather the church planter must carefully nurture the young church and appoint formal leadership only when truly exemplary leaders are available. Such leaders will make the church more attractive to outsiders, while leaders who are less honorable will make the church less attractive. Because the social identity of immigrants is in greater flux than the social identity of nonimmigrants, this phenomenon is amplified among diaspora communities, and leadership selection becomes even more important.

It might be argued that often Paul did not wait long to appoint leaders in many of the churches he planted (at least at the beginning of his ministry). However, it should be noted that many of the converts in Paul's early churches were from synagogues and were already committed to the study of the word of God (e.g., Acts 13:14,15; 14:1; 17:1,2,10,11). At least one synagogue leader, Crispus of Corinth, became a Christian and was most likely a leader in the young church. When highly respected leaders with a knowledge of the word of God come to know Christ early

---

[25] M. A. Hogg, "A Social Identity Theory of Leadership," *Personality and Social Psychology Review* 5 (2001): 184–200.

in a church planting ministry, leadership selection and appointment can advance much more quickly than when this is not the case.

These three models of acculturation each provide unique insights that are useful for church planting among diaspora communities. The melting pot one-dimensional model emphasizes that changes in ministry emphasis need to occur in diaspora churches over time, especially over generations, as the cultural distance between the diaspora group and members of the host culture decreases. The two-dimensional model of acculturation strategies, focusing on the desire to maintain one's home culture and the desire for relationships in the host culture, provides insights into different church planting strategies that may be used according to the needs and values of the diaspora community that is being reached. The social identity model of acculturation accentuates the importance of careful leadership selection in order to enable a young church to be attractive to outsiders and to continue growing.

No single acculturation model is sufficient for understanding the best way to go about planting a church among a diaspora population. Even together, they are insufficient for determining a church planting strategy. However, they provide tools that church planters can use as they seek to obey the leading of the Holy Spirit in obedience to the Great Commission.

Chapter Nine

The "With" of Diaspora Missiology: The Impact of Kinship, Honor, and Hospitality on the Future of Missionary Training, Sending, and Partnership

JACQUES HÉBERT

ABSTRACT

This paper presents a significant development of the current disapora missiology paradigm. This new aspect analyzes the relationship between kinship, transnational networks, and honor-based hospitality, and projects a model for utilizing diaspora missions as a new strategy for sending missionaries into countries that are socially opposed to the gospel. This model integrates traditional missions strategies and fields and diaspora strategies and fields.

Introduction

The postcolonial world is increasingly unsympathetic to the task of world evangelization, discipleship, and church planting. Missionaries going to countries in the 10/40 Window are finding it more and more difficult to acquire and maintain residency permits. One response to this problem is the practice of diaspora missions. Missions *to* the diaspora affords opportunities to reach peoples from closed access countries without the necessary approval from foreign governments. Missions *through* the diaspora mobilizes people who have natural connections to closed access countries. These nationals are able to take the message to people in places where foreigners cannot go even with a visa. Likewise, missions *by/beyond* the diaspora send people who may not raise the same suspicions and animosities as Westerners do. *To*, *through*, and *beyond* are not the complete story. There is one more preposition for the diaspora paradigm: *with*. *With* implies that the job is not finished simply by reaching diaspora groups and sending them back. There is still room in the task of mission for you and me, but we will need the help of the diaspora. Missions with the diaspora can only be achieved once missions to the diaspora is underway. This paper will establish the foundational principles of the *with* category.

Theory

There is a need for new vocabulary if there is to be clarity in defining the *with* dynamic. Within diaspora missions circles, when one speaks of sending a missionary, he is usually referring to either sending one of the diaspora group back to their group in the diaspora or abroad in their homeland (missions through), or he is referring to sending a diaspora missionary to a third ethnic group (missions by/beyond). This chapter will use the designation *exogenous missionary* to refer to the person being sent. This term means a missionary who is not from the diaspora group under discussion. Exogenous missionaries may include citizens of the host nation who share its ethnic identity (e.g., ethnic "whites" in the West or Chinese in China), citizens of the host nation who are from a different ethnic background (e.g., Hispanics in the West), or members of other diaspora groups that are exogenous to the group under discussion (e.g., diaspora Filipinos in the West seeking to reach diaspora Arabs in order to go as missionaries to the Middle East).

With this definition of exogenous missionary in mind, missions *with* occurs: when exogenous missionaries who are participating in missions to the diaspora build relationships with the diaspora group to the depth that they are able to receive invitations to their homeland and go to the diaspora person's family, tribe, or network.

Another term that will be used synonymously as *with* is *kinship bridging*, which is simply the process, practice, and realized phenomena of missions *with*. Table 3 contrasts some common misconceptions regarding the *with* dynamic.

Missions *With* is not...	
Reaching diaspora peoples and reaching the same groups abroad.	Unintegrated
	Not realizing the familial connections between here and there
Using the diaspora as a training ground before going to their home countries	

Missions *With* is...	
Reaching and training among diaspora peoples and then using those relationships, networks, and familial ties as a bridge to specific homes, tribes, villages, and cities in their home countries	Integrated
	Utilizes the regional paradigm
	Fully realizes transitional familial ties and obligations

Table 3: Common Misconceptions

Table 4 delineates and analyzes the levels in integrating and applying ministry and missions between diaspora and natal contexts in existing ministries.[1]

---

[1] These examples are illustrative and not exhaustive as the focus of this research is not to identify and plot every stateside and foreign ministry.

Level of Integration		Examples
1	Traditional mission. Engaging peoples abroad only.	Traditional missions structures. Some churches which participate in foreign missions but do not engage in local diaspora missions.
2	Diaspora missions *To*. Engaging peoples as diaspora only.	Some mono–ethnic churches. Some multi–ethnic churches. Some collegiate ministries.
3	Diaspora mission: *To* and potentially *Through* and *Beyond*. Engaging peoples abroad and in the diaspora.	Some collegiate ministries. Missional mutli–ethnic churches.
4	Diaspora missions: *To*. Engaging peoples in the diaspora in order to train to go abroad.	Several traditional mission agencies have practiced training in diaspora groups prior to departure.

Table 4: Current Diaspora-natal Integration

There are numerous ways in which kinship bridging can help people from various backgrounds overcome cultural, linguistic, ethnic, religious, and geographic differences. Utilizing the religion of Islam juxtaposed against Christianity in the West, table 5 describes the various ways of connecting to diaspora groups and the kinds of networks to which they will be introduced, and provides a matrix for classification as kinship bridging receives further study, analysis, and practice.

The "With" of Diaspora Missiology 151

Designation	Description of the Bridge	Mission Activity
EX–0	(EX–Muslim) + (D–Muslim→N–Muslim) An exogenous Muslim befriends a diaspora Muslim who introduces him to his natal–network.	Not Applicable
EX–1	(EX–Christian) + (D–Christian→N–Christian) An exogenous Christian befriends a diaspora Christian who introduces him to his natal–Christian network.	Partnership with the local church. Discipleship or Leadership training. The hosts help the guest acclimate and receive his ministry.[1]
EX–2	(EX–Christian) + (D–Christian→N–Muslim) An exogenous Christian befriends a diaspora Christian who introduces him to a natal–Muslim network.	Partnership with the local church. Evangelism if possible. The hosts help the guest acclimate and connect him with their Muslim friends and neighbours.
EX–3	(EX–Christian) + (D–Muslim→N–Muslim) An exogenous Christian befriends a diaspora Muslim who introduces him to his natal–Muslim network.	Practices missions to and then with pioneer evangelism and kinship based church planting. The hosts help the guest acclimate and provide him with the social legitimacy in the Muslim community.

Table 5: Types of Exogenous Networking

EX-0 is the baseline. This method of networking is located completely within the structure of the local religion. A Muslim that is exogenous to a particular group befriends a diaspora Muslim who introduces him to his natal network. An example of EX-0 would be a Saudi Arabian Muslim looking for a job in India. He befriends a diaspora Indian Muslim who has family and business connections in India. The Indian Muslim knows someone looking for workers in his home country, and he connects his Saudi friend with the home company. Through his diaspora connection, the Saudi is able to utilize the Indian's natal network and find a job in India.

EX-1 is the mirror of EX-0 with the exception that the participants are all Christian. An exogenous Christian befriends a diaspora Christian who introduces him to his natal-Christian network. An example of EX-1 would be a Western Christian student who befriends a fellow student who is a Christian from Lebanon. Through their friendship, the Lebanese invites his fellow student back to his country to stay with his family and minister with his church. Ministry in this context is partnership with the local body of Christians through discipleship or leadership training. The hosts help the guest acclimate and receive his ministry.

EX-2 is a slight modification of EX-1 in that the point of contact is the same. but the target network is across religious lines. An exogenous Christian networks with a diaspora Syrian Christian in order to reach the Syrian's home network of Muslim friends and acquaintances. This is the first designation to mix Christian and non-Christian networks. The priority, if only initially, is given to the Western Christian's network and contacts rather than the Muslim's network. Rather than focusing only on the Christian community in the natal context, the exogenous missionary also focuses on reaching the Muslim community through his friend's network. Ministry in this context is partnership with the local body of Christians through missions to the neighboring Muslim community, if possible. The hosts help the guest acclimate and connect him with their Muslim friends, neighbors, and contacts.

EX-3 bridges the broadest cultural gap. In an EX-3 scenario, an exogenous Christian befriends a diaspora Muslim who, in turn, introduces him to his natal-Muslim network. An example of EX-3 would be an exogenous Christian who works in an international company alongside migrant workers from around the world. He befriends a Muslim and through that connection is able to transfer to or visit his home country. The exogenous missionary's focus is first on the extended family and then on their network. Ministry in this context is pioneer work within a Muslim network that has probably never heard the gospel. The hosts help the guest acclimate and provide him with social legitimacy in the Muslim community.

Theology

Diaspora peoples can move in four directions. The first two of these directions form the simplest kind of movements: sending and receiving. The second two movements can only occur once these first two have taken place as they build upon the existing movements and connections.

The first direction is from a natal land to the diaspora from an emic perspective. This kind of diaspora is emic because the subject experiences the action of being dispersed (see figure 5), as in the case of the Jewish dispersion.

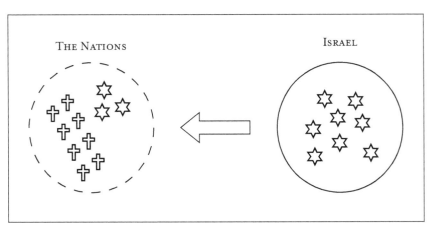

Figure 5: *Emic Diaspora : The Jewish Diaspora*

These kinds of dispersions usually occur under duress with obvious "push" factors motivating and initiating the movement. Israel's exile was forced by military defeat, and captives such as Daniel and Esther lived under these circumstances. Joseph went to Egypt because he was sold into slavery. Joseph's brothers inadvertently followed him there due to the famine in the land. Mary and Joseph fled for Egypt because of imminent danger. The early Christians were scattered throughout Judea and Samaria as a result of persecution. The cause of these emic diasporas is often based initially on some kind of judgment (as in the case of the Jewish exile), but is ultimately rooted in God's plan for redemption. If Joseph had not been sent as a slave to Egypt, his family would have died during the famine. If Esther had not been sent to the king's house, the Jewish nation (at least that part of it) would have been destroyed. Although the persecution of the early church was unfortunate suffering, it provided the impetus for the first missionary movements.

The second direction for a diaspora movement is from a foreign land to one's homeland (see figure 6). This is an etic experience on behalf of the nationals who receive the diaspora peoples as guests in their homeland. Although the majority of the biblical examples are of emic diasporas, due to Israel's geographic position joining three major continents, it is often home to foreigners in its midst. Foreign empires, such as the Greeks and Romans, often had a foothold, or control, in Israel. The Bible gave clear instruction to Israel not to oppress the "sojourner" for they were "sojourners in the land of Egypt" (Ex 22:21 ESV). The presence of foreigners in the land was more than a memorial of Israel's sojourns and more than an opportunity to practice hospitality and be a light to the nations. Solomon indicated that God's glory would be spread through the nations coming to Zion and having their prayers answered (1 Kgs 8:43). Israel as a centripetal light to the nations was realized during Pentecost, when the world gathered in Jerusalem and heard the gospel in their own languages.

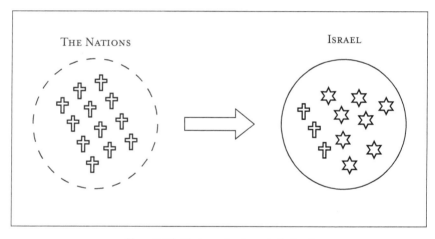

Figure 6: Etic Diaspora : Foreigners in the Land

These first two diaspora trajectories are the same movement but occur in opposite directions and from opposite perspectives, emic and etic. The next two directions use the presence of a diaspora people in their country as bridge to the diaspora's natal land. The exogenous person becomes part of the diaspora group socially and then has the option for moving geographically along relational lines back to the natal land.

The third trajectory occurs when there is an emic diaspora. While Israel was present in the foreign land, there were opportunities for the foreigners to join the Jews socially and religiously. This provided the proselytes the opportunity to move along Jewish geographies (see figure 7).

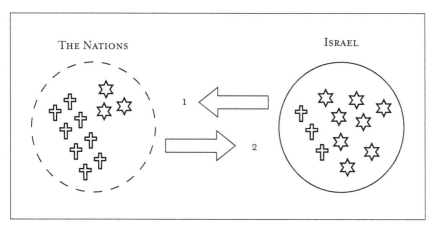

Figure 7: Emic Diaspora as a Bridge to the Natal Land

One instance of this kind of movement occurred during the Exodus. Moses recounts that "a mixed multitude also went up with them" when they left the land of Egypt (Ex 12:38 ESV). These "bridgers" did not achieve much status in the Jewish camp, as Deuteronomy 29:11 suggests they were only used for chopping wood and carrying water. When Nehemiah returned to Jerusalem, there were also some foreigners who traveled with them (Neh 13:3). In the case in Nehemiah, Israel applied the injunction prohibiting Ammonites and Moabites from entering the temple (Deut 23:3–5) to all foreigners in all contexts, and they separated themselves from the foreigners in their midst (Neh 9:2).

The fourth trajectory occurs when there is an etic diaspora. The presence of foreigners in the midst of Israel gives them the opportunity to reach the nations among them. If they utilized the diaspora's networks, they can move according to the geography of the diaspora (see figure 8).

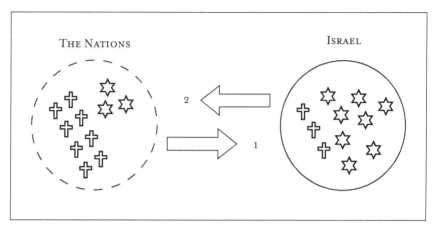

Figure 8: Etic Diaspora as a Bridge to the World

The church in Jerusalem contained Greeks who had converted. This is evidenced by the initial problem the church faced when the Greek-speaking widows were being neglected (Acts 6:1). The disciples urged them to choose men who could serve the widows. The church chose seven men, and all of them bore Greek names, and one, Nicolaus, was from Antioch (Acts 6:5). The presence of these Greeks establishes that there was an etic diaspora present in the early church. The "push" factor of persecution dispersed all of the early disciples except for the apostles, and they fled "as far as Phoenicia and Cypress and Antioch" (Acts 11:19 ESV). Donald McGavran asserts that these impromptu missionaries must have utilized relational connections with family members from the etic diaspora in Jerusalem to share the gospel in Antioch. He says, "This bond of relationship was a bridge over which the faith passed."[2] The church in Antioch was started, in part, by "men of Cyprus and Cyrene" (Acts 11:20 ESV). As reports reached Jerusalem about what was happening there, the church sent Barnabas and Saul to inspect. These two men spent a year working with the church in Antioch (Acts 11:26). McGavran reasoned that Paul was able to network in this church made up of various diaspora peoples and that these relationships served as the basis for his future ministry.[3] This accounts for his speedy reception throughout his journeys, even when his reputation would have warned believers not to receive him. These relationships not only accounted for the hospitality that Paul received but also established where he would go on his journeys. McGavran,

---

2   Donald McGavran, *The Bridges of God*, rev. ed. (New York: Friendship Press, 1981), 24.
3   Ibid., 27.

in answering how Paul chose where to go next, says, "To be accurate we must not say that he did not choose fields. He followed up groups of people who had living relations in the People Movement to Christ."[4]

Culture

The notion of kinship bridging is built upon four cultural patterns: kinship, networks, hospitality, and reciprocal obligation-formed relationships. These four traits and patterns will look different in every culture, and specific ethnographic and anthropological study will be necessary to determine if a given culture is a likely host for kinship bridging.

Kinship

Paul Hiebert defines kinship as the "sets of relatives of which we are a part, who know each other as individuals and who interact in some fashion as a corporate group."[5] This definition lacks certain elements that distinguish the socio-relational characteristics of kinship from the mere function of biological descent.[6] Mayers and Grunlan argue that kinship is more than the nuclear family and their biological relationships:

The family, in its broadest meaning, extends beyond the nuclear family of parents and their children to a whole network of relationships. This larger family network is tied together by kinship. Kinship is more than a network of biological relationships; it is also a network of social relationships. It establishes social ties, patterns of behavior, obligations and responsibilities, and patterns of authority. In short, it is a "road map" or structure of interpersonal relationships.[7]

They go on to say that kinship is built upon three classifications of relationships: affinal, consanguine, and fictive.[8] Affinal ties are formed through marriage. A married couple is not necessarily biologically related (exceptions exist in endogamous cultures) but are joined contractually, socially, and ceremonially through marriage and are now related not only to each other but to their spouse's family. Consanguine ties are formed through blood relationships such as parents to children, and sibling to

---

4   Ibid., 31.
5   Paul G. Hiebert, *Cultural Anthropology*, 2nd ed. (Grand Rapids: Baker Book House, 1983), 223.
6   Christopher Harris agrees that kinship transcends mere biological descent. C. C. Harris, *Kinship* (Minneapolis: University of Minnesota Press, 1990), 27.
7   Stephen A. Grunlan and Marvin K. Mayers, *Cultural Anthropology: A Christian Perspective*, 2nd ed. (Grand Rapids: Zondervan, 1988), 162.
8   Ibid., 163.

sibling. Fictive ties exist where someone is "legally, ceremonially, or religiously" part of a kinship group.⁹ If an outsider is to gain access to a kinship system, presuming marriage is not an option, then the fictive tie is the avenue for such access. Although many cultures do not have the official fictive roles of godparent or blood brother, the culturally and relationally savvy outsider can hope to achieve the status of the honored guest. This is a synthetic relationship, as it is not necessarily formed on the bonds of blood relationship, and can be referred to as synthetic kinship. By achieving this status, an outsider now has an identity through that particular family or clan within the broader community.

Kinship, then, is the patterned interpersonal relationships, bonds, and obligations, ascribed or achieved, that identify a person or family subgroup as part of a given group.

Networks

Similar to the concept of kinship is the concept of network. Harris argues that kinship groups generate networks.¹⁰ Cooke and Lawrence define networks as "the phenomena that are similar to institutionalized social relations, such as tribal affiliations and political dynasties, but also distinct from them, because to be networked entails making a choice to be connected across recognized boundaries."¹¹
Charles Kurzman further refines the definition:

> Networks are not reality; rather, they are a metaphor that privileges certain aspects of reality that are deemed to be of theoretical importance. Networks are not limited: one cannot say that one human institution is a network and another is not. Networks are not new: ancient institutions can be studied through the network lens as easily as contemporary ones. And networks are not inherently egalitarian or liberatory: they may have any structure, including hierarchy, and any ideological content.¹²

---

9   Ibid., 164.
10 Harris, *Kinship*, 64.
11 Miriam Cooke and Bruce B. Lawrence, *Muslim Networks: From Hajj to Hip Hop* (Chapel Hill: University of North Carolina Press, 2005), 1.
12 Quoted in ibid., 7.

Networks consist of nodes, spokes, and structure. Nodes are the persons who make up the network ranging from individuals to tribes and nations. Spokes are the relationships that connect the nodes. Spokes can be economic, technological, media, business, and familial. Finally, "structure is the pattern formed by the nodes and spokes; it is centralized or decentralized, dense or diffuse, homogeneous or riddled with structural holes and bridges, and so on."[13]

The concept of a network is much broader than kinship, although kinship groups form their own networks. Networks can be focused around areas of mutual interest, social action, political opinion, or religious and moral values. Networks transcend natural groupings. For instance, a man's natural group may be his nuclear family and his work environment, both physically located in a foreign land. He might support a particular political movement, even though he no longer resides in the country where the movement is taking place. The people in his natural group may have no idea of his connection to something happening in another place. He uses technological and other media-driven venues to connect to other members, hear news, and give his support.

Arjun Appadurai classifies global cultural movements in five categories: ethnoscapes, technoscapes, financescapes, mediascapes, and ideoscapes.[14] He pairs these categories of people, machinery, money, images, and ideas, with the wordscape to indicate that the shape and location is taking new forms. The ethnoscape, for instance, is no longer merely in one place. People are mobile and are migrating *en masse*. Thus the given people group of Arabs, or the particular nationality of Egyptian, Lebanese, or Moroccan, are no longer to be found only in the Middle East but are now being distributed throughout the world. They are here and there. Due to kinship ties—and other "scapes" such as mediascape and technoscape—these distributed groups are still connected. Furthermore, the rise of technology and its spread to this part of the world enable Arabs to remain connected in ways that were not before possible, not only to their own families but to each other as well. This capacity is forming new networks and "tribes" formed around ideas, movements, places, and interests (see table 6).

---

13 Ibid., 69.
14 Arjun Appadurai, "Disjuncture and Difference in the Global Cultural Economy," in *Theorizing Diaspora: A Reader*, ed. Jana Evans Braziel and Anita Mannur (Malden, MA: Blackwell, 2003), 31.

Category	Example	Location/Context	Networks
Ethnoscape (People)	Dispersed familes Migrant workers Students Refugees	Homeland/new land Businesses Schools Refugee camps	Community center Businesses Ethnic–based social club Kin–based migration sponsoring
Technoscape (Machinery)	Computers Cell Phones	Everywhere Often used to acquire access to other "scapes" (e.g. Mediascape)	Social network sites usually via cell phones Internet chat rooms or cafés
Financescape (Money)	Informal kin–based banking Sending money back to the family Resources and jobs Business and trade routes	Homeland/new land Electronic banking Face–to–face gifts	Kin–based sharing and reciprocity Friendship–based sharing and reciprocity
Mediascape (Images)	Television Satellite Internet Pop art	Homeland/new land Cyberspace	Religio–cultural publications, newspapers, and magazines Foreign pop art consumed via satellite or internet
Ideoscape (Ideas)	Religion Political ideology Revolutions Nationalistic movements	Homeland/new land Cyberspace	Religious center Cultural center Coffee shop Political organizations

Table 6: The Landscape of Relational Networks

Hospitality

Many cultures pride themselves on their hospitality. This is particularly true in Africa, the Middle East, and Asia. Sociocultural traits and cognitive patterns such as honor and shame, negative views on greed and envy, and prioritizing personal relationships and interaction over time, efficiency, and goals has cultivated impositional hospitality in these contexts. Impositional hospitality is a determined focus on the part of a host to meet the needs of the guest, even when the guest refuses (and in such cultures it is polite for guests to refuse so as not to appear envious), in such a way that brings honor to his own family. To refuse to provide hospitality, in all of its demands, would bring great shame on the family and, in some instances, the village, tribe, or broader religious community.

In such a context, the status of *honored guest* carries social significance that transcends simply being invited over for dinner and entertained. This status carries with it the identity, privilege, and status the host family holds within a given context. A host family may not provide a sufficient identity to satisfy the requirements of government offices for residency; however, they do provide the reason for being at the social level in a society that is ruled by personal and familial relationships. In countries that do not provide missionary visas, the identity of being a humanitarian worker—while making sense to the Western mind—may not make as much sense in answering the question, "Who is the foreigner?" as does the simple, relational answer, "He is a friend of the family, and is friends with our relatives overseas."

Obligation and Reciprocity

Mutual obligation and reciprocity are the rules through which relationships are built, maintained, and optimized. Friendship in the non-Western world is a significant relationship. Friends are obliged to help each other out. To refuse to help (the task) would be to refuse the relationship (the person). In these cultural contexts, people are known for their creative and diverse ways of saying "no" in a "yes" way in order to preserve the relationship. Through the course of asking for and receiving help, the relationship is strengthened through reciprocity. The two parties build trust as they have invested significant energy and resources in the other and know the other party is going to act with the same self-interest. Diaspora ministry and mission *to* the diaspora should be holistic. Ministering to the whole person forms the down payment towards future hospitality and reciprocal obligation with an individual and their family, regionally or internationally.

Demographic Trends and Strategic Diasporas

There are a few demographic trends that are bringing in people from cultures and geographies that are likely to practice the four foundational cultural traits for kinship bridging. Two trends, although not entirely new, are on the rise: medical tourists and international students.

Hundreds of thousands of people travel out of their home country to hospitals around the world seeking medical treatment. Between sixty thousand and eighty-five thousand people per year travel to the United States specifically and solely for medical treatment.[15] The opportunity this trend provides is not for Americans alone, as many medical tourists are headed to Thai and Indian hospitals as well. Some medical tourists do not cross the ocean but travel only regionally. In 2010, 180,000 Palestinians received medical treatment in Israeli hospitals.[16]

In 2010 enrollment from international students in the United States rose by 3 percent accounting for 690,923 international students. This was fueled by a 16 percent increase from Middle Eastern students and a 30 percent increase by Chinese students. This makes Chinese students the largest block of all international students in the United States at nearly 19 percent, and Indian students the second largest at 15 percent.[17]

The increase of these two groups and their temporary nature make them great places to begin the process of kinship bridging.

Muslims, Hindus, and Buddhists represent 35 percent of the total global diaspora population, with Muslims accounting for 25 percent of the whole by themselves.[18] Immigrants from these religions span geographically across North Africa all the way to the Pacific Rim and have migrated significantly within their respective regions and to Western countries.

---

15 This study only takes into account those who travel solely for medical purposes. Allison Van Dusen, "U.S. Hospitals Worth the Trip," *Forbes*, May 29, 2008, http://www.forbes.com/2008/05/25/health-hospitals-care-forbeslife-cx_avd_outsourcing08_0529healthoutsourcing.html (accessed July 18, 2013).

16 Khaled Abu Toameh, "Why Arab Leaders Do Not Care About Medical Services in Their Countries," Gaston Institute International Policy, http://www.gatestoneinstitute.org/1741/arab-countries-medical-services (accessed July 18, 2013).

17 Institute of International Education, "International Academic Exchange between the United States and the Middle East on the Rise," December 7, 2010, http://www.iie.org/en/Who-We-Are/News-and-Events/Press-Center/Press-Releases/2010/2010-12-07-Open-Doors-Middle-East-US-Educational-Exchange (accessed July 18, 2013).

18 Pew Research Center, "Faith on the Move: The Religious Affiliation of International Migrants," March 8, 2012, http://www.pewforum.org/2012/03/08/religious-migration-exec/, 11.

Speaking specifically of Muslims, although they have been in America for several hundred years, the majority of the population and institutions are relatively new. More than 75 percent of all mosques have been founded since 1980; 26 percent of mosques have been established since the year 2000.[19] Eighty-four percent of Muslims arrived in America after 1980, with 33 percent and 28 percent arriving during the 1990s and 2000s respectively.[20] To state this negatively, only 16 percent arrived before 1980. Thus 65 percent of Muslims are first-generation immigrants. Due to the nascent nature of Muslims in America, 72 percent of them still have family ties abroad.[21] These Muslims come from sixty-eight nations.[22] Exogenous workers have direct access to many Muslims who are first- or second-generation immigrants from every corner of the Muslim world and who still have ties to their families, friends, and networks back home. Building relationships within the diaspora Muslim community will grant access far into the Muslim world

Conclusion

The *with* of diaspora missiology is relatively unexplored. There is great potential for ethnographic research into many of the diaspora groups and world cultures to determine their potential for such an idea as kinship bridging. There are three categories of mission personnel who would benefit from the study and application of kinship bridging and relational methodology in diaspora missions: individuals, churches, and missions organizations.

With the development of the business as mission (BAM) model there is a renewed emphasis on the opportunities for and responsibilities of individuals to use business as a platform for overseas missions. A person preparing to practice BAM would benefit from the training and networking received during their participation in a diaspora ministry. The relationships built during that time would not only provide cultural preparation but would potentially guide that person to a particular place and job opportunity based on their relationship with the diaspora group. Within any particular diaspora group are a number of subgroups. each with their own needs and benefits. Although refugees may lack the necessary network to be of benefit to the exogenous missionary beyond cultural training, businessmen and students are

---

19 Ihsan Bagby, *The American Mosque 2011: The Basic Characteristics of the American Mosque*, report 1 (Washington, DC: Council on American-Islamic Relations, 2011), 9.
20 Pew Research Center, *Muslim Americans: Middle Class and Mostly Mainstream* (Washington, DC: Pew Research Center, 2007), 15.
21 Ibid., 10.
22 Ibid., 11.

usually well connected and often come from well-to-do and influential families with large business and cultural networks. When they reciprocate the hospitality shown to their family member in another country, these well-connected families are able to provide more than a mere network for an otherwise-unconnected outsider, they provide social legitimacy and support.

As churches trend towards hiring their own mission staff and partnering unilaterally with ministries overseas, kinship bridging will serve as a legitimate avenue to integrate the church's local outreach (missions *to* and *through*) with their international missions (missions *through*, *by/beyond*, and *with*). Local engagement that leads to international engagement will help circumvent some of the problems that result from short-term mission trips. The integrated approach of kinship bridging, which is founded solidly on a series of personal relationships, will promote a healthier outlook and results from short-term trips.

Finally, missions agencies have the resources and the personnel to incorporate kinship bridging as a way of integrating the growing focus on diaspora people while still affirming a commitment to continue to go to the least reached. Many agencies are already focusing on reaching the diaspora but have not yet integrated their diaspora (*to*) activities into their sending strategy. Agencies that employed this strategy would build a seamless relational flow from reaching the diaspora to sending exogenous missionaries to the world.

With the increase of Islamic nationalistic movements in recent days and other nationalistic movements around the world not showing any sign of relenting, traditional mission agencies and tentmakers alike may wish to look towards the longer route of missions *to* the diaspora as training and networking for kinship bridging to the rest of the world.

The increase in human geographic distribution is providing the church in all parts of the world with new opportunities to reach the nations. The people God has put within the church's immediate reach are more than potential new members, they are bridges to the nations.

Part Five:

Case Studies in Diaspora Missions

Chapter Ten

Mission and the Palestinian Diaspora

ANDREW F. BUSH

ABSTRACT

Palestinians are a diaspora community. Christian response to Israel and Palestine is polarized. Often the Christian supporters of Palestinians tend to focus on the political dimension of their plight to the extent that the greater need for support of their spiritual life and mission is neglected. Whereas historically Palestinian mission has been somewhat stunted, this paper will describe and explore the development of a Palestinian Protestant Christian missiology and mission. The author proposes that a valuable service to the Palestinian diaspora is to acknowledge their effort in forming an indigenous missiology, to be constructive listeners and learners as they speak, and to be friends as they search for a better expression of the mission of God in a context of conflict.

Introduction

With the growth of the global Christian movement, innovative and courageous new directions in mission are emerging in quite unexpected places. Such vital mission is developing from the margins of the global Christian community, advanced by Christians from the Majority World who have customarily been viewed as needy recipients of the largesse of Western Christians. These communities on the margins include diaspora Christian communities who are refugees due to famine, war, economic stress, or other hardship. The importance of this mission from the margins, in addition to its obvious importance as a vehicle of the life and message of Christ to those they serve, is that it may be a source of spiritual renewal and insight to Western mission as the latter tries to find its place in the new global mission of the twenty-first century. Western Christians face the challenge of coming alongside diaspora Christians in a way that is at the same time both supportive and open to learn from their mission.

Palestinian Christians in the West Bank, including East Jerusalem, and the Gaza Strip[1] are a diaspora community that is persevering both existentially and in faith in spite of ongoing, intense pressure from several sources. As a diaspora community they are unique in that they must not only face the immediate pressures of their context but also respond to the ambivalence towards them of significant segments of the global Christian community. Despite these pressures, they are exploring new paths for mission both theologically and in praxis; this is especially true of Palestinian Protestant Christians on whom this discussion will focus. It is worthwhile reflecting on their progress, as it offers insights concerning several critical issues facing Western mission. To appreciate their efforts in mission, it is useful to first consider their diaspora status.

The Palestinian People as a Diaspora Community

Most of the Palestinian people, including its Christian community on the West Bank and Gaza, are refugees, having been relocated from their villages during the Arab-Israeli war of 1948. During this war, either as a result of the fear of attack by Israel's military forces, or direct force by the same, Palestinian Arabs fled from almost four hundred villages that were located in what today is the modern State of Israel. Along with this exodus, known as the Nakba, or the Destruction, to Palestinians, Christians transferred en masse to the West Bank, which was at that time under Jordanian Mandate control, or to neighboring countries. Some emigrated further afield to Europe or North or South America.[2] A lesser number relocated within the area that would become the modern State of Israel. The trauma of this uprooting has been told in several autobiographies such as Palestinian Israeli cleric Elias Chacour's *Blood Brothers*.[3]

The 1967 Arab-Israeli war produced further hardship for the Palestinian community. With the defeat of the combined Arab forces by Israel, the West Bank, including East Jerusalem, the Gaza Strip, and the Golan Heights fell under military occupation by Israel. The occupation of the West Bank has remained in effect until

---

1   Palestinians refer to these three areas collectively as "Palestine." Although they do not have full, sovereign national status, as a result of a raised status in the United Nations, the Palestinian National Authority has renamed itself, "The State of Palestine." Israel refers to the land, except for East Jerusalem, which was annexed by Israel to West Jerusalem in 1967, as a "disputed territory," or as the "Palestinian Territories." Israel's annexation of East Jerusalem is not recognized by any international body.

2   *Wikipedia*, s.v. "Palestinian Christians," http://en.wikipedia.org/wiki/Palestinian_Christians (accessed February 1, 2014).

3   Elias Chacour, *Blood Brothers: The Dramatic Story of a Palestinian Christian Working for Peace in Israel* (Grand Rapids: Chosen Books, 1984).

the present. Although Israel has removed its settlements and military from within Gaza, this territory remains under partial Israeli blockade, putting extreme economic stress upon the 1.4 million Palestinians—including its two thousand Christian citizens—who live within its closed borders.

Following the occupation in 1967, Israelis began to colonize the West Bank and Gaza, forming settlements that now range in population from a few dozen to tens of thousands in the largest. In spite of peace negotiations, the presence of Israeli settlers on the West Bank has dramatically increased in recent decades under the protection of the Israeli Defense Forces (IDF) and with the support of the Israeli government. For example, the population of Israeli settlers in the West Bank and East Jerusalem has grown from about ten thousand in 1972 to approximately 530,000 today.[4]

The futility of peace efforts combined with the loss of land that would comprise part of a future Palestinian sovereign state, gave rise to the first and second *intifadas* (uprisings). While the first intifada (1987–91) largely pitted unarmed youth against the Israeli military, the second intifada (2000–2004) was much more violent, resulting in the deaths of more than 3,200 Palestinians and one thousand Israelis.[5] Thousands more were seriously wounded.

The second intifada, and the consequent construction of a separation barrier by Israel, has resulted in greater loss of land as well as freedom of travel for Palestinians, not only into East Jerusalem and Israel but also within the West Bank. Bethlehem, an important center for Palestinian Christians, has suffered significantly due to the wall construction, as it separates people in and around Bethlehem from their work, schools, and hospitals. It also has had the effect of constricting the already fragile economy. The presence of the wall discourages tourist traffic into the city. (Tourists must pass through an imposing Israeli military checkpoint in the wall.)

The dispossession and marginalization of the Palestinian community from 1948 to the present has resulted in the emigration of many Palestinian Christians. In 1948 the population of Palestinian Christians in the West Bank and Gaza numbered about 400,000. At the beginning of the second intifada in 2000 there were approximately

---

4 Foundation for Middle East Peace, "Comprehensive Settlement Population 1972–2010," http://www.fmep.org/settlement_info/settlement-info-and-tables/stats-data/comprehensive-settlement-population-1972-2006 (accessed February 1, 2014).
5 BBC News, "Intifada Toll 2000–2005," http://news.bbc.co.uk/2/hi/middle_east/4294502.stm (accessed March 12, 2014).

eighty thousand Christians remaining in Palestine. The conflict has further reduced the community to about sixty thousand at present.[6]

Not only has the population of the Palestinian Christian community been significantly reduced during the last sixty years since the Nakba, their percentage of Palestinian society continues to dwindle. The total Palestinian population (West Bank and Gaza) was approximately 4.4 million in 2013.[7] Palestinian Christians are now less than 2 percent of this community.[8]

There is significant debate concerning the reasons for the continued emigration of Palestinian Christians from the West Bank. Primarily, it is argued this emigration is a result of the continued pressure on Palestinian society of Israel's occupation of the West Bank and the resultant constriction of the Palestinian economy and the consequent lack of employment possibilities.[9] However, as I mentioned in *Learning from the Least: Reflections on a Journey in Mission with Palestinian Christians,*[10] another factor in the emigration of Palestinian Christians that is often publically downplayed by Palestinian society itself (in what might be an attempt to avoid the painful fact of the reality of tension within its own community) is the tension between Palestinian Christians and Muslims. While there is daily interaction and cooperation, deep friendships, and a shared nationalism among Palestinian Christians and Muslims, there are also sharp prejudices between these communities.[11] The late Palestinian journalist Said Aburish describes this complicated dynamic:

There is an implicit and explicit attempt to deny the existence of a "Christian problem." Christians and Muslims alike practice this denial. On both sides, most people either relegate the problem to a secondary position, behind that of the Israeli

---

6   Abe Ate, "Exodus of Palestinian Christians," *Quaker Life*, March 23, 2003, 6–7. Also, there are 130,000 Palestinian Christians in Israel, and 300,000 scattered throughout the world. In total there are approximately 500,000 Palestinian Christians, who comprise about 7–10 percent of the total global Palestinian population, according to Mitri Raheb, "Sailing through Troubled Waters: Palestinian Christians in the Holy Land," *Dialogue: A Journal of Theology* 41, no. 2 (2002).

7   Palestinian National Authority, Central Bureau of Statistics, June 2013.

8   Before the Nakba there were approximately 1.2 million Palestinians in Israel/Palestine. Almost 500,000 became refugees outside of Israel/Palestine as a result of the Nakba. Thus the Muslim Palestinian community has grown significantly since 1948.

9   Bernard Sabella, "Socio-economic Characteristics and Challenges to Palestinian Christians in the Holy Land," in *Palestinian Christians: Religion, Politics and Society in the Holy Land*, ed. Anthony O'Mahoney (London: Melisende, 1999), 92.

10   Andrew F. Bush, *Learning from the Least: Reflections on a Journey in Mission with Palestinian Christians* (Eugene, OR: Cascade Books, 2013), 60.

11   Rafiq Khoury,"Living Together: The Experience of Muslim-Christian Relations in the Arab World in General and in Palestine in Particular," in *The Forgotten Faithful: A Window into the Life and Witness of Christians in the Holy Land*, ed. Naim Ateek, Cedar Duaybis, and Maurine Tobin (Jerusalem: Sabeel Ecumenical Liberation Theology Center, 2007).

occupation, or dismiss it as transitory and insignificant. This is dishonest, harmful, a mere wish to concentrate on the common enemy, Israel. It is a wish to maintain Palestinian solidarity, or a reflection of the fear that talking about it will make things worse—or a hope that it will disappear.[12]

Some Christian families do not see much hope for their children's success in a society in which they are such a diminished minority and in which they feel there is bias against them. This has resulted in further motivation to emigrate.

In any event, the pressures of the conflict with Israel, the dwindling population of Christians due to emigration, and the historically restricted social status since the rise of Islam in the seventh century have resulted in a psychologically embattled, "hold the fort," nonmissional posture in relation to the majority Muslim community on the part of the majority of the Palestinian Christian community. What mission that does occur frequently is expressed in schools and hospitals that serve the majority Palestinian Muslim population.[13] These are not insignificant efforts by any means. They bring an important service to the Palestinian community; however, engagement with the majority Muslim community with the gospel of Jesus and the related hope of conversion to Christianity is minimal.

If mission to their Muslim neighbors is limited, how much more so is mission to the Jewish community in Israel. Whereas the conflict renders such mission almost impossible, the language and culture barriers in themselves places mission to Israeli Jews beyond the abilities of many Palestinian Christians. There are, however, important exceptions to this withdrawal from mission on the part of some Palestinian Protestant Christians, which will be discussed. In any event, the mission of the international Christian community to the Palestinian diaspora in response to their marginalization has been valued, but has also been problematic.

Mission *to* the Palestinian Diaspora

Mission to the Palestinian diaspora—both its Christian and Muslim communities—is a complex topic that challenges any effort to formulate a concise summary. Nevertheless, as abbreviation is necessary, it should be obvious that the response of the international Christian community to the needs of the Palestinian

---

12 Said Aburish, *The Forgotten Faithful: The Christians of the Holy Land* (London: Quartet Books, 1993), 154.
13 Mitri Raheb, "The Spiritual Significance and Experience of the Churches: The Lutheran Perspective," in *Christians in the Holy Land*, ed. Michael Prior and William Taylor (London: World of Islam Festival Trust, 1995).

diaspora has tended to be polarized. On one hand there has been the response of Christians who interpret God's will for the peoples in the Holy Land through the theological lens of premillennial dispensationalism. The result of this theological perspective is strong support for the State of Israel, which is presumed to be the fulfillment of biblical prophecy, and the consequent casting of the Palestinians, as opponents of Israel, in a negative light. On the other hand, there are those Christians, many of whom adhere to a covenantal theology, who are ardent supporters of Palestinians in the land. They are motivated by the pursuit of justice for Palestinians and support its political objectives of achieving a sovereign state. This approach in turn tends toward a harshly negative view of Israel.

Concerning the former, dispensationalism emphasizes a more or less literal interpretation of biblical prophecies concerning Israel. Essential to these prophecies is the restoration of the Jewish people to the land and the establishment of the state of Israel, which is regarded as a condition for the return of the Lord. This restoration includes the possessing of the land promised to Abraham and his descendants, and the renewal of worship in a rebuilt Jewish temple in Jerusalem.[14] These are key eschatological events that will pave the way for the return of Christ to Jerusalem and to initiate his one-thousand-year reign on earth. Accordingly, those who oppose Israel's possession of all the land of ancient Israel, which of course is the Palestinian position as it claims the West Bank and Gaza for its own sovereign state, are opposing God and are cursed according to the foundational proclamation of God to Abraham, which states, "I will bless those who bless you, and whoever curses you I will curse; and all peoples on earth will be blessed through you" (Gen 12:1–3).

This missional movement, which is often referred to as Christian Zionism, has a tendency to devolve into uncritically promoting nationalism and the marginalization of an indigenous people, the Palestinians, by force.[15] It discounts the authenticity of the Palestinian people as an ethnic group. For example, a leader in the Christian Zionist movement states:

---

14   Andrew F. Bush, "The Implications of Christian Zionism for Mission," *International Bulletin of Missionary Research* 33, no. 3 (July 2009): 144–50.
15   It should be noted that this movement does have various expressions; however, as this movement is depicted in popular Christian media in the United States, it normally depicts Palestinians negatively. A major proponent of such ideas is the organization Christians United for Israel (CUFI), which denies that Palestinians are an authentic nationality, which was a fixture in Israeli propaganda but today is little heard in Israel.

To suggest that "Palestinians have legitimate rights stretching back millennia to the lands of Israel/Palestine," reveals an appalling ignorance of both secular as well as Biblical history. The notion of distinct Palestinian people is the creation of Yasser Arafat's propaganda machine after the 1967 war. The non-Jews in the region have always been Arabs who speak Arabic and whose religion is Islam. There is no such thing as a "Palestinian people."[16]

This represents a type of anti-mission that is contrary to the teachings of Christ. It promotes a colonial posture towards a diaspora community.

Supporters of the Palestinian community and its aspirations represent a wide range of denominational affiliations. Many identify with covenantal theology, which stresses the significance of the New Covenant and the messianic community initiated by Jesus' call for whoever will—either Jews or Gentiles—to follow him. These advocates for Palestine often argue for justice for the Palestinian people by the creation of a sovereign Palestinian state. Some in their zeal to support Palestinians can tend to promote a Palestinian nationalism, which is as equally uncritical as Christian Zionism's support for Israel. For example, Christian movements that support the boycott and divestment of businesses based in Israel—which, by the way, is not supported by the Palestinian Authority leadership—must consider that their actions might have the effect of weakening Israel generally and thus also harming Arab Israelis who constitute 20 percent of the population of Israel. Further, by weakening Israel they also open themselves to the criticism of being anti-Semitic; to threaten Israel's existence is synonymous with removing the national protection of the Jewish people, effectively casting them on the mercy of the nations that have persecuted them for centuries.

While without doubt this support for their political objectives is appreciated by Palestinians, in the retelling of Palestinian grievances and the emphasizing of Israel's offenses toward the Palestinian community, the possibility of Palestinians forging true reconciliation with their Israeli neighbors is hindered. The fact that the Palestinian diaspora community—and especially Palestinian Christians—does not

---

16 James M. Hutchens, "Evangelicals Supporting a Palestinian State?," Special Guests, http://special-guests.com/guests/viewnews.cgi?id=EElVZlpEppBvfZXYMc&style=Full+Article (accessed February 7, 2014).

need more hindrances on its journey toward peace is well expressed by Palestinian Israeli educator and author Elias Chacour who has stated, "We appreciate your friendship. But may your friendship for the Palestinian community not mean hatred of Israel. Our land does not need more hatred."[17]

Clearly all Christian mission to the Palestinian community and its Christians do not fall within extremes that demonize the "other." There are efforts to respond to Palestinian humanitarian needs such as for adequate food and water, education, health care, etc., including the work of the Mennonite Central Committee that supports agricultural research and development, the improvement of wells and water pipes, and the sponsorship of a Palestinian school.[18] The Society of Friends founded and has sponsored the influential Friends Boys School and Friends Girls School in Ramallah since 1905. Christians from many denominations have helped support Bethlehem Bible College in Bethlehem, which educates Palestinian Christians as well as Muslims who are enrolled in its Tour Guide Program.[19] World Vision–sponsored programs assist economic development, education, child welfare, conflict resolution, and more.[20]

Other mission efforts toward Palestinians beyond these include training for Palestinian Christian leaders such as those sponsored by the Palestinian Bible Society (www.pbs.org), support for dialogue efforts between Palestinian Christian and Muslims and Israeli Jews, and the general spiritual support as expressed in the World Council of Churches' Ecumenical Accompaniment Programme in Israel and Palestine (www.eappi.org).

Mission *of* Diaspora Palestinian Protestant Christians

Besides these missional efforts toward diaspora Palestinians, there has been in recent years an increasingly vigorous mission *of* Palestinian Christians. This mission is breaking new ground. It goes beyond the traditional mission of education and other humanitarian services to the Palestinian community. Led especially by Palestinian Protestant Christians, who are the focus of the discussion, new Palestinian mission

---

17 Elias Chacour, "What Things Make for Peace?" (lecture, Eastern University, Saint David's, PA, December 3, 2013).
18 Mennonite Central Committee, "Middle East: Israel and Palestine," http://middleeast.mcc.org/palestine-israel (accessed March 3, 2014; page discontinued).
19 Bethlehem Bible College, "Tour Guide Program," http://www.bethbc.org/academics/tourism (accessed March 3, 2014).
20 World Vision, "Jerusalem, West Bank, Gaza," http://www.worldvision.org/our-impact/country-profiles/jerusalem-west%20bank-gaza (accessed March 3, 2014).

efforts are seeking to creatively engage Palestinian Muslims with the gospel of Jesus, explore avenues of reconciliation with Messianic Jews, promote justice and peace for all who are in Israel/Palestine, and beyond the land, demonstrate to the West mission from below—mission from a posture of weakness, which is especially relevant as Western mission seeks to find its place in the new global mission of the twenty-first century.[21] This mission is being advanced both by missiological writing and praxis.

Their experience of suffering as diaspora Christians has pressed Palestinian Protestant Christians toward a deeper reflection concerning a theology of the land and of Israel, engagement and reconciliation with Messianic Jews, new directions for missional engagement with the Muslim community, and the role of Muslim-background believers, or MBBs, in ministry. While the West historically has attempted to place certain theological frameworks on Arab Christians, the latter is finding today its own theological—and missiological—voice. Much of this missiological reflection comes out of the intense experience of the conflict and efforts to salvage their own humanity and affirm the humanity of those who oppose them. In this way Palestinian missiology also responds meaningfully to triumphal theologies of Western Christians that justify—and even promote—the marginalization of Palestinians, as has been mentioned. Also, from sincere attempts to engage the Palestinian Muslim community with the gospel of Christ Jesus, rich discussion is occurring that is opening new avenues for understanding and witness. Taken together these missiological reflections of Palestinian Protestant Christians represent a significant contextual missiology and point toward creative new directions in mission praxis.

Palestinian protestant Christians have produced a significant body of missional writing. Yohanna Katanacho, a leading Palestinian theologian, in his helpful article entitled "Palestinian Protestant Theological Responses to a World Marked by Violence" identifies four genres of such work. These included autobiographies, apologies, liberation theologies, and reconciliation theologies.[22] Katanacho observes that autobiographies such as Audeh G. Rantisi's *Blessed Are the Peacemakers: A Palestinian Christian in the Occupied West Bank*,[23] and Munib A. Younan's *Witnessing for Peace: In Jerusalem and the World*[24] "are important shapers of Palestinian Protestant theology.

---

21 Bush, *Learning from the Least*, passim.
22 Yohanna Katanacho, "Palestinian Protestant Theological Responses to a World Marked by Violence," *Missiology* 36, no. 3 (July 2008): 289–306.
23 Audeh G. Rantisi, *Blessed Are the Peacemakers: A Palestinian Christian in the Occupied West Bank* (Grand Rapids: Zondervan, 1990), 19.
24 Munib Younan, *Witnessing for Peace: In Jerusalem and the World* (Minneapolis: Augsburg Fortress, 2003).

They also promote peace and human dignity instead of war, advocating a loving God instead of a militant one and making theology relevant to culture."[25]

Younan describes how his cousin, a deaf and dumb carpenter who worked for an Israeli, was a victim of a Palestinian suicide bomber on a bus in Israel. Younan writes that in the suffering of their own community they can empathize with the pain of Israelis who have also lost family members to suicide bombing. He states, "We mourn all victims whenever such an attack occurs, whoever that person may be."[26] With a similar emphasis for the need to empathize with their Israeli neighbors, Rantisi states:

> The deepest lesson I have learned in my life is also the simplest: God loves me and others equally. I may dispute what another does, but he or she is not my adversary. I have suffered, but so have others. I do not want Jews to suffer. Down deep where it is important, my Jewish brother and I are very much alike. We have the same need for security and the same need for acceptance. We must learn to provide for each other's security and well-being.[27]

Concerning apologies, Katanacho notes the formative influence on Arab Christian theology historically of Islam; that is, the fact of Islam's challenge of foundational Christian doctrines such as the Trinity, Christology, and the corruption of biblical Scriptures necessitated a response from Arab Christian concerning those doctrines.[28] These apologetic efforts continue today, as well they should since Islam's doctrinal challenges to Christianity remain. Some contemporary Palestinian Christian writing is evangelistic and sharply critical of Islam; other authors seek to identify common ground and build bridges of rapprochement. Labib Madanat, a leader in the Palestinian Bible Society, whom I will discuss further below, writes movingly of his journey toward a deeper and more empathetic understanding of the Palestinian Muslim community.

Palestinian Protestant liberation theological writing, most notably that of Naim Stifan Ateek in his *Justice and Only Justice: A Palestinian Theology of Liberation*, calls for a rethinking of the modern State of Israel and of the Palestinian people in

---

25 Katanacho, "Palestinian Protestant Theological Responses," 301.
26 Younan, *Witnessing for Peace*, 100.
27 Rantisi, *Blessed Are the Peacemakers*, 19.
28 Katanacho, "Palestinian Protestant Theological Responses," 303.

light of God's justice and of his love, which was ultimately revealed on the Cross.²⁹ Ateek emphasizes the message of the Hebrew prophets of justice for the poor, the outcast, and the stranger or foreigner, and their inclusion into the blessings of God as especially relevant for Palestine and Israel today. In his *A Palestinian Christian Cry for Reconciliation and Peace* he goes on to state that justice must move toward forgiveness. He writes,

> In conflict resolution, whether between individuals or nations, the highest objective is to achieve reconciliation and forgiveness between the conflicting parties. When forgiveness is given and received, healing commences. This constitutes the mountaintop in peaceable relations among the people.³⁰

As a traditionally agricultural society, the identity of the Palestinian people is deeply tied to the land. Already uprooted from their homes and villages in historic Palestine, the present Israel proper, Palestinian Christians are attempting to respond to popular Christian theologies that justify this disenfranchisement. Ateek challenges an exclusive theology concerning the land and argues for a peaceful coexistence of peoples in the land together. Katanacho himself also proposes a new biblical perspective on the land in his article "Christ Is the Owner of Haaretz."³¹ Both authors maintain that the simplistic formula based on Abrahamic texts in the Old Testament (Gen 12:1–3) that God gave the land to Israel, therefore the modern State of Israel has an exclusive claim to it, does not reflect the complexity of the biblical testimony and the difficulties of relating present political realities to the biblical texts. In seeking to develop a contextual Palestinian theology of the land, both Katanacho and Ateek underscore that in speaking of God's will for the land and for both of the communities of Israel and Palestine within it, justice and peace for both peoples must be a priority (Mic 6:8).

Besides their own need to validate their place in the land, Katanacho emphasizes that responding to Western popular dispensational theologies concerning Israel and the land is important because Muslims presume these ideas represent all of the

---

29 Naim Stifan Ateek and Rosemary Radford Ruether, *Justice and Only Justice: A Palestinian Theology of Liberation* (Maryknoll, NY: Orbis Books, 1989).
30 Naim Stifan Ateek, *A Palestinian Christian Cry for Reconciliation* (Maryknoll, NY: Orbis Books, 2008), 183.
31 Yohanna Katanacho, "Christ Is the Owner of Haaretz," *Christian Scholar's Review* 34, no. 4 (Summer 2005).

Christian community. This hinders Palestinian Christians in their witness to their Muslim neighbors in Palestine and beyond.[32]

Finally Katancho discusses reconciliation theologies that seek renewed relationships both within the Palestinian community between Christians and Muslims as well as with Messianic Jews and Israel. Within this genre Salim Munayer's work is important. He suggests that justice is critical for reconciliation between Palestinians and Jews, and that Christians, who know the forgiveness and peace of the Cross, have a critical role to play. He states:

> If I am called a Christian Palestinian, I have a commitment and obligation toward my Palestinian people and their future and welfare. At the same time I have an obligation to my Lord to love my enemies, to break the circle of hatred and enmity and violence, to be a peacemaker, and to look for practical ways for peace between Jews and Arabs. We as Palestinian Christians can play an important role, and be an avenue of peace.[33]

Again, together these Palestinian Protestant Christian texts comprise a significant attempt at developing a coherent contextual missiology. Generally, they seek to advance healing in the land through reconciliation, peace building, and justice. They challenge anti-missional triumphal theologies of exclusion that demonize and diminish Palestinians and their concerns, as well as challenge attempts to justify unjust violence against Israel. As such they share the concerns of important Jewish authors such as Rabbi Michael Lerner[34] and Mark Braverman.[35] Recent Palestinian Protestant Christian missiology recognizes that demonizing Israel falls far short of the mission of God, and only continues the tendency to act destructively from the logic of retribution.

As the theologizing process is not complete without application, so the integrity of the Palestinian Christian mission is demonstrated in their mission through praxis

---

32 Ibid.
33 Salim J. Munayer, "Relations between Religions in Historic Palestine and the Future Prospects: Christians and Jews," in *Christians in the Holy Land*, ed. Michael Prior and William Taylor (London: World of Islam Festival Trust, 1994), 149.
34 Michael Lerner, *Embracing Israel/Palestine: A Strategy to Heal and Transform the Middle East* (Berkeley, CA: North Atlantic Books, 2012).
35 Mark Braverman, *The Fatal Embrace: Christians, Jews, and the Search for Peace in the Holy Land* (New York: Beaufort Books, 2010).

toward both their Jewish and Muslim neighbors. As the task of identifying, however necessarily briefly, several emblematic Palestinian Christian mission efforts could be quite arbitrary, emphasis will be placed on those exceptional Palestinian Christian missions with which this author has had significant acquaintance. These include efforts to bridge the chasm of misunderstanding between Palestinian Christians and their neighbors, both Muslims and Israeli Jews, in the Palestinian Bible Society (PBS), and the attempt to build bridges of understanding with Messianic Jews from Israel and internationally in Bethlehem Bible College's Christ at the Checkpoint Conferences in the West Bank.

The Palestinian Bible Society (PBS) has enjoyed unusually creative leadership. One of its key leaders is Labib Madanat, the general secretary of the Palestinian Bible Society from 1993 to 2007, and now the coordinator of the Palestinian and Israeli Bible Societies. As is mentioned in *Learning from the Least*, Madanat experienced a unique awakening and growing compassion toward his Muslim neighbors as he matured in his faith as a young man and then as a leader in the PBS. He describes several experiences that were pivotal in this spiritual journey. These include experiences with his Muslim roommates in university in Iraq, correspondence with Palestinians in Israeli prisons and their families, encountering the questions of a young Muslim man in Gaza and his father, and more.[36] As a result of these encounters Madanat took action to include Muslims in the PBS's planning and even staff. He states:

> Where friendship and trust and courage are, many fears and taboos simply dissolve. When we were able to know our Muslim neighbours afresh we were able to see through their eyes. When we invited our Muslim neighbours to help us see them the way they see and know themselves, we were able to see ourselves through their eyes.[37]

The significance of this inclusion was summarized by this author in *Learning from the Least*: "Rather than ignore the complexity of the context of Israel/Palestine, this inclusiveness invited the complexity of Palestinian society into the PBS. This unusual partnership provided a way to deepen its relevancy and provide creative

---

36   Bush, *Learning from the Least*, 98–103.
37   Labib Madanat, "Beyond Self: The Story of the Palestinian Bible Society, 1993–2005" (unpublished manuscript, July 2006), quoted in Bush, *Learning from the Least*, 103.

directions in its effort to serve the community."[38] This prophetic leadership gave to other workers in the PBS the freedom to explore deeper relationships with their Muslim community.

Such missional leadership not only serves its immediate context but also opens new possibilities for Western mission's engagement with the global Muslim world. First, it suggests a shift of attitude of the Christian West toward the Muslim world, an attitude historically characterized by hostility. It calls for a change of perspective from seeing Muslims as enemies to seeing them as neighbors on this planet and as potentially close friends. It furthermore calls for creative new directions in working relationship. Mission is not just toward Muslims, but it is also toward ourselves as Muslims help us grasp our own unhealthy attitudes.

Madanat also demonstrated courageous leadership toward the non-Christian Jewish Israelis. During Israel's invasion of Gaza in 2008, hundreds of Palestinian civilians were killed. Madanat described his anger and frustration at this massacre.[39] However, rather than become one more victim of the invasion by succumbing to bitterness, he took decisive action. After loading his car with toiletries and small gifts, he drove to the hospital in the Negev where Israeli soldiers wounded in the invasion were being treated. Entering the ward he visited with soldiers from bed to bed, identifying himself as a Palestinian, praying for them, and wishing them well. He recounts that several broke into tears and expressed their longing for peace between their peoples.[40]

Again such mission forges courageous new paths. Rather than pigeonhole the Jewish people to a role in eschatology—one which ends in a terrible suffering—Madanat was dealing fully with his Jewish neighbors as humans, acknowledging their pain and their hopes. This is mission that is willing to accept the risk of vulnerability. The wounded soldiers could have responded very differently—with anger and resentment.

In a similar direction, Bethlehem Bible College has sought through its Christ at the Checkpoint Conferences (2010, 2012, and 2014) to build bridges of understanding with those whose approach of mission to Israel has fostered—however unintentionally—hostility toward Palestinians.[41] These conferences have provided

---

38   Bush, *Learning from the Least*, 103.
39   Ibid.
40   Madanat, "Beyond Self," quoted in ibid., 104.
41   The author of this paper recalls how, while speaking in a large, traditional, denominational church in Denver, Colorado, concerning the danger of placing more priority on nationalism than reconciliation in

a forum for interaction between ardent supporters of Israel and of Palestine. It has allowed the Palestinian Christians to describe and display the embracing of the humanity and dignity of the other as their mission focus. Through these conferences several questions have been asked including: What is the nature of mission? What is the relationship of mission to nationalism? What is the relationship of mission to eschatology? Who has a right to the land?

Conclusion

While not advocating a heightened sense of sacred geography, it is significant that Palestinian Christian mission is being thoughtfully advanced in the land where Christ Jesus first gave the gospel of forgiveness, peace, and reconciliation to his disciples. Through the mission of Palestinian Christians the mercy and grace of Christ continues as a witness to the world. It is a mission which, carried forward by all-too-human messengers, has embraced the fullness of God's grace as an act of faith, as Palestinians still face on a daily basis the facts of life under occupation—military checkpoints, the death of more Palestinians in the conflict—which could again drag them under the riptide of bitterness and hatred that has already destroyed so many Israelis and Palestinians spiritually, and even physically. As Jack Sara, the president of Bethlehem Bible College, has said, "Still forgiveness is something I must decide every day."[42]

Palestinian Christians are exerting great effort to overcome packaged Western theologies that many seek to place upon them, and to reflect upon their experiences and biblical texts with integrity in order to form an authentic Palestinian missiology. While this missiology may be sharpened by pressing deeper still into Scripture, this is saying no more than what is true of every theology. The great value, though, of emerging Palestinian mission is that it calls all Christians to the heart of the gospel—to value the humanity and dignity of the other; to reconciliation, justice, and peace. It would be well for Western Christian mission to the Palestinian diaspora to recognize the cost—the suffering from the conflict, the loneliness, the pain of being shunned by brothers and sisters in Christ—Palestinian Christians have paid for this mission to emerge and be sustained. It would be well for Western Christians to come alongside this suffering community with respect, laying aside their own agenda to learn from those who are seeking to heal the wounds of the land.

Israel/ Palestine, how a man stood up in the midst of the congregation of eight hundred and started shouting how this idea was just propaganda!

42   Quoted in Bush, *Learning from the Least*, 182.

Chapter Eleven

The Ethiopian Diaspora: Ethiopian Immigrants as Cross-cultural Missionaries; Activating the Diaspora for Great Commission Impact

JESSICA A. UDALL

ABSTRACT

Diaspora believers are one of the American church's greatest assets in effectively reaching the world on their doorstep. This paper examines the great potential of the millions of Ethiopians of the diaspora in the West to participate in the Great Commission by realizing their responsibility and their opportunity to reach other immigrants, as well as those in the host culture, with the gospel of Christ. Practical steps are suggested for how this—or any—immigrant community can begin moving toward increasingly powerful missionary impact wherever they may live.

There have been many voices in recent years calling Christians to evangelize the internationals who immigrate to their countries, and such teaching is good and right. However, it seems to be assumed in conversations about "reaching out to internationals" that all of them are unsaved. Though many immigrants do indeed come from countries or people groups that are minimally evangelized or even unreached, acknowledgement and appreciation of Christian immigrants is needed in order to come to a more nuanced understanding of the international community in America. Believing immigrants may be the American church's greatest asset in effectively reaching the world on their doorstep.

In the process of doing MA thesis research on missiological education in the Ethiopia, the great potential of immigrants—in this case, Ethiopian immigrants—to be a force for tremendous missiological good first became evident to me.[1] The Ethiopian diaspora is widespread, with Washington, DC, being almost the largest Ethiopian city in the world, second only to Addis Ababa, Ethiopia's capital.[2]

---

1 Jessica A. Udall, "Preparing Ethiopians for Cross-cultural Ministry: Maximizing Missionary Training for Great Commission Impact" (MA thesis, Columbia International University, 2013), 3–4.
2 Sam Farzaneh and Bill McKenna, "Little Ethiopia," BBC News, June 12, 2013, http://www.bbc.co.uk/news/magazine-22803973 (accessed March 27, 2014).

Ethiopians also have a significant presence in Canada, Sweden, Saudi Arabia, and many other countries.[3]

This paper examines the great potential of the millions of Ethiopians in the diaspora to participate in the Great Commission by realizing their responsibility and opportunity to reach other immigrants in their countries of residence with the gospel of Christ. Practical steps are suggested for how this—or any—immigrant community can begin moving toward increasingly powerful missionary impact wherever they may live.

The length of this paper necessitates some limitations to make the topic sufficiently narrow. My focus will be on Ethiopians as a potential missions force in the West, as most of my interviewees are Ethiopians with experience living in those regions of the world. I will focus on those immigrants who live and work in communities that are mostly made up of other internationals. I am well aware of the many Ethiopians who have been in America for some time and hold prestigious jobs in academia, medicine, or law, and who generally live surrounded by Americans. These immigrants certainly have great potential to take part in the Great Commission as well, but their level of acclimation to American culture will likely make it easier for them to get sufficient training in evangelism, missions, or cross-cultural issues if they so desire.

Potential

Evangelical Christians make up 19.6 percent of the population of Ethiopia.[4] Unfortunately, getting reliable figures on any aspect of the Ethiopian diaspora living in America is difficult as population estimates and demographic information vary wildly depending on the source. Though there is no way of knowing what percentage of Ethiopians living in America are evangelical, it seems safe to say—since according to the most recent United States Census there are 151,515 people born in Ethiopia who reside in America[5]—that there are many thousands of Ethiopian evangelical

---

3   Aaron Matteo Terrazas, "Beyond Regional Circularity: The Emergence of an Ethiopian Diaspora," *Migration Information Source*, June 1, 2007, http://www.migrationinformation.org/profiles/display.cfm?ID=604 (accessed March 27, 2014).

4   Operation World, "Ethiopia," http://www.operationworld.org/country/ethi/owtext.html (accessed December 16, 2014).

5   US Census Bureau, "Place of Birth for the Foreign-born Population in the United States," http://factfinder2.census.gov/faces/tableservices/jsf/pages/productview.xhtml?pid=ACS_11_5YR_B05006&prodType=table (accessed December 16, 2014).

immigrants who have the potential to be invaluable allies to the American church in Great Commission work among non-Christian immigrants.

In 2013, I wrote my MA thesis on preparing Ethiopians for cross-cultural ministry, focusing on maximizing missionary training for Great Commission impact. My research led me into conversation with seventeen people, fifteen of whom were Ethiopian, who were passionately invested in seeing Ethiopia rise as a major missionary sending nation in the near future. I asked them about what is currently available in terms of missiological education in Ethiopia, and what can be done to enhance what already exists and also to begin new avenues of missionary training. Their responses were insightful and have relevance for this study, but I also did another round of twelve interviews—including some with the same people quoted in the thesis and some whom I had not contacted before—specifically drilling down into how Ethiopians immigrants are or could do cross-cultural ministry in their new countries of residence.[6] If my thesis was largely theoretical, this paper is an intensely practical postscript.

In my thesis research, I concluded that the cultural proximity of Ethiopian missionaries—and, it could be extrapolated, all Majority World missionaries—to other non-Western cultures makes them more natural and possibly more effective messengers of the gospel to these other cultures. Cultural proximity is the number one reason, in my opinion, why the diaspora reaching the diaspora is an idea whose time has come.

The Ethiopian diaspora is in a particularly advantageous position to begin cross-cultural ministry as compared to their counterparts still living in Ethiopia, because they have already overcome the barriers that hold most potential Majority World missionaries back. My thesis discussed several hurdles to cross-cultural ministry that face Ethiopians residing in Ethiopia, including difficulty of obtaining visas and lack of world language fluency. Ethiopians in the diaspora, however, have already obtained a visa and are likely already ensconced in a diverse community—often living in a large apartment complex with immigrants and refugees from various other cultures and working in a similar environment. Though not all immigrants are well versed in the language of the host culture, it will be easier for them to continue learning the language in the host culture than it would have been in Ethiopia, so this is yet another way that the diaspora are a step ahead in terms of getting started in cross-cultural ministry.

---

6   Unless otherwise noted, all quotes are from these interviews.

Diaspora Ethiopians also have a staying power as cross-cultural missionaries living in the West that they might not have in a more "closed" country, and they will likely be surrounded by people from these "closed" countries where they live and work. They will have access to these people who are from countries that are hostile to the gospel and to gospel workers, yet they will likely not get in legal trouble for their witness. Additionally, most have worked long and hard to get to the West, and they are not planning to leave anytime soon. This staying power is an asset and yet another reason why the diaspora reaching the diaspora is too great of an opportunity to miss.

In general, Ethiopian evangelicals are zealous and passionate about their faith. They have no inhibitions—as Westerners often do—about starting or participating in conversations about religion. Religion is a natural part of life for them, integrated into their overall worldview and everyday routine. In cross-cultural conversations, they also have an easy out if they end up coming on too strong and offending someone, because they can "play the foreigner card"—apologizing and blaming cultural differences for any *faux pas* they were perceived to make. Likely offense will not be taken in the first place, however, because most immigrants from non-Western cultures have the same integrated view of religion that Ethiopians do, no matter what religion they are from. Conversations may get heated and loud, but the participants in the conversation will not usually feel intruded upon as many Westerners would if someone brought up so "personal" a topic.

There are some encouraging signs of Ethiopians in the diaspora already taking up the Great Commission mantel and intentionally reaching out to their immigrant neighbors as well as people from their host cultures with the love of Christ. These messengers of the gospel are not generally well known or acclaimed. They simply live their lives as witnesses in their spheres of influence, speaking often and well of Christ.

Diaspora Ethiopians will often "use ceremonial events" for gospel good by sharing the gospel with unsaved attendees at weddings, funerals, and holiday celebrations. They will also sometimes have special conferences with guest speakers and will invite their friends and neighbors to come and hear the message. These conferences often involve intense prayer, deliverance, and healings—God uses these demonstrations of his truth and power to convert some who visit.

An example of diaspora Ethiopians who have been successful in cross-cultural witness are the members of Dallas Ethiopian Bible Church in Garland, Texas, which is active in cultivating connections and sharing the gospel with other cultural groups despite its ethnic distinctness. Another notable diaspora Ethiopian who was mentioned by an interviewee is Daniel Tasaw, who runs International Revival Ministries (IRM) and is based in the United States but is actively preaching the gospel to various cultural groups. Additionally, one Ethiopian couple has begun a ministry that intentionally seeks to strengthen diaspora churches in reaching out to their host communities with the love of Christ.

Challenges

In my thesis, I asked several questions regarding what holds Ethiopia back from being the major missionary sending nation that God desires her to be. When asked, "In what area do you feel your students/disciples need more training [in order to be effective missionaries]?" respondents answered that training in cross-cultural skills was the area that needed the most work. Unfortunately, crossing cultures and living in the West did not change the response by the second round of respondents. Many of them also cited lack of cross-cultural training as a major thing holding even diaspora Ethiopians back from being effective cross-cultural witnesses. How could this be so for people who are already living cross-culturally?

The answer lies in the tight-knit and comfortable nature of the Ethiopian diaspora community. Ethiopians have "a highly defined background and culture" that is dear to them, and they tend to hang on to their ethnic identity even tighter when they are strangers in a strange land. This is of course true of any immigrant group, but Ethiopia as a never-colonized society with tendencies toward isolationism could be classed as an extremely high-context people group, meaning that their attachment to their way of life and culture is perhaps even stronger than that of other groups.

There are many aspects of this love for the motherland that are admirable and allow Ethiopians to have a sense of home and belonging even in a foreign country. There are also some potentially negative manifestations of this mindset, however. First, sometimes pride in one's own culture leads to looking down on and avoiding other cultures. No contact means no converts, so this enclave mentality must be fought against if Ethiopian evangelicals are to be effective in crossing cultures with the gospel. Second, in the name of non-compromise with the world (a commendable and biblical value), Ethiopian immigrants can sometimes close themselves off from the rest of society, fearing the contamination that comes from mixing with unbelievers of any culture. Again, lack of contact with nonbelievers (Ethiopian or those from other cultures) makes it impossible to share the gospel and leads to unfruitfulness and stagnation.

This lack of contact often begins a vicious cycle: because of the limited interaction they have with unbelievers of other cultures, Ethiopians are often not well versed in worldviews that are uncommon in Ethiopia such as new-age thought, atheism, and Eastern religions (though they usually are well aware of the nuances separating Ethiopian Orthodox and Protestant thought). Because of this lack of exposure, many Ethiopians feel insecure in starting evangelistic conversations cross-culturally because of concerns that they will not be able to adequately understand their conversation partner's religious beliefs (or lack thereof). Fear of failure leads to further withdrawal, which leads to deeper fear, and the great potential of Ethiopians as bold cross-cultural evangelists is not realized.

Another result of the enclave mentality is lack of confidence in language. If one mingles almost exclusively with one's own people, there are very few opportunities to learn the language of the host country, much less to intentionally learn the language of another immigrant group. Language is a key in building friendships across cultures—and a bridge language such as English (which both parties have likely at least started studying) can be very helpful, as it can enable two people to communicate sufficiently well without spending years learning the other person's native language. Ethiopians of course tend to favor Amharic or the other native tongues of Ethiopia, but the Lord is calling them to use the bridge language of their new context for the sake of the furtherance of the gospel. He may even call some of them to learn a completely foreign language of another diaspora group in order for them to share even more effectively. Nothing is impossible with God!

A practical concern is that cross-cultural missions is not a priority for the Ethiopian diaspora because other aspects of life are so pressing. Many Ethiopian immigrants are not financially secure, but being in the West gives them a chance for bettering their situation and that of their family. Most are also supporting relatives back home in Ethiopia, so the pressure is great to work harder and longer and more profitably every day. It is easy to become myopic in focusing on the American dream, on getting ahead, on advancing up the ladder of success. The bigger picture of God's plan and purpose in bringing Ethiopians to their country of residence for such a time as this is often lost in the helter-skelter rush of everyday life in the fast lane of Western culture. Though "every migrant is a potential missionary," few realize that potential. Distraction is the name of the game.

The notion of professionalization of ministry is also insidiously at work in the Ethiopian community as it is in so many communities. The idea that the person with the title "evangelist" or "pastor" is the only one who can legitimately do real ministry is a major hindrance to the daily life witness of the majority of titleless (but nevertheless gifted) Ethiopian Christians. The impact of a diaspora church—even a large church—is greatly diminished if the majority of its members are passively waiting for their leaders to do the ministry of the harvest. This is one of the major reasons why the great potential of the Ethiopian diaspora church as a tremendous force for missiological good has not yet been manifested.

Lack of unity is also cited as a problem hindering Ethiopians from sharing cross-culturally. Because of the division that exists between people of the same culture, it is hard to contemplate uniting with people of a different culture. Church politics steal time and energy away from outreach, and inward focus becomes necessary in order to just keep the congregation stable. This is a challenge in every church, but particularly in immigrant churches due to the added stressors of living in a foreign land and having few choices when searching for a culturally appropriate church to call home. People whose only similarity may be their country of birth are thrown together and often have no choice as to which congregation to join if they wish to worship in their native language. Conflicts that might have been swept under the rug in Ethiopia because a discontented family could quietly move to a congregation down the road are not so easily solved in another country, where the next Ethiopian diaspora church (EDC) might be hours away.

Lack of an "introducer" is a final, very surmountable challenge. The concept of a mediator is very important in the Ethiopian culture, and Ethiopians do not tend to plunge into new ventures headlong. As a long-time missionary in Ethiopia stated, "You [Ethiopians] never go alone. You go with someone who knows someone." The Ethiopian church needs partners, those who have some experience in ministry to the diaspora, to be "link people" to connect them to and walk with them into the vast harvest field that awaits them. This is a key way that those in the host culture can get involved in hatching this strategic idea—the diaspora reaching the diaspora—and be part of helping it to take wing and fly!

Where there is great potential, great challenges also crop up, like weeds in a cultivated field of grain. The presence of challenges standing in the way of the Ethiopian diaspora reaching other peoples of the diaspora with the gospel should not be discouraging. Rather, these challenges are opportunities for the worldwide church—particularly the Ethiopian church in the diaspora—to rise up and overcome in order to reach the potential that God has created her for: to reach the nations around her with the gospel of Christ.

Suggestions

Polling the interviewees with the question, "What do you recommend for the Habesha (an alternate term for "Ethiopian" that can also include those from Eritrea) diaspora's evangelistic impact to be maximized?" produced ten insightful suggestions, many of which have application beyond the Ethiopian community to the Christian diaspora at large. I will categorize these suggestions and add a few comments of my own in order to begin brainstorming how Christians in the diaspora can move towards increased Great Commission fruitfulness. I hope this brainstorm will continue and that these words will lead to actions and to new brothers and sisters in Christ from every ethnicity entering the kingdom of God.

Realizing the Bigger Purpose

An Ethiopian seminary leader with experience in the West suggests that Ethiopians in the diaspora "need to realize that they are [in another country] for a bigger purpose than to fulfill their economic needs . . . They need to be missions minded . . . to . . . say that the Lord has brought me here to preach the gospel for others." Despite the fact that several respondents shared that those in the diaspora feel inferior or incapable since they are in an unfamiliar setting, the same leader goes on to say, "There is a lot that the Ethiopian diaspora can give . . . [based on their] previous Christian experience back home." Being empowered by these realizations that they are both called and equipped by God for a purpose will be a key in increasing Great Commission effectiveness among the Ethiopian diaspora.

Church Leaders Catching the Vision

The importance of leadership cannot be overstated in any plan to change. Twenty-five percent of the interviewees responded with some version of this statement, underscoring its importance. If leaders of a church are inspired by the great worth of the good news they believe, the great need of the world around them, and the great responsibility they have to preach the good news to all nations, then it is likely that their congregations will catch the same vision.

Of course, this inspiration of leaders is easy to talk about in vague terms, but it is more complicated when articulating a concrete plan of action. A practical suggestion for enabling this inspiration might be through the Perspectives courses or seminars. Advertisement for this program and others like it could be intentionally extended to leaders of diaspora churches in the hopes that their participation would awaken them—as it tends to do for people from all cultures—to the reality of the unreached world and the commands of Jesus to reach them. As a side note, the Perspectives course has recently been offered in Ethiopia and was very well received, which gives me confidence that this suggestion is culturally appropriate and not too oriented towards a Western audience.

Praying for the Nations

This suggestion is so simple, particularly to the Ethiopian community, which is already very strong in prayer, but a specific focus of praying for the salvation of the nations will likely be a new concept to EDCs. This suggestion is without doubt the most important key to maximizing the Great Commission impact of any community, and I believe it should be the first one implemented in a church after the church leader has caught the vision for reaching the unreached. It is not a new suggestion, for, as an Ethiopian seminary student studying in the West remarked, "The apostles and the church fathers throughout history used prayer as a primary tool in the evangelistic ministry of the church as it proactively encountered various cultures."[7] Taking a cue from the early church and all the generations that have gone before, the EDC cannot but succeed in fulfilling the Great Commission if prayer is the bedrock of her evangelistic efforts.

Training Members

Leaders who love God and love people cannot reach the nations alone. Leading their people in prayer is essential, but they must also inspire, empower, and equip their followers to go and work in the harvest field. An Ethiopian pastor of an EDC shared: "If we dedicate ourselves to teach and train believers to be true disciple[s] of Jesus Christ [rather] than being just member[s] of the church and source[s] of income; we would impact so many people with the message of the gospel." In terms of content, an Ethiopian studying for his MA in the West added some specific suggestions such as "teachings and trainings on [cross-cultural] mission and evangelism" and "personal and group [B]ible studies" that promote "deeper understanding of the [B]ible." It is hoped and expected that the deeper people go in studying the Bible, the more they will understand God's heart for the nations.

---

[7] Abeneazer Gezahegn Urga, *Prayer and Evangelism: Inseparable Elements in Furthering the Gospel* (Addis Ababa: Andnet Printers, 2013), 79.

Collaborating with Other Churches

Two respondents suggested that Ethiopian diaspora churches should consider collaborating with other churches—both Western churches as well as other EDCs and non-Ethiopian diaspora churches—to increase effectiveness through partnership and sharing of information. It is possible, as mentioned in the challenges section, that some Western churches have had valuable experience in reaching out to diverse communities that they could share with the EDC. They could serve as "link people" or "introducers" to connect Ethiopians to opportunities for cross-cultural ministry and to cheer them on and offer advice as needed. Other EDCs could understand the unique challenges that Ethiopians face as well as increase the man power and geographical reach of an EDC, creating a network of connected sister churches with a common Great Commission purpose. Non-Ethiopian diaspora churches could give valuable information to an EDC about the cultures they are trying to reach and could also be a safe place to begin practicing cross-cultural communication in a gracious atmosphere with brothers and sisters in Christ.

Opening Up to Other Cultures

This suggestion goes against the normal human tendency to stay within one's comfort zone and with people who seem familiar. The tendency is exacerbated by the unfamiliar surroundings that come with immigration, which is why most large American cities have a Chinatown and a Little Italy. "Little Addis" is a phenomenon that is growing as more and more Ethiopian immigrants settle near one another and form their own enclaves. In Washington, DC, for example, "There are so many restaurants, shops and businesses catering to Ethiopians that the community has its own 1,000-page telephone book."[8]

As discussed above, there is nothing inherently wrong with loving one's own people, food, products, and customs, but in order to be effective as cross-cultural witnesses, EDCs must guard against the inward gaze and ethnocentrism that sometimes results from overblown patriotism. Compelled by the love of Christ, they must intentionally move out of their comfortable cultural enclaves to seek out friendships with people who are different from them.

Becoming friends across cultural barriers brings with it many difficult requirements, particularly for the Christian who is called to be "all things to all

---

8 Farzaneh and McKenna, "Little Ethiopia."

people" (1 Cor 9:22). Learning different cultures, different customs, and even different languages may be involved. It will require social interactions that are sometimes uncomfortable or awkward, and it will require the delicate art of being in the world but not of it, which has historically been difficult for Ethiopian evangelicals, according to the majority of respondents. Once this opening up of the community has happened, however—fueled by love of Christ and desire to obey him regardless of discomfort—I believe that Ethiopians will be extremely effective in befriending other immigrants because of their warmth, sense of humor, genuineness, and love of conversation.

Evangelizing as a Lifestyle

As one interviewee mentioned above, Ethiopians are well versed at using special occasions—like weddings, funerals, or holiday celebrations—for intentional evangelism. He suggests, however, that Ethiopians in the diaspora should "use [that] boldness" to "address other immigrants or natives on [a] day to day basis instead of occasional[ly]." Indeed, this suggestion would benefit people from any culture: evangelizing "as you go" in daily life rather than viewing it as an event-oriented activity. A pastor of an EDC sees this suggestion as being intertwined with training church members: "If we have well educated, informed and trained [presumably in the necessity of daily-life evangelism] disciples, we can evangelize other immigrants at work, in school and in different social places."

Using Technology

Ethiopians love technology as much as any other culture I have interacted with. As mentioned above, there are great initiatives by groups such as Global Media Outreach who recruit Ethiopians as online missionaries, teaching them to use social media to chat with Ethiopians and those from other countries, sharing the gospel with them. There is still room for many other initiatives of this kind, however, and also for individuals to simply be intentional with using various media to share the gospel. Some examples of this might be posting religious material on social media, hosting neighbors or friends to watch the "JESUS" film, or giving the "JESUS" film to other immigrants in their own language for them to watch.

Equipping the Younger Generation

One of the largest issues facing any diaspora church is how to relate to its younger members who are often second-generation immigrants and who have a bicultural identity. According to an Ethiopian pastor residing in Ethiopia who regularly preaches in EDCs, it is imperative that EDCs "work on equipping [the] young generation spiritually but free them to integrate culturally." Ethiopian-American young people have the potential to be a powerful mission force to reach other bicultural young people; they will understand the unique life experience of one another like few others can. Older Ethiopians who understandably find it nearly impossible to acclimate to a new culture or learn a new language at an advanced age can still find their role in Great Commission work by encouraging and challenging and praying for these young ones as they engage friends from different cultures with the gospel. Younger children also can be used by God to break the ice in new cross-cultural friendships between immigrant families, since they give the parents common ground and a reason to laugh together.

Striving for Unity

This suggestion rings true for any church in any culture, but particularly for the diaspora church. All congregants are under the multiple stressors that come from trying to live and work and raise a family in a cross-cultural environment. The situation makes tension likely, but not inevitable. Ethiopians have a strong and vibrant faith in God and, as an Ethiopian full-time minister living cross-culturally suggests, they should "trust God for the impossible"—for unity that glorifies God and recommends him to a watching world. The exhortation to the diaspora in Peter's day echoes down to present-day EDCs: "Above all, keep loving one another earnestly, since love covers a multitude of sins" (1 Pet 4:8 ESV).

For Further Research

This paper has only scratched the surface in terms of examining the great potential of Christian immigrants to be the most effective way to reach the diaspora in any given country. Ethiopian immigrants, as we have seen, are in a prime position to be used by God as cross-cultural missionaries in the new places in which they live, having already overcome many of the barriers that face Ethiopians who want to be cross-cultural missionaries but who still live in Ethiopia. The challenges that have been mentioned are real but are no match for the Spirit of God and the intentional efforts of his people in the EDC. The suggestions given by my twelve interviewees provide a way forward, making change possible with potential, concrete steps.

These few pages cannot contain all the research that needs to be done. A Western missiologist with extensive experience in Ethiopia responded to the interview questions by commenting that the idea of the diaspora reaching the diaspora is a "huge topic" with "a vast amount of research that could and should be done." I have included three ways in which I hope this research will be deepened and expanded in the future.

Other Christian Diaspora Groups

There are numerous ethnic groups that have a significant diaspora presence in the West, and many of these groups have significant Christian populations. Similar studies could be carried out examining each group and asking its members to consider what is being done and what could be done by their group to reach other diaspora groups around them. This self-reflection might well lead to increased Great Commission impact by the groups studied, so the value of this potential further research is high.

Diaspora Reaching Diaspora in the Majority World

The challenges and suggestions for the diaspora reaching the diaspora in the Majority World will likely be quite different than those for the diaspora in the West, but they are equally deserving of attention and study. Immigrants may be the best hope of reaching the unreached in currently closed countries, because they have already jumped through the legal hoops associated with living and working in the countries without incident. They have a legitimate reason to be there and can be used to share the love of Christ with neighbors, coworkers, and all others they come into contact with in their already established daily routines. Further probing the best practices in this area via case studies would be helpful so as to give an inspirational template to others in similar situations.

Contextualized Training for Diaspora Churches

The Perspectives program and other programs and books like it are excellent and will be helpful in the short run to raise awareness among diaspora churches and train them for cross-cultural ministry, but they are not ideal. Eventually, contextualized training materials should be developed specifically to train Ethiopians and other non-Westerners, approaching missions from their worldview and customized to address the issues that are important to them. Producing this kind of literature in Amharic and other heart languages of diaspora peoples should be the ultimate goal.

Part Six:

The Way Forward

Chapter Twelve

Organizing to Reach the Diaspora:
A Case Study of The International Mission Board, SBC; Changing Its Overseas Structure from Geographic Components to Global Affinity Groups

JERRY RANKIN

ABSTRACT

Mission agencies often make the mistake of seeking to implement changing and innovative strategies while retaining a traditional organizational structure. Recognizing the organization is not an end in itself but a means for fulfilling its mission, the IMB implemented two radical organizational changes in order to support new, contemporary initiatives. This paper describes the rationale, process, and results for moving to a people-group strategy in 1997 and later dissolving a geographical regional structure overseas to function through overlapping global affinity groups in 2009 in order to release missionaries to engage the unreached people groups of the diaspora.

Historically, overseas strategies have not been a significant factor in shaping the organizational structure of missionary-sending agencies. Mission entities have usually focused on the recruitment and training of personnel, mobilizing support and facilitating the missionary fulfilling the call of God to a specific place of deployment around the world. With some stated parameters of core values, accountability to sending churches, and focus on a general objective, field personnel are usually on their own with regard to what they do and whether or not they are successful. An organization might offer some guidance in the formation of field teams and choosing a team leader or field administrator, but the Western agency typically is far removed from the dynamics of strategies guiding cross-cultural witness thousands of miles away.

In the first century of Southern Baptist missions, missionaries functioned with a great deal of autonomy with liberty to organize themselves for the work in whatever way was deemed advisable. In the earlier years it was not anticipated that missionaries would return to the home country, and any communication with the sending agency took months for a letter to be sent and the response to arrive via ocean-going vessels. In 1933, almost ninety years after sending its first missionaries, the Southern Baptist Foreign Mission Board appointed three "area directors," one each for Asia and Latin America and another for Europe, Africa, and the Middle East, but the missionaries themselves continued to organize themselves into autonomous countrywide mission structures.

Post–World War II growth in missionary numbers and changing global conditions necessitated administrative changes. Transoceanic phone calls and airmail enhanced communication, and more direction could be given from headquarters. Administrative areas subdivided as Europe, Northern Africa and the Middle East, Southern Africa, and East Africa became four separate areas. New area directors and field associates were put in place in Middle America and the Caribbean, Eastern South America, and Western South America. The pattern extended globally with the opening of additional fields and continued to be tweaked as determined by the number of personnel in any given area. During my own tenure in Indonesia for more than twenty years I served in field administrative areas designated as Southeast Asia, South and Southeast Asia, and Southern Asia and Oceania—with no change of location!

Unfortunately, mission agencies have traditionally been guilty of confusing organization with strategy. Though field configurations of areas and regions took different shapes and the number of administrative leadership roles increased, these structures were basically designed to provide guidance and support for missionary personnel wherever they were located around the world; the organization did not include areas where there were no missionaries. There have been, and continue to be, a plethora of plans for fulfilling the Great Commission. There is an assumption that establishing missionary units and deploying personnel to pockets of lostness will result in goals of evangelization being met. But the most efficient organizational structure cannot ensure results if it is not shaped to serve the desired strategic objective.

John Kotter, in his book *Leading Change*, spoke of an organization being in decline if it ever finds itself shaping its work to fit the organization. "Sometimes the obstacle [to strategic vision] is the organization itself."[1] The bureaucratic components of any organization usually evolve from a rich history and traditional way of doing things. It is easy to forget that the organization is not an end in itself but a means for serving the purpose of the organization. Attempting to change

---

1   John P. Kotter, *Leading Change* (Boston: Harvard Business School Press, 1996), 10.

traditional ways of doing things and field structures is usually met with resistance and a great deal of trauma; however, change is essential in a world that is rapidly changing in terms of politics, economy, social dynamics, and relative responsiveness to the gospel. The maxim is true: "If the internal changes fail to keep pace with the external changes, an organization is moving toward irrelevance and ineffectiveness." The unprecedented changes in the last decade of the twentieth century are only accelerating as we move further into the twenty-first century, yet the structure of many mission organizations remains the same.

In its 160-year history the International Mission Board, like other mission agencies, followed a geographic field structure. Presuming to be fulfilling the Great Commission as it emerged as the largest Protestant missionary-sending agency in the twentieth century, the IMB was guilty of three flaws as a result of the organization driving strategy. The first mistake was a commitment to concentrate on response—population segments that were responsive to the gospel became the priority for personnel deployment globally and within countrywide strategies. Resources were not to be wasted among the resistant peoples where baptisms and churches would not result. Hence large concentrations of missionaries flowed into Latin America and Africa while massive areas of the world were neglected. A large missionary contingency, of which I was a part, in Indonesia focused on the Javanese and totally ignored the hundreds of more dominant Muslim ethnic groups throughout the densely populated archipelago. We readily agreed with Donald McGavran's advice at the time to concentrate on receptive homogenous peoples while "holding lightly" those who were not open to the gospel.[2]

A second misconception was to assume the assignment of missionaries to a particular country was, in essence, evangelizing that nation without any understanding of the complexities of ethnolinguistic people groups. Our supporting churches pointed with pride each time a new country was colored on our global mission map as if a nation with a population of millions was now being reached with the entry of one new missionary family or team.

A third organizational error that inhibited reaching a lost world—one that is altogether too common among mission agencies—was to organize to administer the work of the missionaries wherever they happened to be serving rather than organizing to penetrate lostness and reach all peoples. Budget and personnel requests came from field structures already in place and always presented compelling reasons

---

2   Donald A. McGavran, *Understanding Church Growth* (Grand Rapids: Eerdmans, 1970), 230.

for more funds and more missionary units. No one represented the unreached. No requests from unengaged people groups crossed the desk of top-level decision makers. If field leaders or area administrators were asked, "Who is reaching the Baluchi in Central Asia or the Zuang in China?" the question would be met with a shrug and the response, "We don't have any missionaries working among them." The implication was that no one was responsible for reaching them since we don't have personnel assigned to them. We were simply administering the work of missionaries where they were serving.

Shift to a People-group Focus

Mission agencies were slow to respond to a growing people-group awareness that emerged in the last two decades of the twentieth century. Noted missiologist Ralph Winter issued a wake-up call at the Lausanne Conference for World Evangelism in 1974 as he challenged the global Christian community to do something about the hidden peoples who had never been engaged with a gospel witness.[3] Mission leaders became incredulous at the fact the Great Commission had been misunderstood and neglected for almost two thousand years of Christian history. In his farewell mandate to his disciples Jesus did not instruct them to make disciples of every geopolitical nation we now know as countries on our modern-day maps, but to disciple the *panta ta ethne* or every ethnic language group on the earth (Matt 28:19 NASB). ROPAL (Research on Peoples and Languages) and other databases have identified anywhere between eleven thousand and sixteen thousand distinct people groups, depending on how they are defined, most of whom are unreached and many unengaged. These are large ethnic population segments where there is no church, no known Christian believers, no Bible in the local language and no one engaging them with a Christian witness. The unengaged peoples represented massive groups who had never heard of Jesus; they were living and dying, generation after generation, without any hope of eternal life.

As a result of this emerging awareness of massive lostness and people-group segmentation, the concept of missions strategy began to radically change. The objective was no longer to send missionaries to as many countries as possible to do whatever good they could accomplish. A global Christian witness was no longer driven by the desire to populate heaven with as many people as possible who could be saved by concentrating on receptivity. Success was no longer reporting more

---

3   Ralph D. Winter, "Seeing the Task Graphically" (Monrovia, CA: MARC, 1974).

baptisms and starting more new churches than the year before but whether or not lost people were being given access to the gospel.

Traditionally missions have been guilty of the Apostle Paul's accusation of "[measuring] themselves by themselves and [comparing] themselves with themselves" (2 Cor 10:12 NASB). If we had more missionaries than five years ago, baptized more converts this year than last year, and started more churches, we considered our work successful. But the strategy now became focused on penetrating lostness and engaging all peoples with the gospel. Some peoples would be responsive and others not, and while harvest was commendable, proclamation of the gospel was intended to give all peoples an opportunity to hear, understand, and respond in their own ethnic, cultural context. The reported perception was generally accepted at the end of the twentieth century that 96 percent of Western missionaries were working in partnership with established churches in places that had been relatively evangelized, and only 4 percent were deployed to the unreached frontiers.

The International Mission Board was no exception. Acknowledging the discrepancy in our strategy and the mission of engaging and evangelizing all peoples, we did not know how many people groups we were currently engaging. We knew we had missionaries in 130 countries, but research revealed in 1995, after 160 years of engaging in foreign missions, we had reached only 338 people groups! *If the strategy was to utilize personnel and resources to engage and disciple all peoples, then the organizational structure had to change to serve that objective!*

In 1997 a radical change was made in organization and strategy that was identified as "New Directions." Areas of field administration had been carved out on the basis of where missionaries were located in order to provide administration and support for fairly even numbers within geographic groupings. A new regional structure was designed that represented not only geographic proximity but cultural and strategic affinity. A new profile for field leaders in each region gave priority to strategic vision and leadership; the previous management roles such as budget disbursement, personnel issues, and policy oversight were relegated to an administrative associate. Each regional leader was given the mandate to seek to engage every people group within one's respective region with the gospel.

It was in that context that the International Mission Board made a paradigm shift to work in partnership with other Great Commission Christians. Previously there had been an attitude of independence; having so many missionaries, there was the perception of exclusivity and not needing cooperation with anyone else. Once the massive challenge of engaging all peoples came into focus, we realized we would never have the resources to do it alone. Strategic thinking resulted in an enlarged concept of the task beyond what IMB missionaries could do alone; it embraced the idea of facilitating national partners and serving other evangelical organizations and partners.

Another change was to dispense with the large, bureaucratic, countrywide organizations that inhibited innovative decision making and consumed an inordinate amount of missionary time. Everyone on the field participated on numerous committees and boards, which existed to serve and manage the life and work of the missionaries themselves, and everyone had to be a part of every decision made in the annual conference. The result was strategic decisions that were satisfying to everyone and threatening to no one, which served to squelch new initiatives and preserve the status quo. In the place of this traditional field structure small, localized missionary teams were organized to target specific people groups and population segments. Mission institutions such as seminaries, publishing houses, and hospitals were nationalized under the responsibility of local conventions and associations of churches, freeing missionary staff to be redeployed to engage lostness.

While partnership continued with established national churches, missionaries themselves shifted to evangelism and church planting, primarily in unevangelized frontiers within countries where they had been assigned. Simultaneously, many personnel took initiative to request transfers to newly emerging opportunities in Eastern Europe and the former Soviet Union. The numbers going to Central Asia, China, and across the 10/40 Window of the Muslim world literally exploded. For the next ten years an average of more than a hundred unreached people groups were newly engaged annually by IMB personnel—one year as many as 192 were reported. Cooperation with other Great Commission agencies resulted in many more people groups being engaged. Ten years after "New Directions" had been initiated the portion of IMB personnel assigned to what was called "the last frontier"—unreached people groups or countries closed to traditional missionaries—had grown from 8 percent to 54 percent.

One reason for the success of such a radical organizational change was a critical displacement of missionary personnel. The 1990s saw a peak in veteran missionary retirements. Those going to the field in an era of post–World War II growth had reached the end of their tenure. They had served faithfully, opened many new fields, planted the seed of the gospel, and seen strong national churches emerge—successful strategies appropriate for that era of missions history. Likewise the IMB had record appointments of new personnel for nine consecutive years, sending out more than a thousand new missionaries in 2001 and 2002. These new recruits were passionate about their call, ready for adventure, committed to a new challenge, and uninterested in nurturing the legacy work of their predecessors.

The Necessity for Additional Change

Along with growth and a successful new strategic thrust to reach the unengaged, several problems began to emerge. The IMB had to deal with the widespread perception of constituent churches that the work was regressing. Southern Baptists had always taken pride in hearing annual reports of impressive statistics related to baptisms and new churches. Now that the majority of missionaries were deployed to plant the gospel among unreached people, fewer were working the responsive fields. Supporters could not understand a strategy that would waste resources on unresponsive Muslim people groups across the 10/40 Window while a vast harvest was being neglected in places like Brazil, the Philippines, and East Africa.

There was a public relations challenge to sustain continued support but also a need to help churches understand sound missiology and give them a sense of ownership in the task. The tragedy of lostness began to sink in and, gradually, responsibility for the Great Commission began to be accepted by the churches rather than it being relegated to a relative handful of missionaries to fulfill on their behalf. The theme that began to resonate with Southern Baptists was declared by the president of the IMB in an annual report to the Southern Baptist Convention as early as 2000.

> It is not the responsibility of the International Mission Board to carry out the Great Commission on behalf of Southern Baptists. The Great Commission was given to every church and every believer. The responsibility of your mission board is to serve, enable, equip and facilitate every church to be obedient to the mandate of our Lord to reach and disciple the nations.[4]

It was evident there would never be enough Western missionaries to reach all the peoples of the world; a challenge was envisioned of mobilizing forty-five thousand churches and 16 million Southern Baptists, believing God had blessed Southern Baptists and raised them up in numbers and resources for the purpose of fulfilling

---

4   Jerry Rankin, *Impact Your World* (Richmond, VA: International Mission Board, 2005), 3.

his mission. However, that vision called for a different strategy, and a different strategy would require a change in organization from simply administering the work of missionaries to mobilizing the larger scope of kingdom resources.

Another trend that led to subsequent organizational changes was the fact that progress in engaging unreached people groups had plateaued and begun to decline. The reason was obvious. Pioneer missionary personnel initiating engagement of a new people group, usually identified as "strategy coordinators," were responsible for mobilizing additional personnel to implement a strategy of engagement. Others may have preceded him in creative access assignments, or the team coordinator may have actually been giving strategic leadership from a nonresidential location. But essential to implementing a strategy of engagement that would result in church planting movements was to expand the number of personnel resources focusing on a particular people group. Personnel on medical or educational platforms, or carrying out humanitarian projects, opened new doors and enlarged the potential of gospel exposure. But beefing up teams where engagement had already been initiated competed with the need for new personnel to engage additional people groups. Engagement strategies had to go beyond IMB personnel to facilitating engagement by anyone, from near-neighbor people groups who had been evangelized to missionaries from third-world countries as well as other partner agencies.

But the factor that created the most compelling need for organizational change came from an awareness of the diaspora. When cooperative research had revealed that a large portion of people groups still unengaged were those with oral cultures, orality strategies had begun to emerge. Likewise, when research revealed that many of the unengaged people groups were large population segments who had migrated and were living outside the location of their cultural origins, changes had to be made in organizational structures in order to provide access to the gospel.

Missionaries had been aware of expatriate population segments of their target people who were living in various places around the world, but their assignments were largely geographic, confined to people groups within a specific city or region. One's team accountability and field structure inhibited the ability to travel and work on another continent, or even to follow people-group relationships to neighboring countries. Even within a specific field, the people-group focus limited the freedom of missionaries to engage other ethnicities they might encounter.

Years earlier during the wars in Indochina, thousands of Cambodian refugees were streaming across the border into Thailand. Missionaries began to respond to the crisis and found a ready response to the gospel. Perceived that they were neglecting their assignment with the Thai, a team decision was made to forbid any missionary personnel assigned to Thailand to work with Cambodians, and an open door of opportunity was forfeited. The people-group-focused strategy perplexed missionaries who found themselves in urban settings in which ethnic distinctions broke down into an amalgamated matrix of diversity. Missionaries in Western Europe worked diligently to find response among indigenous Europeans, oblivious to the fact they were being engulfed by masses of people from South Asia, West Africa, and the Middle East. It became evident that many people considered resistant to the gospel became open when they were separated from family pressures and societal taboos in places or origin. A majority of Japanese Christians actually came to faith in Christ while overseas on business or going to school. Arabs in Argentina, Sudanese in London, Iranians in Germany, or Vietnamese in Paris still have to deal with the social pressures of their community but now live in places where there is no restriction to someone confronting them with the claims of Christ.

As an example, research discovered there were 100,000 Chinese in Zimbabwe, essentially an unengaged people group. Local missionaries were aware there were Chinese throughout the country, but they had been called and trained to contextualize the gospel to an African worldview and evangelize the indigenous peoples of Zimbabwe. How are these Chinese to be engaged and reached if those called by God to the Chinese are all in East Asia? How are churches to be planted among them if Mandarin-speaking Christian workers equipped to reach them are restricted only to places where Chinese are the majority. Migration has changed our world, but our mission strategies have been slow to adapt to the new opportunities this provides. The UN reports there are 550 million migrants displaced from their home environment; almost half of them are refugees who have moved less than five hundred miles from their previous homes. Eighty-nine percent of the population of the United Arab Emirates are noncitizen workers from the Philippines and South Asian countries.

The IMB had moved to a people-group strategy, but a regional organizational structure created two grievous problems inhibiting effective evangelistic impact. People-group teams were not responsible for those who moved out of the region of the core population where the team was assigned, nor were they responsible for other nonindigenous people who migrated into their region. Priority was given to engaging the ethnographic core and refraining from being distracted by those on the fringe. A change had to occur if the neglected fringe groups of the diaspora were to hear and receive the gospel.

Another factor was the realization that creative access assignments in countries restricting a Christian witness are fragile. A missionary who serves in such a context must be discrete in his witness and would be inhibited in being able to make the gospel widely known. Many have frustratingly discovered that presence does not always equal proclamation. However, one's target people have great potential for hearing the gospel if those dispersed abroad are engaged with the good news of salvation in places where the dangers and threats are removed and legal restrictions nonexistent. Creative access assignments found little opening among the Kurds in Iran, Turkey, or Iraq but found a ready response among those in Berlin. Workers in Afghanistan find only rare occasions in which a witness can be discretely shared but more open opportunities to reach these people in Dubai or Toronto. Thousands of Yemeni and Somali are in Minneapolis; Iranian churches are being planted in Cyprus, Dallas, and Los Angeles. But within the IMB structure, when a creative access platform folded in Central Asia, a missionary found it a formidable challenge to get permission to transfer regions in order to work among his target people in Canada or Western Europe.

As Thomas Friedman observed, the world is flat.[5] Borders are archaic as people are no longer confined to places of historic origin. *The IMB Global Research Department reported that of 11,291 people groups in their database, 30.7 percent are outside their country of origin.* But significantly, these diaspora people groups represent only 6.5 percent of the global population.[6] This reality has become apparent in the task of reaching the *panta ta ethne*. If we are to reach and disciple all the ethnolinguistic peoples of the world, we must reach them where they are. But this strategy was inhibited by an organization in which people were assigned and deployed to a geographic region, and strategies were designed and implemented within that confined area. Like the previous paradigm in which the organization was created to guide and administer the work of missionaries only where missionaries were located, we found the current organization was structured to focus on peoples only within geographic areas. Asking, "Who is reaching the Arabs in South America or South Asians in London?" would be met with a shrug and reply: "We are focusing on the Hispanic people groups or indigenous Europeans; we cannot be distracted to work with small, minority groups of migrants." Or local missionary teams might

---

5   Thomas L. Friedman, *The World Is Flat* (New York: Farrar, Straus and Giroux, 2005).
6   Jim Haney, "Church Planting Progress Indicators" (unpublished report, IMB Global Research Department, 2014).

excuse themselves by claiming they did not have sufficient personnel, resources, or training to reach immigrant population segments. Of 711 Muslim people groups with a population more than 100,000, 181 are unengaged; of the 1,314 Muslim people groups with less that 100,000 people, 934 are unengaged. Why? Many of them are like the Egyptian Arabs who are found in twenty-two countries outside of Egypt, but only five of these diaspora groups are being engaged.[7]

A Paradigm Shift to Global Affinity Groups

Once the focus of mission strategies became reaching all peoples, it was a logical step to reorganize in order to reach them wherever they were in the world. It was essential to dispense with a geographic field structure that limited missionaries to a geographic area and assign them to a global affinity group. Following a prototype that had emerged with the identification of major ethnic affinities by researchers, the International Mission Board redesigned field structures into eight affinity groups in 2009. IMB leaders were initially confronted with sixteen global affinities but felt so many would tend to fragment a concerted organizational strategy. Several, such as the Persian, Turkish, and Median peoples were consolidated into the Central Asian Peoples Affinity Group. Instead of a Chinese Affinity Group, the East Asian Peoples Affinity Group included Japanese and Korean peoples as well as Tibetan and Mongolian. Personnel assigned to people groups within these affinities were no longer restricted to a geographic location but were free to engage their peoples wherever they were found. The groups were:

---

7   Jim Haney, "Muslim Unreached People Groups" (unpublished Vision 5:9 report, International Mission board, 2014).

Global Affinity Group	Total People Groups	Diaspora People Groups
Latin American Peoples	1,308	315
European Peoples	942	771
Northern African and Middle Eastern Peoples	845	434
Sub–saharan African Peoples	2,601	771
Central Asian Peoples	469	307
South Asian Peoples	1,580	287
Southeast Asian Peoples	2,725	345
East Asian Peoples	648	236

Table 7: Affinity Groups

Later a Deaf Peoples Affinity Group was added, recognizing that deafness represented a commonality of outreach strategies that superseded ethnicity and cultural identity; they also represented accessibility and responsiveness that was greater than many of the mainstream cultures where they were located.

Several interesting dynamics emerged once regional barriers were removed in having personnel affiliated with nine different organizational components overlapping globally. Two regions had previously focused on the countries of Eastern and Western Europe, respectively, but now the European Peoples Affinity

Group was responsible for work in Canada, Australia, and New Zealand as well as the entire European continent stretching from the United Kingdom across Russia. Those in the Latin American Peoples Affinity Group had the fewest people groups remaining unreached, and the strategic emphasis became mobilizing and equipping Latinos to go to the nations. Sub-Saharan Africa and Southeast Asia had the most people groups but fewer major population segments among migrants abroad, while the fewer, more homogeneous East Asian people groups have massive enclaves all over the world.

Immediately the issue arose as to what proportion of personnel would be deployed to the diaspora relative to those continuing to work within the dominant cultural blocs. Should a missionary leave an assignment to a people group in India with 13 million people to work in Atlanta where three-thousand of them lived? Several personnel in Southeast Asia requested transfers to target small communities of their people group in the more amenable environment of Australia. Two factors were determined to guide deployment decisions.

The first related to potential harvest. Personnel could gain access to Central Asian peoples in Iran or Afghanistan, but open witnessing and discipleship would be severely limited by political restrictions and hostile religious and cultural barriers. Whereas, more open opportunities would exist among Iranian and Afghan immigrants in South Asian or European cities. Planting churches among expatriate believers would inevitably allow the gospel to flow through indigenous believers back to relatives and communities in their native countries that were more restrictive and represented a higher threat level to expatriate missionaries.

The second strategic factor was training and equipping others for the outreach among unengaged diaspora peoples rather than it being dependent on assigned missionaries. Just as personnel were spread extremely thin in the ethnographic core, there would never be enough to reach the migrant segments scattered to the ends of the earth. Most missionary personnel continued to serve with the geographic clusters of people-group teams. Those who were assigned to a diaspora cluster would seek to provide resources and training to local churches, missionaries of other affinity groups, and Great Commission partners to reach the diaspora people group in their community. For example, missionaries in sub-Saharan Africa and churches in Zimbabwe and South Africa would be trained in how to communicate the gospel and plant churches among the Chinese and Indians who had flooded into their cities. Most of the diaspora peoples from throughout the world could be found in the United States, but missionaries from the field would not be reassigned back to America; they would provide research to identify where their people group was settling and then mobilize and equip local churches and associations to reach them. Out of this approach, "Ethni-city" emerged—a partnership between the IMB and the North American Mission Board to cooperatively target the hundreds of ethnic minorities in most of the major cities of the United States.

Another challenge was dealing with the chaos of IMB personnel from practically all affinity groups working in the same city and neighborhood under separate leadership and lines of accountability, such as occurred in London and other European cities. It was determined that a local church planter or team leader in the host culture working in the area would serve as the ad hoc coordinator. For example, someone with the European Peoples Affinity Group in London would be responsible for communication, fellowship, and seeing logistical needs were met among other people-group teams in London.

Previously each geographic region had its own support network for personnel support, business services, and financial management. Would the missionary now relate to these offices where they live or to the administrative support team serving their former region on the other side of the world? Out of the need to economize and streamline these services, missionary support roles were separated from the previous eleven geographic regions and consolidated into four support centers. Located in Santiago, London, Johannesburg, and Chiang Mai, support teams provided logistical support for arranging housing, purchasing vehicles, and processing visas; personnel services provided member care, children's education, and meeting medical needs, while financial services handled disbursements and accounting for all personnel within prescribed continental areas regardless of the affinity group to which they were assigned.

Immediate results of this organizational change were not as effective as had been anticipated, as the implementation took a couple of years due to significant numbers of personnel, both frontline workers and those in support assignments, relocating and getting established. Each affinity group launched more in-depth research in prioritizing assignments and strengthening partnerships. While the scope of engagement has not grown radically, it has not continued to decline, and though most of the newly engaged people groups among the diaspora are not those with a large population, they would have continued to be neglected.

The peak of new people groups engaged by IMB personnel came in the first five years of New Directions, from 1997 to 2002, and then began to decline due to consolidation and strengthening teams as well as fine-tuning what engagement really meant—a long-term commitment to the language and culture that resulted in actual church planting efforts taking place.

The IMB moved from engaging 338 people groups in 1997 to a high of 1,317 in 2003. Because many of these were relatively evangelized, the shift to unreached and unengaged reduced the number of total people groups in 2013 to 907. In the five years since reorganizing into global affinity groups, an average of forty-five unengaged people groups have been engaged each year as well as almost one hundred additional newly engaged unreached people groups annually.[8] Many of these would not be the priority target groups with more than 100,000 population but the smaller groups of the diaspora.

Many mission agencies came out of the Lausanne Conferences of 1974 and 1989 and the influence of the "AD2000 and Beyond Movement" determined to engage all people groups with a million people or more. By the time the twenty-first century arrived the target had become the unengaged with 100,000 people or more. While approximately three hundred of those remain, most of the unengaged people groups are the peoples of the diaspora who continued to be ignored and neglected. They are minorities within their own major cultural blocs, or refugees and migrants resisting assimilation in a foreign land. With the reorganization into global affinity groups the International Mission Board is positioned to lead the effort to research, identify, and engage the remaining unengaged peoples who do not yet have access to the gospel wherever they are dispersed around the world.

---

8   Jim Haney, "CPPI 2014" (unpublished report, IMB Global Research Department, 2014).

Chapter Thirteen
Diaspora Missiology and Beyond: Paths Taken and Ways Forward
ENOCH WAN

ABSTRACT

A quick review of the emergence of diaspora missiology is followed by a brief report on its development as a relatively new focus of research and strategy in Christian mission, concluded by the listing of a few ideas as pointers for the ways forward.

Introduction

In light of the theme of the EMS national conference this year on "Diaspora Missiology," the dual purpose of this chapter is first to look back on the paths taken in the study of diaspora missiology, then look ahead for the ways forward. We shall begin this study with definitions for several key terms.[1]

- Diaspora Missiology—"a missiological framework for understanding and participating in God's redemptive mission among people living outside their place of origin."[2]

- Diaspora Ministry—serving the diaspora in the name of Jesus Christ and for His sake in these two ways: (1) ministering to the diaspora, i.e., serving the diaspora, and (2) ministering through the diaspora, i.e., mobilizing the diaspora to serve others.

- Diaspora Missions—Christians' participation in God's redemptive mission to evangelize their kinsmen on the move, and through them to reach out to natives in their homelands and beyond.[3] There are four types of diaspora missions (see Table 8)[4]:

---

1   With the exception of the first term, the rest are taken from Wan, *Diaspora Missiology* (2014), 6.
2   Lausanne Diaspora Educators Consultation, "The Seoul Declaration on Diaspora Missiology," November 14, 2009, http://www.lausanne.org/content/statement/the-seoul-declaration-on-diaspora-missiology (accessed September 1, 2014).
3   Enoch Wan, "Global People and Diaspora Missiology" (presentation at plenary session, Global Mission Consultation, Tokyo, Japan, May 13, 2010).
4   Adapted from Enoch Wan, "Research Methodology for Diaspora Missiology and Diaspora Missions" (presentation at North Central Regional EMS Conference, Trinity Evangelical Divinity School, Deerfield, IL, February 26, 2011).

DIASPORA MISSIOLOGY

DIASPORA MINISTRY

Type	Ministering to the diaspora	ministering along the diaspora
Means	European Peoples	the Great Commission – imperative and inclusive
Recipient	Northern African and Middle Eastern Peoples	focusing beyond diaspora: mobilizing diaspora Christians to serve other diaspora people or non-diaspora people

DIASPORA MISSIONS

Type	mission to the diaspora	missions through the diaspora	missions by & beyond the diaspora	missions with the diaspora
Means	motivate & mobilize diaspora individuals & congregations to partner with others: the Great Commission, i.e. evangelistic outreach, discipleship, church planting, and global missions			
Recipient	focusing on diaspora		focusing beyond diaspora	
	members of diaspora community	kinsmen in homeland & elsewhere; not cross-culturally	cross-culturally to other ethnic groups in host society & beyond	partnership between diaspora and others in kingdom ministry

Table 8: Diaspora Missiology

- Missions *to* the Diaspora—reaching the diaspora groups in forms of evangelism or preevangelistic social services, then discipling them to become worshiping communities and congregations.
- Missions *through* the Diaspora—diaspora Christians reaching out to their kinsmen through networks of friendship and kinship in host countries, their homelands, and abroad.
- Missions *by* and *beyond* the Diaspora—motivating and mobilizing diaspora Christians for cross-cultural missions to other ethnic groups in their host countries, homelands, and abroad. Missions *wth* the Diaspora—mobilizing nondiasporic Christians individually and institutionally to partner with diasporic groups and congregations.

Paths Taken

The first article bearing the name "Diaspora Missiology" was published in *Occasional Bulletin* of EMS, Spring 2007. It is the two topics of my research at Overseas Mission Study Center (OMSC) as a scholar in residence of Yale Divinity School, Spring 2006, during my sabbatical from Western Seminary. We have come a long way to this point having the theme of the EMS national conference of 2014 on "Diaspora Missiology."

Prior to the 2007 article, I gave a presentation in 2003 at the American Society of Missiology with the title "Mission among the Chinese Diaspora: A Case Study of Migration and Mission," which subsequently was published in *Missiology* 31, no. 1 (January 2003): 35–43.

Personal Efforts

Since the publication of the 2007 article, I had tried to promote the study of diaspora missiology by (a) presentations at national and international conferences (see appendix 1); (b) proposing methodology to conduct research,[5] coaching doctoral students (see appendix 2); (c) publication of articles and books (see appendix 3).

---

5 Listed below are sample efforts proposing an integrative methodology for conducting research in diaspora missiology:
Wan, *Diaspora Missiology* (2014), pt. 3, 111–62; and ch. 10.
Enoch Wan, "The Paradigm and Pressing Issues of Inter-disciplinary Research Methodology," *Global Missiology* 2, no. 2 (January 2005), http://ojs.globalmissiology.org/index.php/english/article/viewFile/97/281.
Wan, "Research Methodology."
Enoch Wan, "Rethinking Missiological Research Methodology: Exploring a New Direction," *Global Missiology* (October 2003).
Enoch Wan and Sadiri Joy Tira, "Diaspora Missiology and Missions in the Context of the Twenty-first Century," *Torch Trinity Journal* 13, no.1 (May 30, 2010): 45–56, Seoul, South Korea.

Personal Journey

My interest in diaspora missiology emerged from my family background and personal journey. My family moved from southwest China to south China and eventually settled down in Hong Kong, where I grew up. My mother was sold as an indentured maid in her teen years by her father, serving in Southeast Asia for a decade. My two paternal uncles emigrated to Burma and Cuba during World War II and eventually died abroad.

In New York, I married a foreign student born in Macau and later we immigrated to Canada and the United States. I conducted my research in New York Chinatown by acquiring two research languages (i.e., the trade language of Chinatown—Toishan—and Mandarin of immigrants from Southeast Asia and Taiwan. My doctoral dissertation in urban anthropology was on the diaspora Chinese community in the lower east side of New York City.[6]

Due to my interest in diaspora studies, my years of missionary service in the Philippines and Australia provided me opportunities to study various diaspora groups (with a focus on Chinese) in two continents. My teaching and pastoral ministries[7] careers in Canada, Hong Kong, and the United States allowed me to continue this pursuit. I started the first "Center of Chinese Study" in North America at Canadian Theological Seminary and served as the director from 1982 to 1988. In 1988 it was expanded to include five diaspora groups at the founding of the Centre for Intercultural Studies (CIS). In 1994 CIS organized the first Intercultural Ministries National Conference of Canada and published the compendium volume *Missions within Reach: Intercultural Ministries in Canada*[8]—a prototype of diaspora missiology.[9]

Conferences and Development[10]

In the past few years, the relatively new diaspora missiology paradigm was introduced to missiologists and missions leaders through a series of activities (e.g., conferences, meetings, and course offerings) as listed below.

---

6 Enoch Wan, "The Dynamics of Ethnicity: A Case Study on the Immigrant Community of New York Chinatown" (PhD dissertation, State University of New York at Stony Brook, 1978).
7 In addition, my experience in diaspora ministry was enriched by church planting ministries among diaspora Chinese in Toronto and Long Island, New York.
8 Enoch Wan, ed., *Missions within Reach: Intercultural Ministries in Canada* (Hong Kong: China Alliance Press, 1995).
9 For a more detailed description, see Wan, epilogue to *Diaspora Missiology* (2014), 315–16.
10 This section is condensed from Wan, *Diaspora Missiology* (2014), ch. 9, 137–41.

The annual meeting of the American Society of Missiology (AMS) in June 2002 chose the theme "Migration Challenge and Avenue for Christian Mission" and the proceedings were subsequently published in the journal *Missiology* (January 2003), covering matters related to ministry to diaspora. In Seoul, South Korea, April 12–15, 2004, at the consultation of the Filipino International Network (FIN), missiologists, theologians, and practitioners reported and explored issues related to diaspora missions with a focus on the global phenomenon of the Filipino diaspora. The proceedings were published in *Scattered: The Filipino Global Presence*[11]—the first book focusing on the study of diaspora missiology with five parts: historical demography, biblical theology, missiological methodology, global strategy (evangelism and discipleship), and personal stories of Filipino "kingdom workers."

In 2004, at the Lausanne Forum held in Pattaya, Thailand, "diaspora" was an issue group for the first time in the Lausanne Committee for World Evangelization (LCWE), and they produced the first-ever Lausanne Occasional Paper on diaspora entitled "The New People Next Door" (LOP 55— a free digital copy is available at http://www.lausanne.org/docs/2004forum/LOP55_IG26.pdf). This booklet provides a discussion on the biblical and theological basis for missions among scattered people and case studies on Chinese, Filipino, South Asian, Persian, and international students. The publication of LOP 55 is significant in that it helped to place diaspora missiology on the global agenda of the church.

The Filipino Diaspora Missions Consultation took place at the Torch Trinity Graduate School of Theology, Seoul, South Korea, April 12–15, 2004. At the conference, Enoch Wan addressed the matter of "The Phenomenon of Diaspora: Missiological Implications for Christian Missions," later published in the multilingual e-journal *Global Missiology*.[12]

At the Philippine Baptist Theological Seminary, Baguio City, Philippines, the Filipino Theological Educators' Consultation on January 4–6, 2006, was attended by dozens of missiologists and theological educators from the United States, Canada, Korea, and the Philippines to strategize ways and means to promote both formal and

---

11 Luis Pantoja Jr., Sadiri Joy Tira, and Enoch Wan, eds., *Scattered: The Filipino Global Presence* (Manila: LifeChange, 2004).
12 Enoch Wan, "The Phenomenon of Diaspora: Missiological Implications for Christian Missions," *Global Missiology* 4, no. 9 (July 2012), http://ojs.globalmissiology.org/index.php/english/article/view/1036. For information regarding this conference, readers are referred to Sadiri Joy B. Tira, "Filipino International Network: A Strategic Model for Filipino Diaspora Glocal Missions," *Global Missiology* 1, no. 2 (October 2004), http://ojs.globalmissiology.org/index.php/english/article/viewFile/123/356 (accessed February 20, 2014).

informal education in diaspora missiology for pastors, missionaries, and Filipino kingdom workers around the world.

Later in the same year, LCWE endorsed the first Global Diaspora Missiology Consultation, sponsored by the FIN, that was held at Taylor University College and Seminary (Edmonton, Alberta, Canada) on November 15–18, 2006.

In 2007, Sadiri Joy Tira was appointed as senior associate for diasporas by LCWE and the following year completed his dissertation entitled "Filipino Kingdom Workers: An Ethnographic Study" (at Western Seminary, Spring 2008, under the supervision of Enoch Wan), which was later published by William Carey Library under the same title in the EMS Dissertation Series, 2011.

At the Lausanne Diaspora Educators Consultation on November 11–14, 2009, at Torch Trinity Graduate School of Theology, Seoul, South Korea, "The Seoul Declaration on Diaspora Missiology" was drafted by a task group and approved on November 14, 2009.[13] And a working committee was formed and tasked to produce an official document for the Cape Town 2010 conference. Consequently the booklet *Scattered to Gather: Embracing the Global Trend of Diaspora* was produced and distributed at Lausanne Cape Town 2010.[14]

Due to a combination of factors, only a few copies of the prepublication version of the booklet *Korean Diaspora and Christian Mission* were available at Cape Town 2010, and a year later it was published by Regnum Books International.[15] Subsequently the Global Diaspora Network (GDN)—a catalytic organization motivating and mobilizing diaspora Christians to partner for global missions—was formed under the auspices of the Lausanne Movement in 2010, and Sadiri Joy Tira serves as both the senior associate for diasporas and chairperson for the GDN.

The GDN headquarters/secretariat office in 2011 was established in Manila and officially registered under the Securities and Exchange Commission of the Philippines providing GDN with a legal identity.[16] And in February 2011 the GDN Advisory Board met for the first time in France to project the "Lausanne Diaspora Missions" for the next five years including the Global Diaspora Forum, March 2015,

---

13 Lausanne Diaspora Educators Consultation, "The Seoul Declaration on Diaspora Missiology."
14 Lausanne Committee for World Evangelization, *Scattered to Gather*.
15 S. Hun Kim and Wonsuk Ma, eds., *Korean Diaspora and Christian Mission* (Oxford: Regnum Books International, 2011).
16 http://www.globaldiaspora.org/about_gdn (accessed February 20, 2014; site discontinued).

in Manila, Philippines.¹⁷ The Global Diaspora Forum was officially announced during the Lausanne Leadership Biennial Meeting in Boston, Massachusetts, June 2011. "The 2015 World Diaspora Forum will be held in the Philippines, March 24–28, 2015, and is sponsored by the Lausanne Committee. The GDN plans to invite 500 people from around the world to participate including church leaders, educators, practitioners and donors . . . The GDN will also publish a compendium about the diaspora and the Kingdom of God with sections on theological foundations, current realities, strategic possibilities of the diaspora, the role of the church, and various case studies."¹⁸

GDN hosted the Far East Asia Educators Forum in Manila, August 11–14, 2011, in order to gather theological educators to a joint effort in developing courses and curriculum to train workers and researchers to advance the cause of diaspora mission and ministry.¹⁹

The eighth Korean Diaspora Forum (KDF) met in Johannesburg, South Africa, February 14–17, 2012, with the theme "Beyond Barrier, Beyond Generations." KDF has a long history tracing back to its birth in Baltimore, Maryland, in 2004, during which Korean diaspora churches worldwide participated. Since 2005 KDF has met annually: Beijing, 2006; Tokyo, 2007; Kuala Lumpur, 2008; Shanghai, 2009; Seol-Ak Mountain, 2010; and Los Angeles, 2011.²⁰

At the Korean Diaspora Forum, May 18–21, 2010, Seoul, South Korea, Enoch Wan presented a paper on "Korean Diaspora: From Hermit Kingdom to Kingdom Ministry," challenging Korean participants from a dozen countries engaging in diaspora ministry among Koreans overseas and in cross-cultural contexts. At the International Forum for Migrant Mission (IFMM, May 25, 2010, Seoul, South Korea), Enoch Wan gave a presentation on "Diaspora Missiology in Action: A Case Study of Chinese Diaspora Missions and CCCOWE."²¹ The Chinese Coordination Centre of

---

17 Ibid.
18 World Evangelical Alliance, "Life on the Road: Updates from the Refugee Highway Partnership," May 31, 2013, http://www.worldea.org/news/4227/life-on-the-road-updates-from-the-refugee-highway-partnership (accessed March 8, 2014).
19 http://www.globaldiaspora.org/content/far-east-asia-disapora-educators-met-manila (accessed February 20, 2014; site discontinued).
20 http://www.globaldiaspora.org/content/gdn-networks-kdf (accessed February 20, 2014; site discontinued).
21 "In July 1974, some seventy Chinese Church leaders, who came together at the International Congress on World Evangelism in Lausanne, were inspired by the Holy Spirit to commence the movement. In August 1976, the 1st Chinese Congress on World Evangelization was convened in Hong Kong; soon after, the Chinese Coordination Centre of World Evangelism was established to mobilize Chinese churches to spread the gospel to nations all over the world." Lausanne Movement, "CCCOWE Overview," http://

World Evangelism is the first ethnic global network in evangelism since Lausanne 1974). He used the case study of CCCOWE to challenge Korean participants to form a global network in diaspora mission.

"On May 22nd, 2012 Eurasian Diaspora Study Center has been opened at Ukrainian Evangelical Theological Seminary. Senior bishops of the Evangelical churches, the rectors of theological schools, scholars, and representatives of public organizations of Ukraine attended the opening ceremony."[22]

The theme "Mission on Our Doorsteps" of the 12th Ethnic Ministries Summit was held in Chicago, April 18–20, 2013. Ethnic America Network (EAN) is "a catalytic coalition of Christian ministries and churches from across the USA and Canada," and "since 2000, we have partnered with local leaders and educators in holding annual Ethnic Ministries Summits, out of which we seek to establish Regional Networks of ethnic ministries."[23] It is interesting to note that it is not hard to draw a parallel between the approach of EAN in ethnic ministry and Donald Anderson McGavran's concept of ethnic diversity of the church in India.[24]

The theme of the Evangelical Missiological Society of 2014 (www.emsweb.org) was "Diaspora Missiology," with many papers presented at regional meetings in the Spring of 2014 and from which some were selected to be included in the national conference and in the EMS annual monograph on diaspora missiology edited by Enoch Wan and Michael Pocock. The theme of the 2014 North American Mission Leaders Conference was "Migration and Mission" with multiple tracks including "Diaspora/Ethnic Ministries" hosted by Missio Nexus, Evangelical Missiological Society (EMS), Ethnic America Network, and Alliance for Excellence in Short-term Mission (AESTM), September 2014, at the Hilton, Atlanta, Georgia.[25]

Recent Researches and Publications

As a newly emerged focus of research and publication, at present there are not many publications. Listed below are an illustrative few for simple reference:

---

www.lausanne.org/en/connect/regions/east-asia/cccowe-overview.html (accessed February 20, 2014; page discontinued).

22   http://www.globaldiaspora.org/content/diaspora-missiology-launched (accessed February 20, 2014; site discontinued).

23   Ethnic America Network, "About the Network," http://ethnicamerica.com/about/ (accessed February 20, 2014).

24   Donald A. McGavran, *Ethnic Realities and the Church: Lessons from India* (Pasadena: William Carey Library, 1979).

25   Missio Nexus, "Mission Leaders Conference," http://www.missionexus.org/mission-leaders-conference/ (accessed March 8, 2014).

- The booklet "The New People Next Door" (Lausanne Occasional Paper 55), produced by the Lausanne Committee for World Evangelization (2004), is a significant document in that it helped place the topic of diaspora missiology on the global agenda of the church.
- R. Stephen Warren and Judith G. Wittner, *Gatherings in Diaspora: Religious Communities and the New Immigration* (Philadelphia: Temple University Press, 1998).
- Gerrie Ter Haar, *Halfway to Paradise: African Christians in Europe* (Cardiff, UK: Cardiff Academic Press, 1998).
- A. F. Walls, "Mission and Migration: The Diaspora Factor in Christian History," *Journal of African Christian Thought* 5, no. 2 (December 2002): 3–11.
- S. Spencer, ed., *Mission and Migration* (Calver, UK: Cliff College Publishing, 2008).
- Jehu J. Hanciles, *Beyond Christendom: Globalization, African Migration, and the Transformation of the West* (Maryknoll, NY: Orbis Books, 2008).
- Claudia Währisch-Oblau, *The Missionary Self-perception of Pentecostal/Charismatic Church Leaders from the Global South in Europe: Bringing Back the Gospel*. Leiden, The Netherlands: Brill, 2009.
- S. Hun Kim and Wonsuk Ma, eds., *Korean Diaspora and Christian Mission* (Oxford: Regnum Books International, 2011).
- F. Ludwig and J. K. Asamoah-Gyadu, *African Christian Presence in the West: New Immigrant Congregations and Transnational Networks in North America and Europe* (Trenton, NJ: Africa World Press, 2011).
- A. Adogame, *The African Christian Diaspora: New Currents and Emerging Trends in World Christianity* (London: Bloomsbury, 2013).
- R. Stephen Warner has presented a convincing argument that "migration is not random with respect to religion." R. Stephen Warner, (2000) "Religion and New (Post-1965) Immigrants: Some Principles Drawn from Field Research," *American Studies* 41, nos. 2–3 (Summer/Fall 2000): 267–86. Along the same line of thought, "Faith on the Move," a recent study by the Pew Research Center's Forum on Religion and Public Life, focuses on the religious affiliation of international migrants, examining patterns of migration among seven major groups: Christians, Muslims, Hindus, Buddhists, Jews, adherents of other

religions, and the religiously unaffiliated. Another important document is "The Global Religious Landscape" (2012), also produced by Pew.[26]

- In reference to Korean diaspora, it is worth mentioning several publications. Chan-Sik Park edited the book *21C New Nomad Era and Migrant Mission* (Seoul: Christianity and Industrial Society Research Institute, 2010). It was distributed to all participants of the Korean Diaspora Forum and the International Forum for Migrant Mission in Seoul, South Korea, May 2010.
- Another book is *Korean Diaspora and Christian Mission*, edited by S. Hun Kim and Wonsuk Ma. Limited copies of a prepublication version were distributed during the Lausanne III (Cape Town 2010) congress in South Africa and later published by Regnum Books International in 2011.
- Two special issues of *Torch Trinity Journal* were designated to the theme of "Diaspora" with Korean, American, and Chinese contributors: vol. 13, no. 1 (May 30, 2010); and vol. 13, no. 2 (November 30, 2010).[27]
- *Strangers Next Door: Immigration, Migration and Mission* by J. D. Payne (Downers Grove, IL: InterVarsity Press, 2012) presents helpful demographic data and calls for Christians to actively engage in diaspora mission by reaching out to incoming migrants and immigrants in our neighborhood.
- Similar to Payne in passion for evangelism and church planting, Tira and Santos use Greenhills Christian Fellowship of the Philippines to showcase the practice of "by and beyond" in diaspora mission extending to Canada. Sadiri Joy Tira and Narry F. Santos, "Diaspora Church Planting in a Multicultural City: A Case Study of Greenhills Christian Fellowship," in *Reflecting God's Glory Together: Diversity in Evangelical Mission*, ed. A. Scott Moreau and Beth Snodderly, EMS 17 (Pasadena: William Carey Library, 2011), 63–90.
- An entire issue of *IJFM* was focusing on diaspora missiology: Brad Gill, ed., "ISFM 2013: Dancing with Diaspora," *International Journal of Frontier Missiology* 30, no. 3 (July–September 2013): 95–131, http://www.ijfm.org/PDFs_IJFM/30_3_PDFs/IJFM_30_3-EntireIssue.pdf.
- Recent publications of the IDS-Diaspora Series, edited by Enoch Wan, are:
- Enoch Wan, ed., *Diaspora Missiology: Theory, Methodology, and Practice*, rev. ed. (Portland, OR: Institute of Diaspora Studies, 2014).

---

26   Pew Research Center, "The Global Religious Landscape," December 18, 2012, http://www.pewforum.org/global-religious-landscape-christians.aspx.

27   The key word "diaspora" may be used to search at http://www0.ttgst.ac.kr:30000.

- Yaw Attah Edu-Bekoe and Enoch Wan, *Scattered Africans Keep Coming* (Portland, OR: Institute of Diaspora Studies, 2013).
- On Vietnamese diaspora—Enoch Wan and Thanh Trung Le, *Mobilizing Vietnamese Diaspora for the Kingdom* (Portland, OR: Institute of Diaspora Studies, 2014).
- Enoch Wan and Ted Rubesh, *Wandering Jews and Scattered Sri Lankans: Viewing Sri Lankans of the Gulf Cooperative Council through the Lens of the Old Testament Jewish Diaspora* (Portland, OR: Institute of Diaspora Studies, 2014).
- On Japanese diaspora— Enoch Wan and Elton S. L. Law, *The 2011 Triple Disaster in Japan and the Diaspora: Lessons Learned and Ways Forward* (Portland, OR: Institute of Diaspora Studies, 2014).
- On diaspora in US urban centers—Enoch Wan and Anthony Francis Casey, *Church Planting among Immigrants in US Urban Centers: The Where, Why, and How of Diaspora Missiology in Action* (Portland, OR: Institute of Diaspora Studies, 2014).
- It is worth mentioning that several additions went into the revised edition of *Diaspora Missiology: Theory, Methodology, and Practice.*

The addition of "Missions *with* the Diaspora" to the paradigm of diaspora missions (chapter 8; especially figures 8.1, 8.3).

The addition of a critique of "managerial missiology" (chapter 7; especially figures 7.1, 8.2).

The addition of a chapter on "Diaspora Missiology in Progress" (chapter 9).

Ways Forward

The interface of diaspora missiology with studies in internal migration (urban mission), international immigration (ethnic studies), globalization, etc., has proven to be fruitful as demonstrated by organizers of national and international conferences on diaspora missiology.

The integration of methodologies borrowed from social sciences (e.g., human geography, cultural anthropology, and migration studies), humanities (e.g., history and religion), service agencies (e.g., refugee work, human trafficking, and advocacy groups) denominations, and mission organizations will be very helpful in the study of the phenomenon of diaspora and the formulation of mission strategy.

The cooperation of experts from diverse fields and the partnership of organizations/institutions will fuel synergy in diaspora study and the practice of diaspora missions. There will be a compendium volume coming out from the proceedings of the Global Diaspora Forum of March 24–27, 2015, Manila, Philippines. It will be the product of collaborative work by experts of various related fields in diaspora missiology.

Conclusion

In this paper, we briefly reviewed the path where diaspora missiology traversed and report the progress in recent years. It is most encouraging to witness the emergence of diaspora missiology as a missiological paradigm for the twenty-first century after the publication of the article on diaspora missiology in 2007. Diaspora missiology has proven to be a missiological paradigm that is contextually relevant for the demographic reality of the twenty-first century and the shifting of Christian centers (i.e., from the Northern Hemisphere to the South, and from the West to the rest).

The future of diaspora missiology is bright, for it has been given a place among practitioners and academicians, in international conferences, major magazines, and mission organizations.

Appendix 1

Presentations at National and International Conferences

2003 June—Enoch Wan, "Mission among the Chinese Diaspora: A Case Study of Migration and Mission." American Society of Missiology, Techny, IL.

2008 April—"The Filipino Experience in Diaspora Missions: A Case Study of Mission Initiatives from the Majority World Churches." North West EMS Regional Meeting, Portland, OR.

2009 June—Sadiri Joy Tira and Enoch Wan, "The Filipino Experience in Diaspora Missions: A Case Study of Christian Communities in Contemporary Contexts." Commission 7: Christian Communities in Contemporary Contexts, Edinburgh, June 12–13.

2010 May—"Korean Diaspora: From Hermit Kingdom to Kingdom Ministry." Korean Diaspora Forum, Seoul, South Korea.

2010 April—"Rethinking Missiology in the Context of the 21st Century: Global Demographic Trends and Diaspora Missiology." Lausanne Diaspora Educators Consultation in Europe, Oxford Centre for Mission Studies, Oxford, UK, April 16.

2010 May—"Global People and Diaspora Missiology: From Edinburgh 2010 to Tokyo 2010." Plenary session at Tokyo 2010, May 11–14. Video clip available at http://www.ustream.tv/recorded/6897559/.

2010 September—Yaw Attah Edu-Bekoe, "Diversity of Ghanaian Diaspora in the U.S.: Ministering to the Diverse Ghanaian Communities through Ghanaian Congregations." 2010 North America Missions Leaders Conference.

2010 October—"Ministering to Scattered Peoples: Moving to Reach the People on the Move." Cape Town 2010. Available at http://conversation.lausanne.org/en/conversations/detail/11438.

2011 January—"Research Methodology for Diaspora Missiology and Diaspora Missions." North Central Regional EMS Conference, Trinity Evangelical Divinity School, Deerfield, IL, February 26.

2011 February—"Global Status of Diaspora Ministry." Web seminar, The Mission Exchange, Global Issues Update. Available at http://www.themissionexchange.org/.

2011 February—"Multitudes Reaching a People-group by Reconciliation." Japan Evangelical Missionary Association (JEMA) Annual Retreat, February14.

2011 February—"The Practice of Diaspora Missions Globally and in Japan Locally." Japan Evangelical Missionary Association (JEMA) Annual Retreat, February 15.

2011 February—"Research Methodology for Diaspora Missiology and Diaspora Missions." North Central Regional EMS Conference, Trinity Evangelical Divinity School, Deerfield, IL, February 26.

2011 September—Larry Caldwell, "Riots in the City: Replacing 19th Century Urban Training Models with Relevant 'Urbanized' Training Models for the 21st Century." Evangelical Missiological Society Annual Meeting, September 29–October 1.

Appendix 2
Research Conducted at Institute of Diaspora Studies[1]

Enoch Wan was instrumental in the founding of the Institute of Diaspora Studies (IDS) in the UK,[2] Asia (IDS-Asia/Pacific),[3] and North America (IDS-USA).

In 2007 Western Seminary (Portland, Oregon) launched an Institute of Diaspora Studies (IDS-USA),[4] a joint effort by researchers and practitioners seeking to understand and minister to people of diaspora.

Since 2007, courses offered are selectively listed below:
- At Western Seminary, Portland, Oregon: courses on diaspora missiology, taught by Enoch Wan, Tuvya Zaresky, Sadiri Tira, Summer 2007, 2009, and April 2010; on Hindu diaspora, taught by Atul Y. Aghamkar, February 2010; on diaspora missiology, taught by Enoch Wan and Sadiri Tira, April 2010, and team taught by Enoch Wan, Thanh Trung Le, Andy Ponce, Mike Holland, and Randy Mitchel, May 2013.
- At Ambrose University College, Calgary, Canada, a course on diaspora taught by Sadiri Joy Tira, February 2010.

Completed doctoral dissertations under Enoch Wan's supervision at IDS-USA, Western Seminary, are selectively listed below:
- Tuvya Zaretsky, "The Challenges of Jewish-Gentile Couples: A Pre-evangelistic Ethnographic Study," Spring 2004. Published as: Enoch Wan and Tuvya Zaretsky, *Jewish-Gentile Couples: Trends, Challenges and Hopes* (Pasadena: William Carey Library, 2004).
- Sadiri Emmanuel Santiago B. Tira, "Filipino Kingdom Workers: An Ethnographic Study," Spring 2008. Published with the same title in EMS Dissertation Series (Pasadena: William Carey Library, 2011).
- Yaw Attah Edu-Bekoe, "Ghanaian Diaspora: An Integrative Study of the Presbyterian Church of Ghana Congregations in the United States of America,"

---

1 In addition to the IDS in UK, Asia, and USA mentioned below, there is also the IDS at Ukraine Evangelical Theological Seminary, Kiev, Ukraine, launched in August 2012.

2 I was the dissertation supervisor of S. Hun Kim in 2007 at the Oxford Centre for Mission Studies, Oxford, UK, where the Korean Institute for Diaspora Studies was launched, which published the seminal work on Korean diaspora: S. Hun Kim and Wonsuk Ma, eds., *Korean Diaspora and Christian Mission* (Regnum Books International, 2011).

3 In April 2007 I gave an address on Abraham as the prototype of subsequent Jewish diaspora at the commencement of Alliance Graduate School in Manila, Philippines, when IDS-Asia/Pacific was launched.

4 Additional info is available at http://www.westernseminary.edu/diaspora.

April 2011. Published as: Yaw Attah Edu-Bekoe and Enoch Wan, *Scattered Africans Keep Coming* (Portland, OR: Institute of Diaspora Studies, 2013).
- Mike Holland, "Diaspora Mission to Hispanics in the USA," February 11, 2013.
- Thanh Trung Le, "A Missiological Study of Vietnamese Diaspora," January 2013. Published as: Enoch Wan and Thanh Trung Le, *Mobilizing Vietnamese Diaspora for the Kingdom* (Portland, OR: Institute of Diaspora Studies, 2014).
- James Mook Sum Lai, "An Ethnography of the Contextual Approach of Community Projects among the Yunnanese Chinese Community in Lashio, Myanmar" (Chinese diaspora), September 15, 2013.
- Paul Kyu-Jin Choi, "Towards a Paradigm of Missional Ecclesiology for Korean Diaspora," April 2014.
- Siu Lun Law, "An Ethnographic Study of the Relief Ministries of the Oasis Chapel and Missiological Implications for Relational Missiology" (Japanese diaspora), January 2014.
- Ted Rubesh, "Wandering Jews and Scattered Sri Lankans: Viewing Sri Lankans of the G.C.C. through the Lens of the Old Testament Jewish Diaspora," February 7, 2014. Published as: Enoch Wan and Ted Rubesh, *Wandering Jews and Scattered Sri Lankans: Viewing Sri Lankans of the Gulf Cooperative Council through the Lens of the Old Testament Jewish Diaspora* (Portland, OR: Institute of Diaspora Studies, 2014).
- Ongoing research projects of IDS-USA at Western Seminary under the supervision of Enoch Wan and about a dozen doctoral dissertations are in progress on various diaspora groups such as Hispanic, Korean, etc.

Appendix 3
Books and Articles by Enoch Wan

Books

Enoch Wan, ed., *Missions within Reach: Intercultural Ministries in Canada* (Hong Kong: China Alliance Press, 1995).

Enoch Wan, ed., *Diaspora Missiology: Theory, Methodology, and Practice*, rev. ed. (Portland, OR: Institute of Diaspora Studies, 2014).

Yaw Attah Edu-Bekoe and Enoch Wan, *Scattered Africans Keep Coming* (Portland, OR: Institute of Diaspora Studies, 2013).

Enoch Wan and Thanh Trung Le, *Mobilizing Vietnamese Diaspora for the Kingdom* (Portland, OR: Institute of Diaspora Studies, 2014).

Enoch Wan and Ted Rubesh, *Wandering Jews and Scattered Sri Lankans: Viewing Sri Lankans of the Gulf Cooperative Council through the Lens of the Old Testament Jewish Diaspora* (Portland, OR: Institute of Diaspora Studies, 2014).

Enoch Wan and Elton S. L. Law, *The 2011 Triple Disaster in Japan and the Diaspora: Lessons Learned and Ways Forward* (Portland, OR: Institute of Diaspora Studies, 2014).

Enoch Wan and Anthony Francis Casey, *Church Planting among Immigrants in US Urban Centers: The Where, Why, and How of Diaspora Missiology in Action*. Enoch Wan and Anthony Francis Casey (Summer 2014)

Articles

Enoch Wan, "Rethinking Missiological Research Methodology: Exploring a New Direction," *Global Missiology* (October 2003), http://www.enochwan.com/english/articles/pdf/Rethinking%20Missiological%20Research%20Methodology.pdf.

Enoch Wan, "Mission among the Chinese Diaspora: A Case Study of Migration and Mission," *Missiology* 31, no. 1 (January 2003): 35–43.

Enoch Wan, "The Phenomenon of the Diaspora: Missiological Implications for Christian Missions," in *Asian American Christianity: A Reader*, ed. Viji Nakka-Cammauf and Timothy Tseng (Castro Valley, CA: Pacific Asian American and Canadian Christian Education project (PAACCE) and Institute for the Study of Asian American Christianity (ISAAC), 2004.

Enoch Wan, "The Paradigm and Pressing Issues of Inter-disciplinary Research Methodology," *Global Missiology* 2, no. 2 (January 2005), http://ojs.globalmissiology.org/index.php/english/article/viewFile/97/281.

On the occasion of Paul Hiebert's passing—Enoch Wan, "Expectation and Reflection," April 2007, http://paul-timothy.net/pages/gm/wan_reflections_on_paul_hiebert_4_2007.pdf/ (page discontinued).

Enoch Wan and Linda Gross, "Christian Missions to Diaspora Groups: A Diachronic General Overview and Synchronic Study of Contemporary USA," *Global Missiology* 3, no. 5 (April 2008), http://ojs.globalmissiology.org/index.php/english/article/view/59.

Enoch Wan, "Core Values of Mission Organization in the Cultural Context of the 21st Century," *Global Missiology* 2, no. 6 (January 2009), http://ojs.globalmissiology.org/index.php/english/article/view/26.

Enoch Wan, "Diaspora Couple Priscilla and Aquila: A Model Family in Action for Mission," *Global Missiology* 3, no. 6 (April 2009), http://ojs.globalmissiology.org/index.php/english/issue/view/34. Originally published in Chinese: *Great Commission Bi-monthly* 79 (April 2009).

Enoch Wan and Sadiri Joy Tira, "Diaspora Missiology and Missions in the Context of the Twenty-first Century," *Torch Trinity Journal* 13, no.1 (May 30, 2010): 45–56, Seoul, South Korea.

Enoch Wan, "Global People and Diaspora Missiology: From Edinburgh 2010 to Tokyo 2010." In *Handbook of Global Mission: Consultation*, 92–106. Celebration in Tokyo, May 11–14, 2010.

Enoch Wan, "Rethinking Missiology in the Context of the 21st Century: Global Demographic Trends and Diaspora Missiology," *Great Commission Research Journal* 2, no. 1 (Summer 2010): 7–20, http://journals.biola.edu/gcr/volumes/2/issues/1/articles/7.

Enoch Wan, "Diaspora Mission Strategy in the Context of the United Kingdom in the 21st Century," *Transformation: An International Journal of Holistic Mission Studies* 28, no. 1 (January 2011): 3–13, http://trn.sagepub.com/content/28/1/3.short.

Enoch Wan and Yaw Attah Edu-Bekoe, "Diversity of Ghanaian Diaspora in the USA: Ministering to the Ghanaian Communities through Ghanaian Congregations," in *Mosaic: Engaging the Beauty of God's Kingdom Diversity*, ed. Scott Moreau and Beth Snodderly, Evangelical Missiological Society Series 19 (Pasadena: William Carey Library, 2011).

Selected Bibliography

Abazov, Rafis. *Historical Dictionary of Turkmenistan: Historical Dictionaries of Asia, Oceania, and the Middle East*. Lanham, MD: Scarecrow, 2005.

———. *The Palgrave Concise Historical Atlas of Central Asia*. New York: Palgrave Macmillan, 2008.

Abu Toameh, Khaled. "Why Arab Leaders Do Not Care About Medical Services in Their Countries." Gaston Institute International Policy. (December 21, 2010), http://www.gatestoneinstitute.org/1741/arab-countries-medical-services.

Abu-Laban, Sharon M., Regula B. Qureshi, and Earle H. Waugh. *Muslim Families in North America*. Edmonton: University of Alberta Press, 1991.

Aburish, Said. *The Forgotten Faithful: The Christians of the Holy Land*. London: Quartet Books, 1993.

Adeney, Miriam. "Colorful Initiatives, North American Diasporas in Mission." *Missiology: An International Review* 39, no. 1 (January 2011): 5–23. http://mis.sagepub.com/content/39/1/5.full.pdf (accessed April 3, 2014).

Adler, Leonore Loeb and Uwe P. Gielen, eds. *Migration: Immigration and Emigration in International Perspective*. Westport, CT: Praeger, 2003.

Adogame, A. *The African Christian Diaspora: New Currents and Emerging Trends in World Christianity*. London: Bloomsbury, 2013.

Alcorn, Randy. *Heaven*. Wheaton, IL: Tyndale (2004): 54.

Alexa. "How Popular Is Facebook.com?" http://www.alexa.com/siteinfo/facebook.com (accessed December 12, 2013).

Alinejad, Donya. "Mapping Homelands through Virtual Spaces: Transnational Embodiment and Iranian Diaspora Bloggers." *Global Networks* 11, no. 1 (2001): 43–62.

Alonso, Andoni, and Pedro J. Olarzabal, eds. *Diasporas in the New Media Age: Identity, Politics, and Community*. Reno: University of Nevada Press, 2010.

Anderson, Benedict. *Imagined Communities: Reflections on the Origin and Spread of Nationalism*. 1983. Reprint, London: Verso, 2006.

Appadurai, Arjun. "Disjuncture and Difference in the Global Cultural Economy." *Theorizing Diaspora: A Reader*, ed. Jana Evans Braziel and Anita Mannur. Malden, MA: Blackwell, 2003: 25-48

———. "Global Ethnoscapes: Notes and Queries for a Transnational Anthropology." *Recapturing Anthropology*. Ed. Richard Fox, 191–210. Santa Fe, NM: School of American Research Press, 1991.

Aristotle. *Politica*. 3.6.4.

Arrianus, *Epict*. 2.9.3.

Aspinall, Peter. "Commentary on 'Trending Now.'" *Journal of Public Health* 36, no. 4 (January 12, 2014): 535–36.

Ate, Abe. "Exodus of Palestinian Christians." In *Quaker Life*, 6-7. 2003.

Ateek, Naim Stifan. *A Palestinian Christian Cry for Reconciliation*. Maryknoll, NY: Orbis Books, 2008: 183

Ateek, Naim Stifan, and Rosemary Radford Ruether. *Justice and Only Justice: A Palestinian Theology of Liberation*. Maryknoll, NY: Orbis Books, 1989.

Azarya, Victor. *Nomads and the State in Africa*. Aldershot, UK: Avebury-Ashgate, 1996.

Back to Europe. "Main Purposes of B2E." http://www.back2europe.org/About-Us/Additional-information.aspx (accessed April 3, 2014).

Backstrom, Lars, Paolo Boldi, Marco Rosa, Johan Ugander, and Sebastiano Vigna. "Four Degrees of Separation." *Proceedings of the 3rd Annual ACM Web Science Conference*, 33–42. Evanston, IL, 2012.

Bagby, Ihsan. "The American Mosque 2011: The Basic Characteristics of the American Mosque." Report 1. Washington, DC: Council on American-Islamic Relations, 2011.

Bakke, Ray. *A Theology as Big as the City*. Downers Grove, IL: InterVarsity Press, 1997.

Banerjee, Padmini, and Myna German. "Migration and Transculturation in the Digital Age: A Framework for Studying the Space Between." *Journal of International and Global Studies* 2, no. 1 (2010): 23–35.

Barry, F. R. *Recovery of Man*. New York: Charles Scribner's Sons, 1949.

Barth, Fredrik, ed. *Ethnic Groups and Boundaries: The Social Organization of Cultural Difference*. 1969. Reprint, Long Grove, IL: Waveland, 1998.

Basch, Linda, Nina Glick Schiller, and Christina Blanc-Szanton, eds. *Nations Unbound: Transnational Projects, Postcolonial Predicaments, and Deterritorialized Nation-states*. New York: Routledge, 1994.

BBC News. "Intifada Toll 2000–2005." http://news.bbc.co.uk/2/hi/middle_east/4294502.stm. (accessed March 12, 2014).

Benitez, Jose. "Transnational Dimensions of the Digital Divide among Salvadoran Immigrants in the Washington DC Metropolitan Area." *Global Networks* 6 (2006): 181–99.

Bernal, Victoria. "Diaspora, Cyberspace and Political Imagination: The Eritrean Diaspora Online." *Global Networks* 6, no. 2 (2006): 161–79.

Bernard, H. Russell. *Research Methods in Anthropology: Qualitative and Quantitative Approaches*. 3rd ed. Walnut Creek, CA: AltaMira, 2002.

Berry, J. W. "Acculturation: Living Successfully in Two Cultures." *International Journal of Intercultural Relations* 29 (2005): 697–712.

———. "Immigration, Acculturation, and Adaptation." *Applied Psychology* 46 (1997): 5–34.

———. "A Psychology of Immigration." *Journal of Social Issues* 57 (2001): 615–31.

———. Y. H. Poortinga, M. H. Segall, and P. R. Dasen. *Cross-cultural Psychology: Research and Applications*. Cambridge: Cambridge University Press, 2002.

Bethlehem Bible College. "Tour Guide Program." http://www.bethbc.org/academics/tourism. (accessed March 3, 2014).

Blow, Steve. "Migrant Policy is a Puzzler." *Dallas Morning News*, July 16, 2005.

Bourhis, R. Y., L. C. Moise, S. Perreault, and S. Senecal. "Towards an Interactive Acculturation Model: A Social Psychological Approach." *International Journal of Psychology* 32 (1997): 369–86.

Bourhis, R. Y., E. Montaruli, S. El-Geledi, S. P. Harvey, and G. Barrette. "Acculturation in Multiple Host Community Settings." *Journal of Social Issues* 66 (2010): 780–802.

Boyd, Dana, and Nicole Ellison. "Social Network Sites: Definition, History, and Scholarship." *Journal of Computer Mediated Communication* 13, no. 1 (2007): 210–30.

Braverman, Mark. *The Fatal Embrace: Christians, Jews, and the Search for Peace in the Holy Land*. New York: Beaufort Books, 2010.

Brinkerhoff, Jennifer M. *Digital Diasporas: Identity and Transnational Engagement*. New York: Cambridge University Press, 2009.

Brown, Francis, S. R. Driver, and Charles A. Briggs. *A Hebrew and English Lexicon of the Old Testament*. Oxford: Clarendon (1970): 853

Brown, Rick. "Biblical Muslims." *International Journal of Frontier Missions* 24, no. 2 (Summer 2007): 65–74.

Bruce, F. F. *The Acts of the Apostles: The Greek Text with Introduction and Commentary*. Grand Rapids: Eerdmans (1990): 181.

Brummell, Paul. *Turkmenistan: The Bradt Travel Guide*. Guilford, CT: Globe Pequot, 2005.

Bush, Andrew F. "The Implications of Christian Zionism for Mission." *International Bulletin of Missionary Research* 33, no. 3 (July 2009): 144–50.

———. *Learning from the Least: Reflections on a Journey in Mission with Palestinian Christians*. Eugene, OR: Cascade Books, 2013.

Bustamant, Javier. "Tidelike Diasporas in Brazil: From Slavery to Orkut." *Diasporas in the New Media Age: Identity, Politics, and Community*, edited by Adoni Alonso and Pedro J. Oiarzabal (2010): 170–89.

Caldwell, Larry W. "Reconsidering Our Biblical Roots: Bible Interpretation, the Apostle Paul and Mission Today," parts 1 and 2. *International Journal of Frontier Missiology* 29, no. 2 (April–June 2012): 91–100; vol. 29, no. 3 (July–September 2012): 113–21.

Campbell, William S. *Paul and the Creation of Christian Identity*. London: T & T Clark, 2008.

Camilleri, C., and H. Malewska-Peyre. "Socialization and Identity strategies." *Handbook of Cross-cultural Psychology*. Vol. 2, *Basic Processes and Human Development*, edited by J. W. Berry, P. R. Dasen, and T. S. Saraswathi (1997): 41–67.

Carroll R., M. Daniel. *Christians at the Border: Immigration, the Church and the Bible*. 2008. Reprint, Grand Rapids: Brazos, 2012.

———. *Thinking Christianly about Immigration*. Denver: Vernon Grounds Institute of Public Ethics, 2011.

Chacour, Elias. *Blood Brothers: The Dramatic Story of a Palestinian Christian Working for Peace in Israel*. Grand Rapids: Chosen Books, 1984.

———. "What Things Make for Peace?" (lecture, Eastern University, Saint David's, PA, December 3, 2013).

Chan, Kim-Kong. "Missiological Implications of Chinese Christians in Diaspora." Wan, *Diaspora Missiology* (2011): 179–95.

Checa, Francisco, and A. Arjona. *Las Migraciones a Debate: De las Teorias a las Practicas Sociales* [The Debate about Migration: From Theories to Social Practice]. Barcelona: Institut Catala d'Anthropologia-Icaria, 2002.

Clayman, Chris, and Meredith Lee. *ethNYcity: The Nations, Tongues, and Faiths of Metropolitan New York*. New York: Metro New York Baptist Association and Baptist State Convention of North Carolina, 2010.

Cooke, Miriam, and Bruce B. Lawrence. *Muslim Networks: From Hajj to Hip Hop*. Chapel Hill: University of North Carolina Press, 2005.

Cooper, Rod. "People Just Like Me: Does the Bible Give Us Freedom to Build Deliberately Homogeneous Churches?" *Building Unity in the Church of the New Millennium*, edited by Dwight Perry (2002): 156.

Cueva, Samuel. "Mission, Missionaries and the Evangelization of Europe." *Evangelical Review of Theology* 34, no. 4 (October 2010): 9. http://www.back2europe.org/getattachment/7af255e3-a83b-4e38-8098-c2ba12978547/Resource-2.aspx (accessed April 4, 2014).

Danker, Frederick William, ed. *A Greek-English Lexicon of the New Testament and Other Early Christian Literature*. Chicago: University of Chicago Press, 2000. Accordance electronic edition.

Davey, Andrew. *Urban Christianity and Global Order: Theological Resources for an Urban Future*. Peabody, MA: Hendrickson, 2002.

Denny, Frederick Mathewson. *An Introduction to Islam*. 2nd ed. New York: Macmillan, 1994.

DeYmaz, Mark and Harry Li. *Ethnic Blends: Mixing Diversity into Your Local Church*. Grand Rapids: Zondervan, 2010, 100–11.

DeYoung, Curtiss Paul, Michael O. Emerson, George Yancey, and Karen Chai Kim. *United by Faith: The Multiracial Congregation as the Answer to the Problem of Race*. Oxford: Oxford University Press, 2003.

Dimangondayao, Lorajoy. "To All People: Samples of Diaspora Filipinos Making a Kingdom Impact." Pantoja, Tira, and Wan, *Scattered*.

Dodd, C. H. *The Apostolic Preaching and Its Developments: Three Lectures*. 3rd ed. London: Hodder & Stoughton, 1963.

Dunch, Ryan. "Beyond Cultural Imperialism: Cultural Theory, Christian Missions, and Global Modernity." *History and Theory*, 41, no.3 (October 2002):301–25.

Dunn, James D. G. *Baptism in the Holy Spirit: A Re-examination of the New Testament Teaching on the Gift of the Spirit in Relation to Pentecostalism Today*. 2nd ed. London: SCM, 2010.

———. *The Theology of Paul the Apostle*. Grand Rapids: Eerdmans, 1998. Kindle edition.

Edu-Bekoe, Yaw Attah and Enoch Wan. *Scattered Africans Keep Coming* OR: Institute of Diaspora Studies, 2013.

Embassy of Turkmenistan, "Turkmenistan at a Glance." http://turkmenistanembassy.org/turkmenistan-at-a-glance/ (accessed March 26, 2014).

Ethnic America Network. "About the Network." http://ethnicamerica.com/about/ (accessed February 20, 2014).

Evangelical Immigration Table. "I Was a Stranger." http://evangelicalimmigrationtable. com/iwasastranger; Religious News Service, "One More Time, Evangelicals Head to Hill in Immigration Reform," April 29, 2014.

Evans, Craig A., and Stanley E. Porter. *Dictionary of New Testament Background*. Downers Grove, IL: InterVarsity Press, 2000. Accordance electronic edition, version 1.2.

Farzaneh, Sam, and Bill McKenna. "Little Ethiopia." BBC News. June 12, 2013. http://www.bbc.co.uk/news/magazine-22803973 (accessed March 27, 2014).

Fatehi, Merhdad. *The Spirit's Relation to the Risen Lord in Paul: An Examination of Its Christological Implications*. Vol. 28. WUNT 2. Tübingen, Germany: Mohr Siebeck, 2000.

Fee, Gordon D. *God's Empowering Presence: The Holy Spirit in the Letters of Paul*. Peabody, MA: Hendrickson, 1994.

Foltz, Richard. *Religions of the Silk Road: Overland Trade and Cultural Exchange from Antiquity to the Fifteenth Century*. New York: St. Martin's Press, 1999.

Foundation for Middle East Peace. "Comprehensive Settlement Population 1972–2010.http://www.fmep.org/settlement_info/settlement-info-and-tables/stats-data/comprehensive-settlement-population-1972-2006 (accessed February 1, 2014).

Friedman, Thomas L. *The World Is Flat*. New York: Farrar, Straus & Giroux, 2005.

Gill, Brad ed. "ISFM 2013: Dancing with Diaspora" *International Journal of Frontier Missiology* 30, no. 3 (July–September 2013): 95–131.

Graham, Mark, and Shahram Khosravi. "Reordering Public and Private in Iranian Cyberspace: Identity, Politics, and Mobilization." *Identities: Global Studies in Culture and Power* 9, no. 2 (2002): 219–46.

Gramada, Costel. "Festivitate la Seminarul Biblic 'Emmanuel' din Arganda del Rey, Spania." *Cuvântul Adevărului* (January 2006).

Graves, T. D. "Psychological Acculturation in a Tri-ethnic Community." *Southwestern Journal of Anthropology* 23 (1967): 337–50.

Green, Michael. *Evangelism in the Early Church*. Grand Rapids: Eerdmans, 2004. Kindle edition.

Greeson, Kevin. *Camel Tracks: Discover the Camel's Secret*. Bangalore: WIGTake Resources, n.d.

Grunlan, Stephen A., and Marvin K. Mayers. *Cultural Anthropology: A Christian Perspective*. 2nd ed. Grand Rapids: Zondervan, 1988.

Hanciles, Jehu J. *Beyond Christendom: Globalization, African Migration, and the Transformation of the West*. Maryknoll, NY: Orbis Books, 2008.

Haney, Jim. "Church Planting Progress Indicators." Unpublished report, IMB Global Research Department, 2014.

———. "CPPI 2014." Unpublished report, IMB Global Research Department, 2014.

———. "Muslim Unreached People Groups." Unpublished Vision 5:9 report, International Mission Board, 2014.

Harris, C. C. *Kinship*. Minneapolis: University of Minnesota Press, 1990.

Hausfeld, Mark. *Islam in America: Understanding and Engaging Diaspora Muslims through the Local Church*. Springfield, MO: Assemblies of God Theological Seminary, 2009.

Hengel, Martin. *Between Jesus and Paul: Studies in the Earliest History of Christianity*. London: SCM, 1983.

———. *The Four Gospels and the One Gospel of Jesus Christ: An Investigation of the Collection and Origin of the Canonical Gospels*. Harrisburg, PA: Trinity Press International, 2000.

Hiebert, Paul G. *Cultural Anthropology*. 2nd ed. Grand Rapids: Baker Book House, 1983.

———. *Transforming Worldviews: An Anthropological Understanding of How People Change*. Grand Rapids: Baker Academic, 2008. Kindle edition.

Higgins, Kevin. "Identity, Integrity and Insider Movements: A Brief Paper Inspired by Timothy Tennent's Critique of C-5 Thinking." *International Journal of Frontier Missions* 23, no. 3 (Fall 2006): 117–23.

Hofstede, G., G. J. Hofstede, and M. Minkov. *Cultures and Organizations: Software of the Mind*. 3rd ed. New York: McGraw-Hill, 2010.

Hogg, M. A. "Social Identity Theory." *Contemporary Social Psychological Theories*, edited by P. J. Burke (2006): 111–36.

———. "A Social Identity Theory of Leadership." *Personality and Social Psychology Review* 5 (2001): 184–200.

———. and D. I. Terry. "Social Identity and Self-categorization Processes in Organizational Contexts." *Academy of Management Review* 25 (2000): 121–40.

Human Rights Watch, "I Already Bought You." www.hrw.org/zh-hans/node/129797/section/5 (accessed May 21, 2015).

Human Rights Watch, "Turkmenistan." http://www.hrw.org/world-report/2013/country-chapters/turkmenistan?page=1 (accessed March 26, 2014).

Humes, Karen R. "Overview of Race and Hispanic Origin: 2010." Census Briefs. http://www.census.gov/prod/cen2010/briefs/c2010br-02.pdf.

Hurtado, Larry W. *How on Earth Did Jesus Become a God?: Historical Questions about Earliest Devotion to Jesus*. Grand Rapids: Eerdmans, 2005. Kindle edition.

Hutchens, James M. "Evangelicals Supporting a Palestinian State?" Special Guests, http://special-guests.com/guests/viewnews.cgi?id=EElVZlpEppBvfZXYMc&style=Full+Article (accessed February 7, 2014).

Ilie, Cristina. "Criminality among Romanian Emigrants in Spain." *International Journal of Academic Research in Business and Social Sciences* 4, no. 3 (March 2014): 509–17. http://hrmars.com/hrmars_papers/Criminality_among_Romanian_Emigrants_in_Spain.pdf (accessed April 3, 2014).

Institute for War and Peace Reporting, "Rising Emigration from Turkmenistan." October 8, 2012, http://iwpr.net/report-news/rising-emigration-turkmenistan (accessed March 26, 2014).

Institute of International Education. "International Academic Exchange between the United States and the Middle East on the Rise." December 7, 2010. http://www.iie.org/en/Who-We-Are/News-and-Events/Press-Center/Press-Releases/2010/2010-12-07-Open-Doors-Middle-East-US-EducationalExchange (accessed July 18, 2013).

———. "International Education Matters," *Open Doors* 2005 Report, www.udel.edu/iepmedia/economy_opendoors05.html (accessed December 1, 2006).

The Internal Displacement Monitoring Centre, Geneva. UNHCR, "Internally Displaced People Figures," http://www.unhcr.org/pages/49c3646c23.html (accessed June 5, 2014).

———. "International Labour Migration and Development: The ILO Perspective," 2006, http://www.ilo.org (accessed December 5, 2006).

———. "International Labour Organization (ILO) and the 2013 High Level Dialogue on International Migration and Development," p. 3, http://www.un.org/esa/population/meetings/eleventhcoord2013/ILO_Paper_UN_11th_CM_on_Migration_2013_15022013.pdf (accessed June 5, 2014).

Issa-Salwe, Abdisalam M. "The Internet and the Somali Diaspora: The Web as a Means of Expression." *Bildhaan: An International Journal of Somali Studies* 6, no. 8 (2008): 54–67.

Jan, Muhammad Ayub. "Current Unrest and the Ensuing Debates about Identity among the Pakhtuns in Cultural and Virtual Spaces." In *Proceedings of the International Conference of the Department of Political Science: Dynamic of Change in Conflict Societies; Pakhtun Region in Perspective*, 120–47. Peshawar, Pakistan: Peshawar University, 2011.

Jenkins, Philip. *The Lost History of Christianity: The Thousand-year Golden Age of the Church in the Middle East, Africa, and Asia and How It Died*. New York: HarperOne, 2008. Kindle edition.

———. *The Next Christendom*. New York: Oxford University Press, 2002. Johnson, Luke Timothy. *Religious Experience in Earliest Christianity: A Missing Dimension in New Testament Studies*. Minneapolis: Fortress, 1998. Kindle edition.

Johnstone, Patrick. *Future of the Global Church*. Colorado Springs: Biblica, 2011.

———. Robyn Johnstone, and Jason Mandryk, eds. *Operation World*, 21st Century ed. Carlisle, UK: Paternoster Lifestyle, 2001.

———. and Jason Mandryk, eds. *Operation World*. Milton Keynes, UK: Authentic Media, 2001.

Katanacho, Yohanna. "Christ Is the Owner of Haaretz." *Christian Scholar's Review* 34, no. 4 (Summer 2005).

———. "Palestinian Protestant Theological Responses to a World Marked by Violence." *Missiology* 36, no. 3 (July 2008): 289–306.

Keener, Craig S. *Acts: An Exegetical Commentary*. Vol. 1, *Introduction and 1:1–2:47*. Grand Rapids: Baker Academic, 2012. Kindle edition.

Khoury, Rafiq. "Living Together: The Experience of Muslim-Christian Relations in the Arab World in General and in Palestine in Particular." In *The Forgotten Faithful; A Window into the Life and Witness of Christians in the Holy Land*, edited by Naim Ateek, Cedar Duaybis, and Maurine Tobin. Jerusalem: Sabeel Ecumenical Liberation Theology Center, 2007.

Kim, S. Hun, and Wonsuk Ma, eds. *Korean Diaspora and Christian Mission*. Oxford: Regnum Books International, 2011.

King, Martin Luther, Jr. *A Knock at Midnight*. Edited by Clayborne Carson and Peter Holloran. New York: Warner Books, 1998.

Kingsway International Christian Centre. "The KICC Vision." http://www.kicc.org.uk/Church/Vision/tabid/45/Default.aspx (accessed April 3, 2014).

Kisskalt, Michael. "Cross-cultural Learning: Issues of the Second Generation of Immigrant Churches." *Ethnic Churches in Europe: A Baptist Response*, ed. Peter F. Penner Prague: International Baptist Theological Seminary (2006): 120.

———. "Immigrant Churches in the German Baptist Union." *Ethnic Churches in Europe: A Baptist Response*, edited by Peter F. Penner (2006): 188–91.

Koehler, Ludwig, and Walter Baumgartner. *Lexicon in Veteris Testamenti Libros*. Grand Rapids: Eerdmans (1953): 2:804

Kotter, John P. *Leading Change*. Boston: Harvard Business School Press (1996):10.

Kraft, Charles. "Dynamic Equivalence Churches in Muslim Society." *The Gospel and Islam: A 1978 Compendium*, edited by Don McCurry (1979): 114–24.

Lausanne Committee for World Evangelization. "The New People Next Door." Lausanne Occasional Paper 55. Pattaya, Thailand: Lausanne Committee for World Evangelization, 2004. http://www.lausanne.org/docs/2004forum/LOP55_IG26.pdf (accessed April 4, 2014).

———. *Scattered to Gather: Embracing the Global Trend of Diaspora*. Manila: LifeChange, 2010. http://www.jdpayne.org/wp-content/uploads/2010/10/Scattered-to-Gather.pdf.

Leary, M. R. "Responses to Social Exclusion: Social Anxiety, Jealousy, Loneliness, Depression, and Low Self-esteem." *Journal of Social and Clinical Psychology* 9 (1990): 221–29.

Lee, Samuel. *Blessed Migrants: God's Strategy for Global Revival*. Bloomington, IN: iUniverse, 2008.

Lerner, Michael. *Embracing Israel/Palestine: A Strategy to Heal and Transform the Middle East*. Berkeley, CA: North Atlantic Books, 2012.

Lewin, K. *Resolving Social Conflicts*. New York: Harper & Row, 1948.

Lewis, Donald M. ed., *Christianity Reborn: The Global Expansion of Evangelicalism in the Twentieth Century* Eerdmans, 2004.

Lewis, Rebecca. "Insider Movements: Honoring God-given Identity and Community." *International Journal of Frontier Missions* 26, no. 1 (Spring 2009): 16–19.

———. "Promoting Movements to Christ within Natural Communities." *International Journal of Frontier Missions* 24, no. 2 (Summer 2007): 75–76.

Lima, Fernando. "Transnational Families: Institutions of Transnational Social Space." *New Transnational Social Spaces: International Migration and Transnational Companies in the Early Twenty-first Century*, edited by Ludger Pries (2001): 77–93.

Lopez, Hugo. Pew Research Center Hispanic Projects. http://www.cnn.com/2013/09/24/us/undocumented-immigrants-population/ (accessed May 19, 2014).

Lopez, Robert F. K. "The Philippine Missions Association (PMA) Tentmaking Agenda: Raising an Army of Outstanding Filipino Witnesses." *Scattered*, 197–208.

Lorance, Cody C. "Reflections of a Church Planter among Diaspora Groups in Metro-Chicago: Pursuing Cruciformity in Diaspora Missions." Wan, *Diaspora Missiology* (2011): 261–85.

Loukili, Amina. "Moroccan Diaspora, Internet and National Imagination: Building a Community Online through the Internet Portal Yabiladi." Paper presented at Nordic Africa Days, Nordic Africa Institute, Uppsala, Sweden, October 5–7, 2007.

Ludwig, F., and J. K. Asamoah-Gyadu. *African Christian Presence in the West: New Immigrant Congregations and Transnational Networks in North America and Europe*. Trenton, NJ: Africa World Press, 2011.

Lund, Hans. "Migrant Churches in Europe." Presentation at the Diaspora Consultation, Amsterdam, September 24–25, 2013.

Luter, A. B., Jr. "Gospel." *Dictionary of Paul and His Letters*, edited by Gerald F. Hawthorne, Ralph P. Martin, and Daniel G. Ried, Kindle locations 4623–52. Downers Grove, IL: InterVarsity Press, 1993. Accordance electronic edition.

Mahapatra, Lisa. "The 25 Most Miserable Places in the World." *Business Insider*, February 22, 2013, http://www.businessinsider.com/most-miserable-countries-in-the-world-2013-2?op=1 (accessed March 26, 2014).

Mandryk, Jason, ed. *Operation World*. 7th ed. Downers Grove, IL: InterVarsity Press, 2010.

Manzano, Jojo, and Joy C. Solina, eds. *Worker to Witness: Becoming an OFW Tentmaker*. Makati City, Philippines: Church Strengthening Ministry, 2007.

Martin, Jimmy. "International and Multiethnic Churches." *Ethnic Churches in Europe: A Baptist Response*, edited by Peter F. Penner. Prague: International Baptist Theological Seminary (2006).

Martin, Philip, Manolo Abella, and Christine Kuptsch. *Managing Labor Migration in the 21st Century*. New Haven, CT: Yale University Press, 2006.

Massey, Joshua. "God's Amazing Diversity in Drawing Muslims to Christ." *International Journal of Frontier Missions* 17, no. 1 (Spring 2000): 5–14.

McGavran, Donald. *The Bridges of God*. Rev. ed. New York: Friendship Press (1981).

———.*Understanding Church Growth*. Grand Rapids: Eerdmans (1970): 230.

———. *Ethnic Realities and the Church: Lessons from India*. Pasadena: William Carey Library, 1979.

McIntosh, G., and A. McMahan. *Being the Church in a Multi-ethnic Community: Why It Matters and How It Works*. Indianapolis: Wesleyan Publishing House, 2012.

McKnight, Scot. *The King Jesus Gospel: The Original Good News Revisited*. Grand Rapids: Zondervan, 2011. Kindle edition.

Missio Nexus. "Mission Leaders Conference." http://www.missionexus.org/mission-leaders-conference/ (accessed March 8, 2014).

Moore, Natallia."Turkmenistan Domestic Developments," Eurasianet.org, August 2, 2012, http://www.eurasianet.org/node/65742 (accessed March 26, 2014).

Mouw, Richard. *When the Kings Come Marching In*. Grand Rapids: Eerdmans, 1983.

Munayer, Salim J. "Relations between Religions in Historic Palestine and the Future Prospects: Christians and Jews." *Christians in the Holy Land*, ed. Michael Prior and William Taylor. London: World of Islam Festival Trust (1994): 149

Murthy, Dhiraj. "Digital Ethnography: An Examination of the Use of New Technologies for Social Research." *Sociology* 42, no. 5 (2008): 837–55.

Nasser, Haya El. "U.S. Hispanic Population to Triple by 2050."*USA Today*, February 12, 2008). http://www.usatoday.com/news/nation/2008-02-11-population-study_N.htm#11.

Nur-Muhammad, Rizwangul, Giles Dodson, Evangelia Papoutsaki, and Heather Horst. "Uyghur Facebook Use and Diasporic Identity Construction." IAMCR 2013 Conference, Dublin, June 25–29, 2013.

Obama, Barack. "Remarks by the President on a New Beginning." Speech presented at Cairo University, Cairo, Egypt, June 4, 2009. http://www.whitehouse.gov/the_press_office/Remarks-by-the-President-at-Cairo-University-6-04-09/ (accessed December 1, 2013).

OC International, and Misiunea Mondială Unită. *God's Heart for Romania*. Bucharest, Romania: OC International and Misiunea Mondială Unită, 2001. http://ocresearch.info/sites/default/files/Romania%20National%20Church%20Census%20Report%202001.pdf.

Olofinjana, Israel. *Reverse in Ministry and Missions: Africans in the Dark Continent of Europe*. Central Milton Keynes, UK: AuthorHouse, 2010.

———. ed. *Turning the Tables on Mission*. Watford, UK: Instant Apostle, 2013.

Operation World. "Ethiopia." http://www.operationworld.org/country/ethi/owtext.html (accessed December 16, 2014).

Organisation for Economic Co-operation and Development, "Migration and the Brain Drain Phenomenon," http://www.oecd.org/social/poverty/migrationandthebraindrainphenomenon.htm (accessed June 5, 2014).

Ott, Craig. "Diaspora and Relocation as Divine Impetus for Witness in the Early Church." Wan, *Diaspora Missiology* (2011): 73–94.

———. and Gene Wilson. *Global Church Planting: Biblical Principles and Best Practices for Multiplication*. Grand Rapids: Baker Academic, 2011, 46.

Padilla, A. M., and W. Perez. "Acculturation, Social Identity, and Social Cognition: A New Perspective." *Hispanic Journal of Behavioral Sciences* 25 (2003): 35–55.

Palestinian National Authority. Central Bureau of Statistics. June 2013.

Pantoja, Luis, Jr., Sadiri Joy Tira, and Enoch Wan, eds. *Scattered: The Filipino Global Presence*. Manila: LifeChange, 2004.

Parfit, Michael. "Human Migration." *National Geographic*, October 1998.

Park, Chan-Sik ed. *21C New Nomad Era and Migrant Mission*. Seoul: Christianity and Industrial Society Research Institute, 2010.

Payne, J. D. *Strangers Next Door: Immigration, Migration and Mission*. Downers Grove, IL: InterVarsity Press, 2012.

Pennington, Jonathan T. *Reading the Gospels Wisely: A Narrative and Theological Introduction* Grand Rapids: Baker Academic, 2012, 34.

Pérez-Latre, Francisco Javier, Ioia Portilla, and Cristina Sanchez-Blanco. "Social Networks, Media and Audiences: A Literature Review." *Comunicación y Sociedad* 24, no. 1 (2011): 63–74.

Persons, S. *Ethnic Studies at Chicago, 1905–45*. Urbana: University of Illinois Press, 1987.

Pew Research Center, "Catholics, Other Christians Support Immigration Reform, But Say Faith Plays Small Role." April 1, 2014. http://www.pewresearch.org/fact-tank/2014/04/01/catholics-other-christians-support-immigration-reform-but-say-faith-plays-small-role/.

———. "Faith on the Move: The Religious Affiliation of International Migrants." March 8, 2012. http://www.pewforum.org/2012/03/08/religious-migration-exec/.

———. "The Global Religious Landscape." December 18, 2012. http://www.pewforum.org/global-religious-landscape-christians.aspx.

———. *Muslim Americans: Middle Class and Mostly Mainstream*. Washington, DC: Pew Research Center, 2007.

———. "Muslim Americans: No Signs of Growth in Alienation or Support for Extremism." August 30, 2011. http://www.pewforum.org/2011/08/30/muslim-americans-no-signs-of-growth-in-alienation-or-support-for-extremism/.

Phinney, J. S. "Ethnic Identity in Adolescents and Adults: Review of Research." *Psychological Bulletin* 108 (1990): 499–514.

Pocock, Michael. "Christian Perspectives on Immigration." Presentation at University Christian Church, Austin, TX, April 22, 2007. Available from author.

———. "Good Migrations!" *Kindred Spirit*. Spring/Summer 2010, Dallas Theological Seminary.

———, and Joseph Henriques. *Cultural Change and Your Church*. Grand Rapids: Baker Books, 2002.

———, Gailyn Van Rheenen, and Doug McConnell. *The Changing Face of World Missions*. Grand Rapids: Baker Academic, 2005.

Porter, W.J. "Creeds and Hymns," in *Dictionary of New Testament Background*, ed. Craig A. Evans and Stanley E. Porter (Downers Grove, IL: InterVarsity Press, 2000), Accordance electronic ed., version 1.2.

Portes, Alejandro, Luis Guarnizo, and Patricia Landolt. "The Study of Transnationalism: Pitfalls and Promise of an Emergent Research Field." *Ethnic and Racial Studies* 22, no. 2 (1999): 217–37.

Pritchard, James B. ed. *Ancient Near Eastern Texts Relating to the Old Testament*, 3rd ed. Princeton: Princeton University Press (1969): 93.

Rah, Soong-Chan. *The Next Evangelicalism*. Downers Grove, IL: InterVarsity Press, 2009.

Raheb, Mitri. "Sailing through Troubled Waters: Palestinian Christians in the Holy Land," *Dialogue: A Journal of Theology* 41, no. 2 (2002).

———. "The Spiritual Significance and Experience of the Churches: The Lutheran Perspective." *Christians in the Holy Land*, ed. Michael Prior and William Taylor (1995).

Randeree, Kasim. "Workforce Nationalization in the Gulf Cooperation Council States," Center for International and Regional Studies, Georgetown University School of Foreign Service in Qatar, Occasional Paper 9, http://www12.georgetown.edu/sfs/qatar/cirs/KasimRandereeCIRSOccasionalPaper9.pdf, 2–3.

Rankin, Jerry. *Impact Your World*. Richmond, VA: International Mission Board, 2005.

Rantisi, Audeh G. *Blessed Are the Peacemakers: A Palestinian Christian in the Occupied West Bank*. Grand Rapids: Zondervan, 1990.

Redfield, R., R. Linton, and M. J. Herskovits. "Memorandum for the Study of Acculturation." *American Anthropologist* 38 (1936): 149–52.

Rhys-Williams, Stefan. "Educating Nomads: Ethiopia's Afar and the Fight for Learning," Institute of Opinion, http://www.instituteofopinion.com/2013/11/educating-nomads-ethiopias-afar-and-the-fight-for-learning/; *Wikipedia*, s.v. "Mongolia," http://en.wikipedia.org/wiki/Mongolia (accessed June 5, 2014).

Robbins, Joel. "The Globalization of Pentecostal and Charismatic Christianity." *Annual Review of Anthropology* 33 (2004): 117–43.

Ross, Alan P. *Creation and Blessing: A Guide to the Study and Exposition of Genesis*. Grand Rapids: Baker, 1988.

Ryder, A. G., L. E. Alden, and D. L. Paulhus. "Is Acculturation Unidimensional or Bidimensional? A Head-to-head Comparison in the Prediction of Personality, Self-identity, and Adjustment." *Journal of Personality and Social Psychology* 79 (2000): 49–65.

Sabella, Bernard. "Socio-economic Characteristics and Challenges to Palestinian Christians in the Holy Land." *Palestinian Christians: Religion, Politics and Society in the Holy Land*, edited by Anthony O'Mahoney. London: Melisende (1999).

Schnabel, Eckard J. *Early Christian Mission: Paul and the Early Church*. Downers Grove, IL: InterVarsity Press (2004): 923–27.

Schermerhorn, R. A. *Comparative Ethnic Relations: A Framework for Theory and Research*. Chicago: University of Chicago Press, 1978.

Schiller, Nina. Linda Basch, and Cristina Blanc-Szanton, "From Immigrant to Transmigrant: Theorizing Transnational Migration," *Anthropological Quarterly* 68, no. 1 (1995): 48–63.

Severson, Lucky. "Interview with Michael Emerson." *Religion and Ethics Newsweekly* (December 19, 2008), http://www.pbs.org/wnet/religion and ethics/episodes/december-19-2008/interview-with-michael-emerson/1736/.

Shiraev, E., and D. Levy. *Cross-cultural Psychology*. 4th ed. Boston: Pearson Education, 2009.

Snodgrass, Klyne R. "Introduction to a Hermeneutics of Identity;" "Jesus and Identity;" "Paul's Focus on Identity;" "Pauline Perspectives on the Identity of a Pastor. In *Bibliotheca Sacra*. 3–19; 131–45; 259-73; 387-401. 2011.

Socialbakers, "Top 10 Fastest Growing Facebook Languages," http://www.socialbakers.com/blog/1064-top-10-fastest-growing-facebook-languages (accessed March 14, 2014).

Sökefeld, Martin. "Alevism Online: Re-imagining a Community in Virtual Space." *Diaspora: A Journal of Transnational Studies* 11, no. 1 (2002): 5–38.

Song, Minho. "The Diaspora Experience of the Korean Church and Its Implications for World Missions." *Korean Diaspora and Christian Mission*, edited by S. Hun Kim and Wonsuk Ma, 117–28. Eugene, OR: Wipf & Stock (2011).

Spencer, S. ed. *Mission and Migration*. Calver, UK: Cliff College Publishing, 2008.

Stark, Rodney. *The Rise of Christianity: How the Obscure, Marginal Jesus Movement Became the Dominant Religious Force in the Western World in a Few Centuries*. San Francisco: Harper, 1997.

Steele, C. M. "The Psychology of Self-affirmation: Sustaining the Integrity of the Self." *Advances in Experimental Social Psychology*, vol. 21, edited by L. Berkowitz, 261–302. San Diego: Academic Press (1988).

Stevens, David. *God's New Humanity: A Biblical Theology of Multiethnicity for the Church*. Eugene, OR: Wipf & Stock, 2012.

Sturge, Mark. *Look What the Lord Has Done: An Exploration of Black Christian Faith in Britain*. Queensway, England: Scripture Union, 2005.

Suinn, R. M., K. Rickard-Figueroa, S. Lew, and P. Vigil."The Suinn-Lew Asian Self-identity Acculturation Scale: An Initial Report." *Educational and Psychological Measurement* 47 (1987): 401–7.

Tajfel, H., and C. J. Turner. "The Social Identity Theory of Intergroup Behavior." *Psychology of Intergroup Relations*, 2nd ed., edited by S. Worchel and W. G. Austin, 7–24. Chicago: Nelson-Hall (1986).

Tellbe, Mikael. *Christ-believers in Ephesus: A Textual Analysis of Early Christian Identity Formation in a Local Perspective*. Tübingen, Germany: Mohr-Siebeck, 2009.

Ter Har, Gerrie. *Halfway to Paradise: African Christians in Europe*. Cardiff, UK: Cardiff Academic Press, 1998.

Terrazas, Aaron Matteo. "Beyond Regional Circularity: The Emergence of an Ethiopian Diaspora." Migration Information Source. June 1, 2007. http://www.migrationinformation.org/profiles/display.cfm?ID=604 (accessed March 27, 2014). "Thousands Adrift without a Country," *Dallas Morning News*, May 15, 2015, 12A.

Tira,Sidiri, ed. *The Human Tidal Wave*. Manila: LifeChange, 2014.

Tira, Sidiri and Narry F. Santos."Diaspora Church Planting in a Multicultural City: A Case Study of Greenhills Christian Fellowship." *Reflecting God's Glory Together: Diversity in Evangelical Mission*. Ed. A. Scott Moreau and Beth Snodderly, EMS 17 Pasadena: William Carey Library, 2011, 63–90.

Toameh, Khaled Abu. "Nomadic Pastoralists Meet in Addis Ababa." Gatestone Institute, December 28, 2006. http://afrol.com/articles/15594 (accessed December 29, 2006).

Travis, John. "The C1 to C6 Spectrum: A Practical Tool for Defining Six Types of 'Christ-centered Communities' ('C') Found in the Muslim Context." *Evangelical Missions Quarterly* 34, no. 4 (October 1998): 407–8.

———. "Messianic Muslim Followers of Isa: A Closer Look at C5 Believers and Congregations." *International Journal of Frontier Missions* 17, no. 1 (Spring 2000): 53–59.

Tynes, Robert. "Nation-building and the Diaspora on Leonenet: A Case of Sierra Leone in Cyberspace," *New Media and Society* 9, no. 3 (2007): 497–518.

Udall, Jessica A. "Preparing Ethiopians for Cross-cultural Ministry: Maximizing Missionary Training for Great Commission Impact." MA thesis, Columbia International University, 2013.

UNESCO Institute for Statistics, "Global Flow of Tertiary-level Students." http://www.uis.unesco.org/Education/Pages/international-student-flow-viz.aspx (accessed June 5, 2014).

UNHCR. "Convention and Protocol Relating to the Status of Refugees." http://www.unhcr.org/protect/PROTECTION/3b66c2aa10.pdf (accessed December 6, 2006).

———. "UNHCR Statistical Online Population Database." 2012, http://popstats.unhcr.or/PSQ_POC.aspx (accessed June 5, 2014).

UN International Migration and Development, "International Migration Facts and Figures." 2006, http://www.unmigration.org.

United Nations Development Agenda. "Integrating Migration in the Post-2015 UN Development Agenda Position Paper." October 2013. http://www.ilo.org/wcmsp5/groups/public/---ed_protect/---protrav/---migrant/documents/genericdocument/wcms_242561.pdf (accessed June 5, 2014).

United Nations Department of Economic and Social Affairs and the Organisation for Economic Co-operation and Development, "World Migration in Figures," October 3–4, 2013, http://www.un.org/en/development/desa/population/

publications/pdf/migration/migration/World_Migration_Figures_UNDESA_OECD.pdf (accessed May 20, 2014).

Urga, Abeneazer Gezahegn. *Prayer and Evangelism: Inseparable Elements in Furthering the Gospel*. Addis Ababa: Andnet Printers, 2013.

U.S. Census Bureau. "Nation's Foreign-born Population Nears 37 Million." http://www.census.gov/newsroom/releases/archives/foreignborn_population/cb10-159.html.

———. "Place of Birth for the Foreign-born Population in the United States." http://factfinder.census.gov/faces/tableservices/jsf/pages/productview.xhtml?pid=ACS_11_5YR_B05006&prodType=table (accessed December 16, 2014).

U.S. Department of Energy, "Turkmenistan." Updated July 2014, http://www.eia.gov/countries/ beta/international/country.cfm?iso=TKM.

Van den Bos, Matthijs, and Liza Nell. "Territorial Bounds to Virtual Space: Transnational Online and Offline Networks of Iranian and Turkish-Kurdish Immigrants in the Netherlands." *Global Networks* 6, no. 2 (2006): 201–20.

van der Veer, Peter. *Conversion to Modernities: The Globalization of Christianity*. Psychology Press, 1996.

Van Dusen, Allison. "U.S. Hospitals Worth the Trip." *Forbes*, May 29, 2008. http://www.forbes.com/2008/05/25/health-hospitals-care-forbeslifecx_avd_outsourcing08_0529healthoutsourcing.html (accessed July 18, 2013).

Van Hear, Nicolas. *New Diasporas: The Mass Exodus, Dispersal and Regrouping of Migrant Communities*. Seattle: University of Washington Press, 1998): 2.

Wagner, C. Peter. *Your Spiritual Gifts Can Help Your Church Grow*. Ventura, CA: Regal Books, 1980.

Währisch-Oblau, Claudia. *The Missionary Self-perception of Pentecostal/Charismatic Church Leaders from the Global South in Europe: Bringing Back the Gospel*. Leiden, The Netherlands: Brill, 2009.

Walls, A. F. "Mission and Migration: The Diaspora Factor in Christian History." *Journal of African Christian Thought* 5, no. 2 (December 2002): 3–11.

Wan, Enoch, ed. *Diaspora Missiology: Theory, Methodology, and Practice*. Portland, OR: Institute of Diaspora Studies, 2011.

———. "Diaspora Missiology." *Occasional Bulletin* (Spring 2007): 3.

———. ed. *Diaspora Missiology: Theory, Methodology, and Practice*. Rev. ed. Portland, OR: Institute of Diaspora Studies, 2014.

———. "The Dynamics of Ethnicity: A Case Study on the Immigrant Community of New York Chinatown." PhD diss., State University of New York at Stony Brook, 1978.

———."Filipino International Network: A Strategic Model for Filipino Diaspora Glocal Missions."*Global Missiology* 1, no. 2 (October 2004), http://ojs.globalmissiology.org/index.php/english/article/viewFile/123/356 (accessed February 20, 2014).

———. "Global People and Diaspora Missiology." plenary session, Global Mission Consultation, Tokyo, Japan (May 13, 2010).

———. "Mission among the Chinese Diaspora: A Case Study of Migration and Mission." *Missiology* 31, no. 1 (January 2003): 35–43.

———. ed. *Missions from the Majority World: Progress, Challenges, and Case Studies*. EMS 17, Pasadena: William Carey Library, 2009.

———. ed. *Missions within Reach: Intercultural Ministries in Canada*. Hong Kong: China Alliance Press, 1995.

———. "The Paradigm and Pressing Issues of Inter-disciplinary Research Methodology." *Global Missiology* 2, no. 2 (January 2005). http://ojs.globalmissiology.org/index.php/english/article/viewFile/97/281.

———. "The Phenomenon of Diaspora: Missiological Implications for Christian Missions." *Global Missiology* 4, no. 9 (July 2012) http://ojs.globalmissiology.org/index.php/english/article/view/1036.

———. "The Phenomenon of the Diaspora: Missiological Implications for Christian Missions." *Asian American Christianity: A Reader*, edited by Viji Nakka-Cammauf and Timothy Tseng. Castro Valley, CA: PAACCE and ISAAC (2009).

———. "Research Methodology for Diaspora Missiology and Diaspora Missions." North Central Regional EMS Conference, Trinity Evangelical Divinity School, Deerfield, IL (February 26, 2011).

———. "Rethinking Missiological Research Methodology: Exploring a New Direction." *Global Missiology* (October 2003).

———, and Anthony Francis Casey. *Church Planting among Immigrants in US Urban Centers: The Where, Why, and How of Diaspora Missiology in Action*. Portland, OR: Institute of Diaspora Studies, 2014.

———, and Elton S. L. Law. *The 2011 Triple Disaster in Japan and the Diaspora: Lessons Learned and Ways Forward*. Portland, OR: Institute of Diaspora Studies, 2014.

———, and Thanh Trung Le. *Mobilizing Vietnamese Diaspora for the Kingdom.* Portland, OR: Institute of Diaspora Studies, 2014.

———, and Michael Pocock. *Missions from the Majority World: Progress, Challenges, and Case Studies.* EMS 17 Pasadena: William Carey Library, 2009.

———. and Ted Rubesh. *Wandering Jews and Scattered Sri Lankans: Viewing Sri Lankans of the Gulf Cooperative Council through the Lens of the Old Testament Jewish Diaspora.* Portland, OR: Institute of Diaspora Studies, 2014.

———. and Sadiri Joy Tira. "Diaspora Missiology and Missions in the Context of the Twenty-first Century." *Torch Trinity Journal* 13, no.1 (May 30, 2010): 45–56, Seoul, South Korea.

Warner, Stephen R. "Religion and New (Post-1965) Immigrants: Some Principles Drawn from Field Research." *American Studies* 41, nos. 2–3 (Summer/Fall 2000): 267–86.

———. and Judith G. Wittner. *Gatherings in Diaspora: Religious Communities and the New Immigration.* Philadelphia: Temple University Press, 1998.

Wenham, Gordon J. "Genesis 1–15." *Word Biblical Commentary.* Waco, TX: Word (1987): 213.

Whitehead, James D., and Evelyn Eaton Whitehead. *Method in Ministry: Theological Reflection and Christian Ministry.* (Minneapolis: Seabury, 1980): 21–26.

Wickeri, P.L. "Mission from the Margins." *International Review of Mission* (2004), Wiley Online Library.

Wilkens, Steve and Mark L. Sanford. *Hidden Worldviews: Eight Cultural Stories That Shape Our Lives.* Downers Grove, IL: InterVarsity Press Academic, 2009, 20.

Williams, K. D. "Ostracism." *Annual Review of Psychology* 58 (2007): 425–52.

Winter, Ralph D. "Seeing the Task Graphically." Monrovia, CA: MARC (1974).

Woo, Rodney. *The Color of Church: A Biblical and Practical Paradigm for Multiracial Churches.* Nashville: B&H Academic, 2009.

Woodberry, J. Dudley. "To the Muslim I Became a Muslim?" *International Journal of Frontier Missions* 24, no. 1 (Spring 2007): 23–28.

World Evangelical Alliance. "Life on the Road: Updates from the Refugee Highway Partnership." May 31, 2013, http://www.worldea.org/news/4227/life-on-the-road-updates-from-the-refugee-highway-partnership (accessed March 8, 2014).

———. "Refugee Sunday 2009 Resource Pack." June 21, 2009. http://refugeehighway.net/downloads/wrs/refugee_sunday_resource_pack_complete.pdf.

The World Factbook. "Geography: Turkmenistan." https://www.cia. gov/library/publications/the-world-factbook/geos/tx.html (accessed March 26, 2014).

World Vision. "Jerusalem, West Bank, Gaza." http://www.worldvision.org/our-impact/country-profiles/jerusalem-west%20bank-gaza (accessed March 3, 2014).

Wright, N. T. *The New Testament and the People of God: Christian Origins and the Question of God* Minneapolis: Fortress, 1992, Kindle location 3113.

———. *Pauline Perspectives: Essays on Paul, 1978–2013*. Minneapolis: Fortress, 2013, 218.

Yen, Hope. "Census Estimates Show Big Gains for U.S. Minorities." *The Oregonian* (February 4, 2011): A10.

Younan, Munib. *Witnessing for Peace: In Jerusalem and the World*. Minneapolis: Augsburg Fortress, 2003.

Contributors

Andrew F. Bush, Associate Professor and Chair of the Missions and Anthropology Department, Eastern University

Rev. Dr. Andrew Bush is associate professor and chair of the Missions and Anthropology Department at Eastern University. Before coming to Eastern in 2005, Andrew and his wife, Karen, served internationally for twenty years. They began their mission service in 1987 as church planters in the Philippines, where they established a network of congregations that serve both the business sector and the inner-city families who are living in deep poverty. In 1998 they entered a new phase of their service in the Palestinian territories, where Andrew has worked with the Palestinian Bible Society until the present. There they established an outreach to students and families—Living Stones Student Center on the West Bank—that conducts summer camps for kids, evening programs for university students, family wellness programs, and more. Between semesters you will find Andrew there. Andrew has recently published *Learning from the Least: Reflections on a Journey in Mission with Palestinian Christians* (Eugene, OR: Wipf & Stock, 2013). He may be reached at abush2@eastern.edu.

Larry W. Caldwell, Director of Training and Research, Converge Worldwide; and Professor of Intercultural Studies, Sioux Falls Seminary

Larry W. Caldwell, PhD, recently completed twenty years teaching missions and Bible interpretation at Asian Theological Seminary in Manila, Philippines. He has now relocated to the United States and is director of training and strategy for Converge Worldwide (formerly Baptist General Conference), as well as professor of intercultural studies at Sioux Falls Seminary, Sioux Falls, South Dakota. He continues to teach at seminaries worldwide as well as researching and writing on missions.

Trevor Castor, Associate Director of the Zwemer Center for Muslim Studies, Columbia International University

Trevor, Katie, and their three children live in Columbia, South Carolina, where Trevor serves as the associate director of the Zwemer Center for Muslim Studies. He is also a professor of intercultural studies at Columbia International University (CIU). Prior to coming to CIU, he and his wife served with Youth With A Mission (YWAM) for seven years. During their missionary service, they worked in a 100-percent Muslim country in South Asia. Trevor's undergraduate work is in Bible and humanities. He has a master's degree in Muslim studies and is a PhD candidate at the Australian College of Theology. In addition to his missionary and academic ministries, he served for five years as a youth and college pastor where he discovered his love of preaching and teaching.

Stan Downes, Assistant Area Director—Europe, One Challenge

Stan and his wife, Donna, joined OC in 1983 and served in Kenya for eleven years. Following that they served for twelve years in Romania, where Stan was the team leader. Stan served as the area director for Europe from 2000 to 2004. His interest in diaspora issues came from seeing many Romanians emigrating to the West and starting churches and ministries. Prior to his career in missions, Stan was a manager with Arthur Andersen & Co. and an auditor for the Coca-Cola Bottling Company. David R. Dunaetz, Assistant Professor of Organizational Leadership, Chicago School of Professional PsychologyDavid's research focuses on organizational processes in churches and missions. He recently completed an empirical study on pastoral attitudes that predict numerical church growth, which appeared in the *Great Commission Research Journal*. He and his wife spent seventeen years in evangelism and church planting in France, where they started two churches.

Fred Farrokh, Missionary, Elim Fellowship

Rev. Fred Farrokh is an Iranian-American of Muslim family background. Born in the United States, Fred met Jesus Christ as Savior in 1983 while reading through the Bible. He is an ordained missionary with Elim Fellowship. His life call is serving Muslim people with the gospel. He became ambassador-at-large with Jesus For Muslims Network, after serving as executive director with JFM from 2006 to 2013. Fred graduated with a PhD in intercultural studies from Assemblies of God Theological Seminary in 2014. He has also ministered in Egypt, Lebanon, Israel, Cyprus, Bangladesh, Ukraine, Uzbekistan, Malaysia, Morocco, and the Philippines.

Mark Hausfeld, International Director, Global Initiative

Global Initiative: Reaching Muslim Peoples is a ministry established to collaborate with Assemblies of God World Missions regions and with US missions to equip and mobilize the church to reach Muslims everywhere. Hausfeld is also associate professor of urban and Islamic studies and the director of the Center for Islamic Studies at Assemblies of God Theological Seminary, Springfield, Missouri.

Jacques Hebert, Director of Training and Strategy, Urban Catalyst
Michael Pocock, Senior Professor Emeritus of World Missions and Intercultural Studies, Dallas Theological Seminary

A native of England who spent his formative years in the United States, Dr. Pocock always has subscribed to an intercultural approach to the gospel. Before joining Dallas Theological Seminary's world missions faculty in 1987, he pastored a culturally diverse church in Chicago. He holds the MDiv, ThM, and DMiss degrees from Trinity Evangelical Divinity School. He and his wife Penny also ministered for sixteen years with The Evangelical Alliance Mission (TEAM), first in Venezuela and later as mobilization director in Wheaton, Illinois. He continues to travel extensively to participate in missions ministries and conferences. Dr. Pocock has researched and written on the development of multicultural churches in America (2002) and the impact of globalization on missions (2005). He currently is researching human migration in Scripture and the implications for ministry worldwide. Dr. Pocock has been a visiting professor at Christian colleges and seminaries around the world. Since its founding in 1991, he has served as a board member of Evergreen Family Friendship Services—China. He continues to teach as an adjunct professor at Dallas Theological Seminary.

Jerry Rankin, President Emeritus, International Mission Board, Southern Baptist Convention; and Director, Zwemer Center for Muslim Studies, Columbia International University

Jerry Rankin served as a missionary in South and Southeast Asia for twenty-three years, including tenure as area director for the region. For seventeen years prior to retirement he served as president of the Southern Baptist International Mission Board. Rankin is a graduate of Mississippi College and Southwestern Baptist

Theological Seminary and has been awarded three honorary doctorates. He currently lives in Mississippi and serves as director of the Zwemer Center for Muslim Studies at Columbia International University. He has written eight books and is adjunct professor of missions at Mississippi College, William Carey University, and CIU. In 2013 he received the Missio Nexus Lifetime Achievement Award.

David Stevens, Senior Pastor of Central Bible Church

David Stevens is senior pastor of Central Bible Church in Portland, Oregon.

Established in its present location in 1957, Central Bible is in full metamorphosis as it reaches an increasingly diverse urban demographic. David's vision for multiethnic ministry was birthed during his fifteen years as a missionary-pastor in France (1985–2000). He is a graduate of Dallas Theological Seminary (1982, ThM) and of the Faculté Libre de Théologie Évangélique (1999, ThD) near Paris, France. He also authored the recently released *God's New Humanity: A Biblical Theology of Multiethnicity for the Church* (Eugene, OR: Wipf & Stock, 2012). David and his wife, Mary Alice, are the parents of four children—Jonathan (now with the Lord), Rebecca, Mary Lynne, and Justin—and grandparents to three grandchildren. In his spare time, David loves to read French, snow
ski, travel, and hang out with family members.

Esther J. Stewart, Equip International, Missionary Appointee

Esther holds an MA in intercultural studies from Columbia International University and serves as professor at the Evangelical Theological College, Addis Ababa, Ethiopia. She and her husband recently moved to a large New England city to work among the diaspora community there. They plan to return to her husband's native Ethiopia in 2015 as missionary trainers, equipping Ethiopians for cross-cultural ministry to the unreached within Ethiopia and in other nations.

Enoch Wan, President, Evangelical Missiological Society; and Director, Doctor of Intercultural Studies Program, Western Seminary

Dr. Wan (PhD) is the research professor of intercultural studies and director of the doctor of intercultural studies program at Western Theological Seminary. He has served as president of the Evangelical Missiological Society (EMS), and is currently V.P. for publications of the society. He founded the Institute for Diaspora Missions Studies at Western, serves on the advisory board of the Global Diaspora Network, and is cofounder/editor of the multilingual electronic journal at www.globalmissiology.org. He is a researcher with interest in missiology, research methodology, sinology, and intercultural studies. His multitude of contributions to missiology can be found at www.enochwan.com. One of the earliest contributors to the discipline of diaspora missiology, he edited *Diaspora Missiology: Theory, Methodology, and Practice* (2011; repr., Portland, OR: Institute of Diaspora Studies, 2014).

Index

A

Abu-Laban, Sharon, 69
accommodation, 126, 132
acculturation, 130–32, 135–37, 142–45
   psychological, 131
   social identity model of, 142
   three models of, 131
   two-dimensional model of, 136
AD2000 and Beyond Movement, 213
Adeney, Miriam, 83
Affinity Groups, 122, 199, 209–12, 213
Afghanistan, 32, 34, 44, 208, 211
   Afghans, 55, 68, 211
Africa, 8, 14, 32, 82, 86, 108, 118, 161, 200–201
   African, 6, 15, 29, 109, 207
Alcorn, Randy, 122
Alonso, Andoni, 24
America(n). See United States of America.
American Community Survey (ACS), 67–68
American Society of Missiology (AMS), 217, 219
Angola, 32
   Angolan, 138–39
Annan, Kofi, 3
Appadurai, Arjun, 159
Arabic, 22, 26, 34, 173
Argentina, 207
Arizona, 6
Asia, 5, 7–8, 14, 32, 79, 82, 86, 161, 200
   Asian, 6, 29, 108–9
Asia Minor, 118
Assemblies of God Theological Seminary, 61
Assemblies of God World Mission (AGWM), 42
assimilation, 64, 68, 126, 130–39, 142, 213
asylum, 18
Ateek, Naim Stifan, 176–77
Athens, 4, 98–102
Australia, 12, 211, 218
Austria, 86
   Austrian, 86

B

Bangladesh, 32, 61, 63, 67, 70–71, 74
   Bangladeshi, 68, 70
Barrett, C. K., 50
Barry, F. R., 110
Bedouins, 14
Beijing, 8, 221
Belgium, 31–32
Berber Arabs, 14, 23, 34
Bernal, Victoria, 24, 27–28
Bernard, Russell, 71
Berry, John, 136, 140
Bethlehem Bible College, 174, 179–81
bicultural, 91–94, 108–9, 133, 136, 139–40, 193–94
Blow, Steve, 7
Bolshevik Revolution, 43
Botswana, 32
Brazil, 205
Brown, Rick, 63
Burkina Faso, 32, 74
Burma, 218
   Burmese, 16
business as mission (BAM), 163

C

Cameroon, 32
Campus Crusade, 13
Canada, 7, 14, 31, 184, 208, 211, 218–20, 222, 224
　Canadian, 10
　Canadian Theological Seminary, 218
Caribbean, 5, 86, 200
Central America, 13
　Central American, 16
Chacour, Elias, 168, 174
Chad, 9, 16
Chan, Kim-Kong, 80
Chicago Council on Global Affairs, 17
China, 14, 32, 35, 79, 87, 148, 202, 204, 218
　Chinese, 12, 22, 78, 80, 83, 148, 162, 207, 209, 211, 217–19, 221, 224
Christ at the Checkpoint Conferences, 179–80
Christianity, 13–15, 43–44, 83, 150, 171, 176
Chronological Bible Storying, 48
church planting, 49, 79, 83–87, 125, 129–35, 137–45, 147, 151, 204, 206–08, 211–12, 213, 216, 224
　cross-cultural, 129–32
Church World Service, 10, 17
Clayman, Chris, 67
computer mediated communication (CMC), 21, 24–25
conversion, convert, 44, 49, 52–54, 62, 65–66, 73, 93, 96–98, 144, 156, 171, 186–87, 203
Cooke, Miriam, 158
Cote d'Ivoire, 32
creative access, 206, 208

Cuba, 218
Cuban, 16

D

Democratic Republic of Congo, 33
　Congolese, 79
Denny, Frederick Mathewson, 38
diaspora
　believers, 59, 77–81, 83–85, 88, 183
　case studies in, 86, 88, 195, 199, 217–18, 222
　Chinese, 80, 217–18, 221
　churches, 78–82, 84–85, 88, 112, 123, 129, 133, 135, 138, 141, 187, 189–90, 192–95, 221
　communities, 25, 28, 31, 59–60, 62–65, 71, 74–75, 80, 82–84, 88, 130, 132, 134–35, 137–39, 144–45, 167–68, 173, 216, 218
　digital, 21–22, 24–25, 27–28, 31
　Eritrean, 27
　Ethiopians, 183–90, 192
　　Ethiopian Diaspora Church (EDC), 189, 191–94
　Filipino, 4, 148, 219
　global, 162, 220–21
　Korean, 80, 220–21, 223–24
　literature, 24
　missiology, 59–60, 62, 75, 77–78, 88, 91, 147, 163, 215–26
　Muslim, 37–55, 60, 62–65, 134, 151–52
Dimangondayao, Lorajoy, 4
discipleship, 47–48, 53–55, 62, 147, 151–52, 211, 216, 219
　narrative, 55
diversity, 32, 65, 68, 71, 75, 111, 114–15, 118–21, 124–26, 217, 22, 224

Du Toit, Andries B., 92

E

East Africa, 63, 200, 205
Eastern Michigan University, 40
economically active migrants, 10–11
Egypt, 32, 61, 74, 94, 153–55, 209
 Egyptian, 37, 67–68, 159, 209
emic, 153–55
enclave mentality, 187–88
enculturation, 130–31
Eritrea, 27, 190
eschatology, 52–53, 180–81
Ethiopia, 14, 32, 125, 183–85, 187–89, 191, 194
 Ethiopian, 183–95
ethnographic research, 24, 163
etic, 154–56
Eurasia, 37, 41–42
 Eurasian Diaspora Study Center, 222
Europe, 5, 7–8, 15, 41, 67, 77–79, 81, 83, 86–87, 134–35, 168, 200, 204, 207–08, 210, 223
 European, 5–6, 21, 86–87, 133–34, 140, 207–08, 210–12, 216
Evangelical Immigration Table, 17
evangelicals, 4, 13, 17–18, 81, 87–88, 184, 186–87, 193, 204
evangelism, 47, 49, 51, 53, 55, 59, 62, 88, 151, 184, 191, 193, 204, 217, 219, 222, 224
 direct, 47, 54–55
evangelist, 45, 49, 51, 88, 188
EX-03, 151–52
expatriate, 206, 211

F

Facebook (FB), 21–35
 Graph Search, 21, 28–29, 31–32, 35
 limitations of, 32–35
Filadelfia Movement, 15
Filipino Diaspora Missions Consultation, 219
Filipino International Network (FIN), 11–12, 219–20
Finland, 14
France, 17, 31, 107, 116, 126, 220
Fulani, 30–32
Fulbe, 14

G

Germany, 78–79, 82, 142, 207
 German, 22, 84, 86, 142
Ghana, 32
 Ghanaian, 79
Global Affinity Group, 199, 209–10, 213
Global Diaspora Missiology Consultation, 220
Global Mapping International (GMI), 23
Global Pastoralist Gathering, 15
globalization, 12, 225
Google, 22, 28, 35
Great Britain, 12
Great Commission, 4, 59–60, 145, 183–86, 190–92, 194–95, 200–05, 211, 216
Greek, 4, 39, 51, 92–93, 99–100, 102, 116, 118–19, 121, 154, 156
Green, Michael, 52
Greeson, Kevin, 63
Grunlan, Stephen, 157
Guinea, 31
Guyana, 74
Gypsies (Romani), 15

H

Hausfeld, Mark, 69
Hebrew, 92, 96, 110, 115, 177
Hengel, Martin, 51
hermeneutical method, 97–98
Hiebert, Paul, 52, 157
Higgins, Kevin, 63
Hinduism
  Hindu, 5, 79, 162, 223
Hispanic, 7, 17, 79, 108, 148, 208
Holland, 82
  Dutch, 82
honor, 147, 161
hospitality, 48, 147, 154, 156–57, 161, 164
human trafficking, 11, 18, 41, 225
Hunter, Malcolm, 15

I

identity formation, 123–24
Ilie, Christina, 81
Imago Dei, 110, 112
India, 5, 32, 67, 74, 87, 152, 211, 222
  Indian, 12, 152, 162, 211
Indonesia, 61, 63, 71, 200–01
  Indonesian, 22, 67, 82
Instagram, 35
integration, 85, 136–40, 150, 225
International Justice Mission, 15
International Labour Organization (ILO), 10–12
International Mission Board (IMB), 23, 31, 199, 201, 203–09, 212, 213
International Revival Ministries (IRM), 187
international students, 3, 12–14, 23, 29, 162, 219
International Students Incorporated, 13–14

internet communities, 22, 25
InterVarsity Christian Fellowship, 13
intifada, 169
Inuits, 14
Iran, 27, 44, 60, 67, 74, 208, 211
  Iranian, 27, 55, 60, 62, 67–68, 79, 207–08, 211
Islam, 32, 39–40, 43–45, 61–62, 65–66, 69–70, 150, 171, 173, 176
Israel, 12, 61, 94–95, 108, 115–16, 153–56, 167–81
Israeli Defense Forces (IDF), 169
Issa-Salwe, Abdisalam, 25
Italy, 31, 87

J

Japan, 82, 225
  Japanese, 12, 207, 209, 225
Jenkins, Philip, 109
Jerusalem, 43, 49, 92–95, 119, 154–56, 168–69, 172, 175
JESUS film, 193
Jewish, 5, 84, 91–94, 97, 100, 116, 153, 155, 171–73, 176, 178–80, 225
Jew, 39, 43, 67, 91–93, 96–100, 104, 108, 115–16, 118–19, 121, 155, 171, 173–76, 178–79, 223, 225
JFM Network, 62
Jordan, 74
Joshua Project, 23
Judaism, 96–98

K

Kairos courses, 87
Katanacho, Yohanna, 175–78
Kazakhstan, 44, 74
Kenya, 8, 125

King, Martin Luther, 109
Kingsway International Christian Centre, 82
kinship, 147-48, 150-51, 157-59, 162-64, 217
Kisskalt, Michael, 85
Kolkata, 8
Korea, 219
Korean, 12, 80, 82, 125, 209, 220-24
Kotter, John, 200
Kraft, Charles, 63
Kurzman, Charles, 158

L

Lagos, 8
Latin America, 5, 8, 12, 22, 210-11, 79, 81-82, 200-01
Latin American, 6, 79, 82, 109
Lausanne, 78, 82, 202, 219-24
    Conference, 213
        Cape Town 2010, 220, 224
Lawrence, Bruce, 158
Lebanon, 32, 61, 74, 152
Lee, Meredith, 67
Lee, Samuel, 82
Leonenet, 26
Lerner, Michael, 178
Lewis, Rebecca, 63
Liberia, 32
Libya, 32
Lifewater International, 15
LinkedIn, 35
Londono, Jesus, 86
Lorance, Cody, 83

M

Madanat, Labib, 176, 179-80
Majority World, 82, 86, 167, 185, 195

Martin, Jimmy, 84
Martin, Philip, 16
Masai, 14
Massey, Joshua, 63
Mauritania, 31
Mayers, Marvin, 157
McGavran, Donald, 156, 201, 222
Mediascape, 159-60
mediator, 189
melting pot, 60, 132
    one-dimensional model, 131-32, 144
Mennonite Central Committee, 174
Mexico, 6, 12
Mexican, 10, 16
Middle East, 14, 67, 79, 118, 148, 159, 161, 200, 207
migration
    global, 3, 5, 7, 18, 40
    human, 3-4, 8
    internal, 8, 225
    international, 3, 8, 16
    secular and Christian opinions on, 17
"Minutemen", 6
missiology, 63, 70, 167, 175, 178, 181, 205
    diaspora. See diaspora.
Missional Helix, 42
    Cultural Analysis (CA), 42
    Historical Perspective (HP), 42-43
    Strategy Formation (SF), 42, 53
    Theological Reflection (TR), 42, 48
missionary
    exogenous, 148, 152, 163
    pioneer, 206
Mongolia, 14
    Mongolian, 209
Morocco, 32, 61, 74
    Moroccan, 26, 78, 159
Muhammad, 39, 74

multiethnic, 85, 88, 107, 122, 125, 138, 140–41
Munayer, Salim, 178
Muslim, 5, 17, 32, 35, 37–40, 42, 47, 51, 59–75, 134–35, 151–52, 162–63, 170–71, 174–80, 201, 204–05, 209, 223
Sufi, 44, 73
Sunni, 45, 60, 73
Muslim-Background Believer (MBB), 37, 73, 175
Muslim-Background Christian, 59–60, 62–63, 65, 68, 71–74
Myanmar, 9, 83

N

Nairobi, 8
Nestorians, 44
New Humanity, 107, 110, 114–17, 119–26

New Testament, 39, 49, 51, 53, 104, 110, 118, 125
New York (NY), 59, 61, 64, 218
New Zealand, 12, 211
Nigeria, 8, 32, 108
Nigerian, 82, 86
Niyazov, Saparmurat, 45
nomads, 3, 14–15
nongovernmental organizations (NGO), 10, 15
North Africa, 67, 87, 162
North America, 8, 13, 16, 18, 63, 69, 139, 168, 218, 223
North American, 12, 125
Nwaobasi, Ike, 86

O

Obama, Barack, 66
OC International, 78, 86

Oiarzabal, Pedro, 22, 24
Old Testament, 39, 94, 97, 101, 103, 115, 177, 225
Olofinjana, Israel, 86, 88
Organization for Economic Cooperation and Development (OECD), 13
Ott, Craig, 49, 77, 91, 100
outreach, 42, 125, 164, 189, 210–11, 216
Overseas Mission Study Center (OMSC), 217

P

Pakistan, 5, 32–33, 67, 73–74
Pakistani, 16, 68, 73
Palestine, 61, 74, 167, 170, 173–75, 177–79, 181
Palestinians, 68–69, 162, 167–81
Christians, 168–71, 173–79, 181
Palestinian Bible Society (PBS), 174, 176, 179–80
Pashto, 34
pastoralists, 15
Pennington, Jonathan, 52
Pentecost, 43, 114, 117–18, 119, 154
People Group Focus, 202–03, 206–07
Perry, Rick, 6
Peru, 87
Pew Foundation, 17, 22, 65–67, 70–72, 75, 223–24
Philippine Council of Evangelical Churches, 83
Philippine Missions Mobilization Movement, 85
Philippines, 4–5, 9, 32, 61, 79, 85, 205, 207, 218–19, 221, 224, 226
Filipinos, 4–5, 11, 82, 148, 219–20
Philippines Missions Associations, 82–83
Pinterest, 35

Portuguese, 22, 138–39
Protestant, 107, 126, 167–68, 171, 174–76, 178, 188, 201

Q

Queen's University, 136
Qur'an, 28, 32, 39
Qzone, 35

R

Rantisi, Audeh G., 175–76
Rasmussen, Lars, 28
Redfield, Linton, 133
Reformation, 107
refugee, 3, 5, 9–10, 17–18, 40, 65, 131, 160, 163, 167–68, 185, 206–07, 213, 225
Refugee Highway Partnership, 18
Research on Peoples and Languages (ROPAL), 202
Rojas, Daniel Carroll, 18
Roman Catholic, 4–5, 107, 126
Romania, 78, 86–87
 Romanian, 77, 80–81, 83, 86–88, 125
Russia, 14, 211
 Russian, 14, 43, 45, 79
Ryder, A. G., 135

S

Sahara Desert, 14
Sahel, 14
Sami, 14
Saudi Arabia, 8, 32, 74, 184
 Saudi Arabian, 152
  desert, 14
Senegal, 31–32
 Senegalese, 68

sex
 sexual
  abuse, 11
  exploitation, 11
  favors, 46
 shame, 143, 161
Shari'a, 68
Sierra Leone, 32, 74
 Sierra Leoneans, 26
Silvoso, Ed, 79
Sina Weibo, 35
Social Identity Model, 131, 141–42, 145
social media, 21–25, 28, 35, 193
Somalia, 9
 Somalis, 15, 25
Song, Minho, 80
South Africa, 78, 211, 221, 224
South Carolina, 32
South Korea, 219–21, 224
Southern Baptist Foreign Mission Board, 200
Spain, 15, 78, 81, 83, 87–88
Spanish, 22, 81, 83, 87, 108
sub-Saharan Africa, 13, 17, 67, 79, 210, 211
Sudan
 Sudanese, 9, 16, 207
Sweden, 184
Syria, 32
 Syrians, 118, 152

T

Taiwan, 218
Tasaw, Daniel, 187
Technological University of Monterrey, 12
Texas, 6, 186
Thailand, 16, 206–07, 219
Tibet
 Tibetan, 14, 209

Travis, John, 63
Trinidad, 74
Turkana, 14
Turkey, 32, 71, 74, 208
Turkish, 29, 44, 142, 209
Turkmen, Turkmenistan, 37, 40-48, 54-55
Twitter, 35, 104
Tynes, Robert, 26

U

Uganda, 32
Ukraine, 61, 222
umma, 64, 71
United Arab Emirates, 8, 16, 207
United Kingdom (UK), 12, 23, 31, 86, 88, 211
United Nations High Command for Refugees (UNHCR), 9-10
United States of America, 7, 65, 69, 126, 163, 183-84, 212
    American, 7, 11, 17, 40-41, 47, 66, 70, 72, 108-09, 122, 133, 162, 183-85, 188, 192, 194
    Congress, 6, 17
University of British Columbia, 135
University of Chicago, 132
unreached people group (UPGs), 21, 23, 34-35, 60, 103, 129, 183, 191, 195, 199, 202- 06, 211, 213
US Immigration Act, 6
Uzbekistan, 43-44, 46, 61, 69, 74
    Uzbeks, 43, 55

V

Van Rheenen, Gailyn, 42
virtual
    communities, 22, 25
    space, 21-22, 24-27

W

West Africa, 14, 207
Wilson, Gene, 49
Winter, Ralph, 202
World Council of Churches
    Ecumenical Accompaniment Programme, 174
World Evangelical Alliance, 18
World Vision, 15, 174

X

xenophobia, 12

Y

Yale Divinity School, 217
Younan, Munib A., 175-76

Z

Zimbabwe, 32, 207, 211
Zuckerberg, Mark, 28, 35

CPSIA information can be obtained
at www.ICGtesting.com
Printed in the USA
LVHW080109010522
716679LV00021B/276